WOMEN
in WORLD
RELIGIONS

McGill Studies in the History of Religions
A Series Devoted to International Scholarship
Katherine K. Young, Editor

WOMEN
in WORLD
RELIGIONS

edited by
ARVIND SHARMA

introduction by
KATHERINE K. YOUNG

State University of New York Press

Published by
State University of New York Press, Albany

© 1987 State University of New York

Printed in the United States of America

For information, address State University of New York Press, State University Plaza,
Albany, N.Y., 12246

Library of Congress Cataloging-in-Publication Data

Women in world religions.

  (McGill studies in the history of religions)
  Bibliography: p.
  Includes index.
  1. Women and religion.   1. Sharma, Arvind.
II. Series.
BL458.W57   1987   291′.088042   87-6475
ISBN 0-88706-374-8
ISBN 0-88706-375-6 (pbk.)

10 9 8 7 6

CONTENTS

To my daughter

"Men and women equally compose mankind"

Dabistān-i-Mazāhib
(a seventeenth century Indian text)

Arvind Sharma

PREFACE

THIS book has been edited by me, but it has been written by others. My attitude to it is marked by the satisfaction one might feel at the birth of a brain child after a gestation period of several years; my attitude to its contributors is marked by silent gratitude on account of the deficiency of language which affects the grateful.

An enterprise such as this can only succeed with the help of many, too numerous to mention. Yet, even at the risk of appearing invidious, I must gratefully acknowledge the following for their interest in the project and their optimism regarding its eventual completion: Alaka Hejib, formerly of McGill; Diana Paul of Stanford; Nancy Falk of Western Michigan University-Kalamazoo; Julia Ching of Toronto; Priscilla Ching Chung and Cynthia Y. Ning of Hawaii; Chun-Fang Yü of Rutgers; Katie Carlitz of Pittsburg; Irene Bloom of Columbia; Ellen Ch'en of St. John's University; Judith Plaskow of Manhattan College; Judith A. Berling of Indiana University; Sheila McDonough and Lynn Teskey of Concordia, and Cornelia Dimmitt of Georgetown University.

This book represents the application of the phenomenological stance, with its respect for the insider's view, to the study of women in world religions. That a man should put together a book written by women scholars is potentially male chauvinistic; that none of the women scholars should have even raised an eyebrow is proof that the academia is concerned not with the gender but with what is engendered.

Katherine K. Young

INTRODUCTION

I met Arvind Sharma in 1973 at Harvard. I was a visiting doctoral student and he was a resident at the Center for the Study of World Religions. The lively interest in the issue of women and religion at Harvard Divinity School across the street proved contagious, and we decided to give a course on women and world religions at the Cambridge Center of Adult Education. Though the signs of emerging scholarly interest were easily discernible, we soon discovered that the enthusiasm for the topic was not anchored securely in adequate scholarship and pedagogic materials, especially where Asian religions were concerned.

Our initial efforts that year led to the publication of a bibliography and subsequently a course outline on women in Hinduism and Buddhism. The speed with which this tentative bibliography was sold out and afterwards outdated was a barometer of the changing intellectual climate. Women's studies had now not only entered the curricula of North American universities, but were on their way to becoming established. A growing, vibrant, and diversified literature was emerging on the topic; primary sources were being combed, historical developments were being traced, and anthropological fieldwork was being directed to the woman's domain. While at the beginning of the 1970s we may have been in danger of dying of thirst, by the middle of the next decade we were looking for that proverbial drop to drink in the copious waters of scholarship.

A word about the choice of the expression *world religions*. By world religions is meant primarily the major religions—Hinduism, Buddhism, Confucianism, Taoism, Judaism, Christianity, and Islam—and secondarily the tribal religions, which have been receiving increased attention in their own right. Accordingly, this volume discusses the religions listed above and also one representative of the tribal religions, that of the Australian Aborigines, for purposes of comparison.

I wish to point out the special features of this book. As is well known, one of the basic breakthroughs in the method of the study of religion is represented by the creatively ambiguous expression: the phenomenology of religion. Among other things, this method emphasizes a sympathetic but not submissive attitude towards the insider's view. It has hitherto been confined to the study of individual religions. This book extends this method to the study of women in world religions by inviting contributions from women scholars who start not only with an attempt to appreciate the religion from within its own framework but also begin from within their own feminine perspective and so may have a good perception of what a woman's experience entails.

But just as any empathetic approach to a religion must be grounded in a firm knowledge of the milieu, so too it is necessary to be aware of the differences in women's experiences across various religions, cultures, and time periods. One must give rigorous attention to the differences that mold a woman's sphere of influence and world of meaning. The authors of these various essays are not only women who espouse the phenomenological method, but also adept historians who ground their analyses in publicly verifiable facts. While the results may well be open to debate, these essays may nonetheless be appreciated for their attempt to strike a delicate balance between hard fact and fine perception in the best tradition of the phenomenology and history of religions.

The difficulty of this task becomes especially apparent when one realizes that the subject of women has been greatly distorted by the editorial lens of history, which has been focused largely by men. In her essay on tribal religion, Rita Gross challenges us to move beyond "androcentric methodologies, biases, and values in reporting, organizing, and interpreting the materials being studied". Yet it is difficult to meet this challenge. Despite the fact that the climate of feminism has made us sensitive to androcentrism, we find such androcentrism so built into our sources that we often have difficulty discovering what, in Gross's words, "women actually do, think, or feel." Her insistence that we shift to a "two-sexed or androgynous" view of humanity gives us an important starting point, but we quickly discover that because there are so few writings by women—the problem of "silent history"—we cannot avoid the androcentric text which muffles our stethoscope and prevents us from hearing the heartbeats of real women.

We now know better than to think that women have always been of marginal importance, but as historians who must labor against the constraint of textual evidence we have less opportunity than anthropologists and other interpreters of contemporary societies, who document women's actual lives, to recover the feminine perspective. We are limited, in other words, by the written word and can probably never meet Gross's agenda that "we will have accounts of societies and religions in which full information about women is integrated into all discussions." Therefore, her desire to understand the "totality of any tradition" may well remain an ideal. However, we are certainly moving toward a point when historical studies will be complemented by anthropological research and primary accounts written by contemporary yet traditionally religious women, so that some day we will have both the written and oral sides of a tradition to further our understanding.

In the meantime, we must still attempt to meet Rita Gross's challenge—to understand sex roles and their patterns of complementarity, which together constitute the whole pattern of a tradition. We must examine textual materials to see whether they will yield more information with a different approach, and we must determine whether complementarity really does exist at the core of the major world religions, as Gross has discovered in tribal religions. This volume provides opportunities to reflect on these issues.

If scholarship on women and religion is coming of age in the form of methodological sophistication, its growth towards maturity is also reflected in its treatment of history. Gone are the days when concern over how patriarchal religions adversely affect women presented a uni-dimensional view of the relation of religion and women as one of subjugation. In the sense that gynocentrism was the obverse of androcentrism, it distorted the view of reality. Many people would agree that the radical critique of women's traditional roles was an extremely important phase and that our very consciousness has been permanently altered by what this new perspective revealed. Since stereotypes do contain a measure of truth—indeed may capture the most extreme aspects of religion as it affects women—a focus on them may be an important catalyst for reform. Yet many thinkers may also be ready to return to a consideration of the great variety that exists within and among the various world religions, despite their common feature of being patriarchal. It cannot all be summed up by the descriptions of Chinese footbinding, Hindu *sati*, Muslim *purdah*, and Christian witchcraft.

The essays in this volume show that flexibility, ambivalence, and alternatives existed within the religions, sometimes at the core, sometimes at the margins. There were opportunities for "degrees of human freedom, of options taken and refused, of the exercise of aspiration and will—even if sometimes within patterns of severe constraints."[1] Jane Smith, in her chapter, tackles the problem of stereotypes directly. Other scholars represented here demonstrate the intricate patterns and deep structures that emerge through the historian's attention to detail and change. Just as the starting point, explicit or implicit, may be a concern with patriarchal religion, so the final point may be a return to the issue of what to do today about those aspects of religion that have affected women negatively. Meanwhile, our task is to study a history that is rich with the nuances of human life, ideals, and realities.

If we decide to put aside, for a moment, the contemporary critiques of patriarchal religion regarding the subordination of women, then this variety is indeed striking. Sometimes, for instance, we find that male authority and power are not always found together. Whereas the male may represent authority in the household, it is the female who exercises the real power in the domestic domain. Sometimes the same religious concept may be appropriated differently by men and women, and while the male version may appear oppressive for the female, it is not always the male version which is foremost in women's minds. Then, too, there may be a difference between precept and practice. Or what may appear as a male exclusion of women from a certain aspect of the religion may actually be a consequence of something other than misogyny or may have a parallel in female exclusion of men from certain religious activities.

The essays represented here also demonstrate how much religions may vary over time. What may be true of one period is not necessarily true of another. The variety within and among the world religions comes to the foreground when we examine the evidence carefully. The negative effects of patriarchy were at times like low-level, at times like high-level, radiation. But despite our institutionalized amnesia of the role of women, and depsite the fact that women were physically included within recorded history but were often emotionally and intellectually outside it, we can nevertheless recover some of the complexity of the past.

It is significant that the present authors are not just historians but historians of religions. Accordingly, they are well aware of how the religious domain, if it is to be understood, must be approached on its own terms. Interpretation, in other words, must take religion seriously, not bypass it. Each of the chapters relates the soteriology and the transcendental aspects of a religion to the lives of women. The results of this point of departure are often dramatically different from those reached by scholars who approach religion and women from the disciplines of psychology, sociology, and history itself. Herein lies another important contribution of this collection of essays.

It is perhaps a legitimate question to ask what general insights these essays have made available to us which otherwise would have remained inaccessible. I have noted the rich variety that appears so striking and which may lead to qualifications, if not reversals, of earlier views, judgments, and theories. But what generalizations can be gleaned from these essays?

The most obvious answer lies within the essays themselves: each must deal with a complex history and also provide an overview of women in a particular religion—an awesome task, as each contributor knows only too well. The exercise of locating and tracing dominant religious ideas and institutions as they pertain to women or women to them is in itself a generalizing activity. To avoid repetition I shall leave the overviews of the different traditions to the reader's perusal of this book and turn instead to generalizations of a comparative nature.

As it is not possible to generalize about women in world religions on the basis of just one religion, a comparative study of the position of women in the major religious traditions may yield valuable insights. All generalizations, of course, are subject to many dangers. If the facts are too rigorously considered, they escape generalization, and if they are too loosely considered, they allow the generalization to cover too much ground.

I shall begin this discussion by searching for the reasons behind the rise of patriarchal religions and the conditions under which the relative status of women changes within the history of such a religion. In this task I draw upon the work of Peggy Reeves Sanday entitled *Female Power and Male Dominance: On the Origins of Sexual Inequality*, which is based on a cross-cultural, large-sample approach to questions of power and dominance in 150 tribal societies. I shall also draw on Eli Sagan's *At the Dawn of Tyranny: The Origins of Individualsim, Political Oppression, and the State*, which is a cross-cultural study of the phenomenon of the rise of kingdoms based on Polynesian and African data.

The world religions have been called patriarchal religions. What is meant by this expression? Is the religion itself solely a creation or projection of male concerns and imagery and a legitimation of male desire to subjugate women and have power over them? Or does the adjective patriarchal merely refer to "a system of social organization in which descent and succession are traced through the male line"?[2] Or does the expression refer to a more complex social and historical reality that involves not only the differentiation of the sexes but also the symbolization of creation and its relation to the organization of sex roles with reference to such factors as geography, economics, and psychology?

Sanday begins her study by noting that different cultures choose from a variety of behavioral possibilities and this involves selecting a sex-role plan to organize behavior between the sexes:

> Such plans help men and women orient themselves as male and female to each other, to the world around them, and to the growing boys and girls whose behavior they must shape into a commonly accepted mold.
>
> In addition to guiding behavior, sex-role plans solve basic human puzzles. Human beings seek answers to such questions as where did we come from; how did we get here; how did others get there . . . and what are we to do about the powerful forces within any of these categories not fully understood. Confronted with the obvious, generally accepted, but frequently ignored facts that babies come out of females and female genitals differ from male genitals, people seek to solve the puzzle of sex differences by sorting out how and why the differences came about, what is to be done about the differences, and how the two kinds of people resulting from the differences are to relate to one another and to their environment (Sanday 1981, 3-4).

While sex-roles are chosen by a culture, this choice is not random; rather it relates to factors of environment, human subsistence activities, physical and emotional needs, as well as primary sex differences. Sex-role plans have their symbolic as well as behavioral component. "Sacred symbols are not . . . an [sic] epiphenomena of secular roles but secular power roles are derived from ancient concepts of sacred power" (Sanday 1981, xv). The symbolic manifestations of a people's sex role plan are found in the symbols of creative power, for there is:

> a congruence between the gender of a people's creator god(s), their orientation to the creative forces of nature, and the secular expressions of male and female power. Scripts for female power . . . accord feminine symbolism and women a prominent role in the sacred and secular domains. . . . Generally speaking, when males dominate, women play an inconsequential role in the sacred and secular domains. Almost always in male-dominated societies, the godhead is defined in exclusively masculine terms (Sanday 1981, 6).

If male dominance is correlated with supreme male deities as Sanday's evidence suggests, then we should predict the same in patriarchal religions if we find male dominance. An overview of the world religions, however, does not initially support this correlation based on tribal data. One finds, in fact, that transcendence is imaged or conceived in a variety of ways in that male, female, and androgynous deities are viewed as unique, dual, and multiple or that transcendence is beyond form, gender, and number altogether. Moreover, the imagery of transcendence occasionally changed in the history of a world religion. At the same time, the world religions maintained male social dominance in the prevailing social structure.

The lack of correlation between the gender of the deities and male dominance in world religions may be explained by suggesting that there was once such a correlation of male deities and patriarchal social structure at a formative stage of the religion or the antecedent or dominant religion in the area, but such a correlation did not always continue to exist.

Early Buddhism, for example, viewed transcendence as *nibbāna*, but refused to conceptualize nibbāna with reference to gender, form, or place. Yet early Buddhism had a patriarchal organization of society for its laity, and even nuns had to be deferent to monks. If we look to the antecedents of Buddhism in early Brahmanism, we find a predominantly male pantheon and the rise of supreme deities along with male social dominance. It may be argued, then, that Buddhism inherited this male dominance, but transformed the understanding of transcendence. A similar argument may be made for Hindu and Buddhist Tantra. While they expressed transcendence with female symbolism and even allowed for degrees of female religious power and leadership, they inherited a male-dominated society, which they never fundamentally challenged. Though Taoism's roots may have been deep in ancient agricultural religions with female symbolism, in some real sense, it too was formed in interaction with the male-dominance of Confucianism. Behind Confucianism lurked Shang-Ti, the male ancestral spirit of the Shang dynasty, who was transformed by the Chou dynasty into a supreme male god and identified with heaven, which was *yang* or masculine. Thus the Tao Te Ching, which was edited into is present form in a century of upheaval (250-150 B.C.E.), proposed to compensate male domination by the feminine trait of passivity in order to bring about a real reconciliation of opposites, the ideal of androgyny, and harmony in the kingdom (Ames 1981, 32-40). It was about the same time, however, that Confucianism was accepted as a state system by the Han dynasty as a way to bring order to the society. Order according to the state system of Confucianism involved the "three female submissions (*san-ts'ung*) to father, husband and mature son" and regulation "by the *yang* qualities of the male" so that the all-important harmony of family and cosmos would not be upset (Guisso 1981, 53). Since this concept of order came to prevail in China, Taoism never managed to change the patriarchal organization of society.

Hence, it is possible to locate a correlation of male gods and male dominance in the world religions by resorting to antecedent or dominant religions in a territory. The enduring factor, however, was male dominance. What was responsible for this male dominance that characterized the world religions? Sanday finds that male dominance is by no means a universal in tribal religions.[3] Rather, male dominance develops where there exist the antecedent conditions of an outer orientation and a separation of the sexes and where there is a situation of stress. These factors together generally result in male aggression as a response to stress in a negative environment. An outer orientation, according to Sanday, is when one pursues the power "out there" be it animals as in the hunt and pastoralism or dominion through war. Such cultures have religious symbols related to the stars, the sky, animals, and otiose deities (p. 110) or some expression of the power beyond. Because such activities take men away from the camp or home, there develops a male bonding and a separation of the sexes. The stress of war exacerbates the separation of the sexes, for male bonding is particularly strong under the severe stress created by the possibility of death in battle. Sanday thinks that real male dominance developed at a relatively late point in human history; by contrast the simpler societies have:

> a rather basic conceptual symmetry, which is grounded in primary sex differences. Women give birth and grow children; men kill and make weapons. Men display their kills (be it an animal, a human head, or a scalp) with the same pride that women hold up the newly born. If birth and death are among the necessities of existence, then men and women contribute equally but in quite different ways to the continuance of life and hence of culture. The evidence ... suggests that, all other things being equal, the power to give life is as highly valued as the power to take it away (Sanday 1981, 5).

Rita Gross in her study of the Australian Aborigines in this volume notes that women's life crisis ceremonies chiefly revolve around menstruation and childbirth; menstruation, for instance "is generally the most significant event in a woman's ritual progression ... to the religiously significant status of womanhood" and the ritual pattern "is identical to that found in men's rituals," which does "not bear out an interpretation that women are 'profane' creatures with only very limited religious practices," as some earlier scholars thought. The tribal symmetry noted by Sanday and Gross needs to be compared to the data from the world religions, which has complementarity situated within the asymmetry of male dominance.

From this discussion, we should see if the world religions (or at least their antecedent or dominant religions) had an outer orientation involving a strong separation of the sexes as their prior conditions and whether their formative period occurred during a period of great stress and strong male dominance.

A quick survey shows that the formative period of the older world religions—Judaism, early Brahmanism, and Confucianism—which influenced the others by defining the prevailing social structure, did indeed develop extreme male dominance at a time of great stress, which was preceded by the outward orientations of pastoralism, migration, or wars. This observation takes us to the work of Eli Sagan, whose cross-cultural study of societies engaged in warfare and building kingdoms provides some important clues for why we find supreme male deities and extreme male dominance at this moment of history.

Sagan's thesis is that societies pass through a state of development from the social cohesion provided by kinship and the confederation of tribes to a centralized monarchy, which is organized by loyalty to the king and fear of his power to oppress. These societies develop a hierarchically ordered social system, rich cultures full of imaginative and differentiated cultural forms such as epic poetry and theatre, and a religious orientation based on a sacrificial complex. The period of Indian history from about the ninth to third centuries B.C.E., for instance, reflects the same diagnostic features discovered by Sagan for a number of Polynesian and African societies when there was a radical transformation of the value system as kingdoms or "complex societies" developed. While the development of kingdoms arose earlier in ancient Israel and China, there continued to be warfare and power struggles, for the early kingdoms were fragile in structure and easily collapsed by wars among chiefs or vassals or neighboring powers extending their empires. For instance, during the Babylonian captivity preservation of ethnic identity became a problem for Jews and theories of dualism prevalent in Babylonia led to a tendency to view the cosmos in terms of conflicting good and evil forces. When the Jews returned to their homeland and had to reestablish the kingdom with all the tensions that entailed, there was increasing anxiety about women, increasing rigidification of their role definition and sometimes even a tendency to view them as evil, men as good. Similarly, "China's classical age was militaristic and masculine, characterized among other things by inter-state rivalries which often used women as instruments of alliance or subversion ... As she came to be seen in the age of Confucius more and more as a commodity, and as the thrust toward societal order began to gain momentum after his death, women became less free, and lost status" (Guisso 1981, 42-51). If we extend Sagan's thesis from the initial rise of kingdoms to a subsequent period when the stability and strength of early kingdoms remained an issue, then a formative stage in the consolidation of kingdoms, nations, and empires may be related to an increase in male dominance, and to a formative stage in the development of the world religions. It is my contention that understanding some of the features of the rise of kingdoms will shed light on certain aspects of the patriarchal world religions, but that the world religions represent an attempt to introduce moderation, values, and above all a sense of order to the political and social turbulence that surrounded the rise of kingdoms.

The development of kingdoms was an extremely violent stage of history. Kings and warriors fought for territory and dominion. The ideal of the king was omnipotence; "License is implicit in omnipotence ... the two great licenses are the sexual and the aggressive, and early kings were expected to exercise both" (Sagan, 1985, 320). With sexual license, "every woman in the world—save one—is food for the sexual appetite" (p. 319) and the man "who has the power to take a woman away from another man exercises a double tyranny ... the wishes of the woman involved play no part in the drama" (p. 291). The king expressed his omnipotence by demanding women as tribute from his chiefs. Harems developed; the issue was "ownership, not sexual pleasure or variety" (p.291). Sagan's description is similar to Sanday's diagnostic features for extreme male dominance: there is exclusion of women from political and economic decision making and there is "the expectation that males should be tough, brave, and aggressive; the presence of men's houses or specific places where only men may congregate; frequent quarreling, fighting, or wife beating; the institutionalization or regular occurrence of rape; and raiding other groups for wives" (Sanday, 1981, 164). These factors taken together indicate extreme male dominance in a society.

With the rise of kingdoms came an increase in male authority. According to Sagan, men expressed their dominion over their wives (and children) by being authoritarian: "'He had the best of the food, which was prepared to his special liking and kept waiting at his wish. Some say that the wife did not normally eat with her husband.... She was a minor at law in that she was under the control of her father, her brother, or her husband as regards the conduct of court cases.'" (from the King's Men by L.A. Fallers; see Sagan, 292). While this quotation is about an African kingdom, it resonates with expressions of extreme male authority from the time of the rise of kingdoms in India. There was a parallel between politics and family life.

Sagan also argues that along with extreme male authority, separation and individuation were features of the rise of kingdoms: "The crucial tabus had to do with women and eating. Men and women were not allowed to eat together. The burden of maintaining this separation fell on both sexes" (p. 90). The development of schools, according to Sagan, was a feature of the rise of kingdoms, and male schools extended the segregation of the sexes to education so that schools became exclusive male spheres and with this exclusivity developed male specialization. This was the birth of intellectualism, esoteric learning to keep the wares scarce and prices high, teaching by chanting, a concern with language and symbols that made the world "fuller, deeper, rounder, more ambiguous, more invested with meaning" (p. 105). Individualism, personality, self-advertisement, command, curiosity, competitiveness, and a sense of the dramatic also developed.

Sagan's psychoanalytic look at this phenomenon of separation and individuation is helpful in exploring male dominance and female subordination. Relating Mahler's discussion of the separation-individuation stage with its four substages of differentiation (six to ten months); practicing (ten to eighteen months); rapprochement crisis (eighteen to twenty-one months), and consolidation of individuality (twenty-two to thirty months)(p. 356) to the social development of the rise of kingdoms, Sagan notes that the third stage of the process of separation-individuation from the child's point of view is fraught with ambiguity and increased anxiety. This stage is difficult for both female and male children, but probably more difficult for the latter who must form a separate identity:

'As the toddler's awareness of separation grows—stimulated by his maturationally acquired ability to move away physically from his mother and by his cognitive growth—he seems to have an increased need, a wish for mother to share with him every one of his new skills and experiences, as well as a great need for the object's love.' The child is now face to face with one of the great ambiguities of human existence: separation, which is a necessary and life-enhancing experience [which] results in an intensity of separation anxiety.

[The rapprochement crisis] is the critical pivot of the whole separation-individuation process, critical because it also offers the possibilities of regression, of *undoing* what has been accomplished. . . .

As separation anxiety grows, the child entertains the idea of regression to the symbiotic stage as a mode of lessening anxiety. But his impulse, in turn, leads to a fear of re-engulfment by the mother, so that the child becomes trapped between two conflicting anxieties. . . .

In the traditional family situation, the child attempts to solve his fear of re-engulfment by the mother by turning to the father

. . . . We begin to understand why it is the king who leads the attack on the kinship system and becomes the bulwark against the fear of re-engulfment by it. For the small child, the mother is an omnipotent being—an all-powerful, all-providing, all-protecting, all-loving, all-hating entity. As the child begins to separate and individuate from the mother it begins to recognize that she is not a divinity but a person. This is frightening news, because the child thinks it must now stand completely on its own. The panic of having to live without omnipotent support drives the child back toward the symbiotic stage, but here again the fear of re-engulfment, the fear of loosing all the gains of individuation, keeps the average child from total retreat. One solution appropriate for this stage of development, something Mahler does not discuss, is to transfer the old omnipotence from the mother to the father. He now becomes the all-powerful provider of life's necessities, and since he is not the mother, he does not present the same threat of symbiotic re-engulfment. In the father, the child seeks to discover what we all long for: omnipotent support without the threat of symbiotic regression. That is why all kings, especially those in advanced complex societies, where the separation from the mother-kinship system is so recent, assume an omnipotent stance. And that is why most supreme divinities, especially in advanced religions, are fathers (Sagan, 1985, 357-60).

Sagan relates this male omnipotence to tyrannical men who protect themselves against re-engulfment and annihilation by "mothers [who] will eat you if you leave our protection" (p. 360). Boys identify with the father, a process aided in youth by initiation into male society and exclusive male domains, which helps them to disengage themselves from the mother. Sagan adds:

In my view, the male bonding that ultimately brings us tyranny against children, women, and deprived classes has its genesis at this moment. Fearing the mother's power to re-engulf not only their individuality but also their unique maleness, fathers and sons join together in the attempt to make females harmless through degradation. The society that males create reveals this intention (Sagan, 1985, 360).

Extrapolating from Sagan's analysis, I may add that girls, by contrast, had less opportunity for individuation because they remained in the home and their behavior tended to be defined by role models with personality relegated to the background.

If anxiety was increased during the rise of kingdoms and this anxiety was analogous to the anxiety experienced during the stage of separation-individuation in childhood development as Sagan suggests, then it should not surprise us to find that the mother represented this security par excellence, but because she was held sacrosanct by incest taboos, not to mention primal attachment, the anxiety regarding re-engulfment was not directed to her. Rather, it was directed to the wife or generalized to all women.

One finds male incorporation of womb symbolism in male initiation rituals, for the womb represented the attraction of re-engulfment, especially at the moment of initiation into manhood and individuation. To be sure this was a kind of womb envy. But womb envy may also be found in the warrior himself, who constantly had to face death and so may have envied the privileged position of women who, because of their primary role in the reproductive process, had to be protected and so could enjoy the positive role of supporting life through birth rather than death. An observation of Sanday's is helpful here:

> Though a few women have died fighting for the women's world ... the female role is not conceived in terms that make the acceptance of death in combat a possibility. Because the male role is conceived in these terms, the social body is sometimes entrusted to men as reward for being the expendable sex. Obviously, if women willingly embraced mass slaughter, there would be no social body to preserve.
> In cases of severe social stress or cultural disruption, the fighting takes on a different flavour. Instead of fighting the external oppressor, men band together and turn aggression against women. In these cases male dominance seems extreme because the whole of public life, that is, life that does not revolve around child rearing and family activities, becomes synonymous with the male collective. These primordially based male solidarities exhibit an uneasy strength because they are usually held together by fear of women (Sanday, 1981, 9).

Now we are in a position to understand why the rise of kingdoms is so relevant to understanding the position of women in patriarchal religions. Male authoritarianism, exclusive spheres, and anxiety regarding separation and individuation all contributed to extreme male domination. Male domination went hand in hand with the desire to regress to the security of the womb and with that went envy of women's own security and life-affirmation based on their role in reproduction. There are similar statements of envy in tribal cultures.

> The Mundurucu believe that women once had all the power in the days when the sex roles were reversed. Mundurucu men took the symbol of power from women; today they keep it carefully guarded and hidden in an inner chamber of the men's houses. This symbol turns out to represent the generative capacities of women (Sanday, 1981, 50).

What seems to be different between tribal religions and the world religions is that envy and fear of women is mythically expressed and ritually enacted in tribal religions, which may have contributed to their greater symmetry through recognition of women's power and the need for men to steal it. But envy was deeply repressed in world religions, which had as its corollary the asymmetry of male dominance and deep ambivalence regarding women.[4] Consequently, the envy of women was categorically denied by men and yet can be decoded in cultural images and stories in the patriarchal societies of the world religions.[5]

The source of this deep ambiguity regarding women can be traced to the conflicts created by male experimentation and wagers with death surrounding the rise of kingdoms or their aftermath. This ambiguity was especially prevalent with the new tensions between monogamy and large-scale prostitution. We have already noted how the king expressed his omnipotence by his posession of women he fancied. But the king also had need of legitimate succession to ensure his dynasty; succession had to be stabilized by insistence on monogamy by his wives along with primogeniture. Moreover, because the king became a model for society, extreme male domination and the ideal of monogamy on the part of the wife developed in the society at large. I have argued that Sagan's analysis of the rise of kingdoms is helpful to understand the development of extreme male dominance and that this development is related to the formation of patriarchal religions. The religions, however, are by no means a mere product of the rise of kingdoms, for they often try to eliminate the extremism associated with omnipotent kings and men and to restore values and balance to the society.

A case in point is the fact that all world religions are concerned with family stability. Whether marriage is sacred or contractual, whether it is mandatory or based on a choice, whether asceticism is "higher" and marriage is "lower," whether prostitution is legitimized or not, a stable family is recognized as extremely important for society and figures in the constellation of religious sanctions. A stable family was an attempt to bring order to a time of tremendous social upheaval and to provide for male security, identity, and above all continuity in the face of death. Patriarchal social structures became particularly significant at this time, for patrilineality, or descent and succession through the male line, ensured this continuity just as it reflected male authority, power, and control over other key social institutions.

Patrilineality was also a male way of harnessing to male ends the power of women to bear children and to render that power less threatening. In the past, women rarely challenged male control or attempts at exclusivity, for with these elements also came male protection, both physical and economic, which was supportive of women's biological role. Moreover, it was advantageous to women who wanted male support to accept the general patriarchal restriction of one husband so that the paternity of a child could be established and a woman could bind a man to her through his identification with his male progeny, his investment in male descent, and his transferral of property to his son(s). Because men asserted their status by relationships with multiple women in the experimental age of the rise of kingdoms, women probably needed the help of religion to ensure male commitment. Thus, in response to male licentiousness, women attempted to ensure male support. Even with the asymmetry posed by male domination, that asymmetry still had a kind of complementarity: dominance was exchanged for economic and physical protection.

This exchange, however, was not enough to overcome the deep tension between absolute control over women through patriarchal structures inclusive of monogamy on the part of women at the same time that men enjoyed polygamy and prostitutes. This split in attitudes to women and the tension between chastity and sexual license characterizes much of the history of patriarchal religions.

With a correlation between society, family, and the psychodynamics of child-rearing practices, we should expect a correlation with images of creative power. In fact, it was at the time when there was the rise of kingdoms that there emerged the concept of a supreme male deity, who transcended the cosmos and represented dominion over all, just as the king did in his kingdom and the man did in his home. For example, during the Babylonian captivity, Yahweh, who had been considered the particular deity of the Jews and associated with the temple at Jerusalem, became mobile, so to speak, as he continued to be associated with the people in Babylon; moreover, according to Isaiah, Yahweh was now God for all the people of the world, not just the Israelites. In short, by the time the second temple was re-established in Jerusalem, Yahweh had become a supreme deity. Similarly Viṣṇu and Śiva, who emerged as supreme deities in India, and Shang-Ti who became such a god sometime earlier in China are also cases in point. The extreme transcendence of these anthropomorphic and energetic "Divine Kings" stood in contrast to the older concept of deity as higher than humans but nonetheless on the model of kin and associates.

One discovers that despite the strong male dominance so fundamental to patriarchal religion, the world religions almost always have had at least one prominent soteriology that is gender inclusive. Salvation is available to both men and women. Indeed, were it not for this appeal to humanity and this ability to speak to the human condition, there probably would have been no religion worthy of the status of a major world religion that could endure to the present. It is no doubt this soteriological equality that sustained women in patriarchal religions throughout the centuries. Speaking of Judaism and Christianity, Sanday remarks: "The inclusion of other possibilities, no matter how buried these may be, is one of the reasons that Judaism and Christianity have survived as great traditions. If a people can find alternatives within their cultural tradition enabling them to meet current exigencies, they are strengthened and so is their culture" (p. 321). Thus, there is no necessary correlation between how transcendence is imaged or conceived and soteriology in the world religions. While the transcendent may or may not have a gender component, the prominent soteriology of a world religion is always gender inclusive, even when the transcendent is a supreme male being. And even in the latter case, women found a number of ways by which to express their spirituality and gain inspiration from the scriptures.

Now that the conditions for the development and continuity of patriarchal religion have been explored, I shall survey the world religions discussed in this volume on a continuum between male dominance (outside the home) and female power (outside the home).

MALE DOMINANCE: JUDAISM, HINDUISM[6],
CONFUCIANISM, ISLAM, CHRISTIANITY,
BUDDHISM, TANTRA, TAOISM: FEMALE POWER.

At the outset I note that Judaism, Hinduism, and Confucianism share certain features because they were ethnic religions in their early phase; as a group they generally acknowledge male dominance outside the home. Islam, Christianity, and Buddhism have similarities as universal religions; women were active in the initial phase, but later the traditions reverted to male dominance outside the home or were divided on the question of female power and leadership. Tantra and Taoism resemble each other because of their metaphors from nature and female symbolism as well as greater recognition of real female power outside the home, albeit with some degree of male deference.

Ethnic religions were associated with a special status "on the basis of complex, often variable traits including religious, linguistic, ancestral, or physical characteristics."[7] Their social structure was based on kinship relations with reference to family, clan, tribe, or confederation of tribes, and they were often associated with a certain territory. When ethnic populations migrated or when they were threatened by other migrants seeking assimilation to their culture, they attempted to preserve their identity as fundamental to their concept of cosmic order by emphasizing birth into and marriage within the ethnic group. Because marriage was generally mandatory and women were central to the preservation of ethnic identity, their religious significance was based on their role as mothers to provide continuity from the male ancestors who were worshiped in ethnic religions. Women were dominated to ensure the purity of the bloodline; strict male control over women at each stage of life by father, husband, and then son prevented miscegenation. The refusal or reluctance to allow a woman to divorce her husband or a widow to remarry were familiar practices in ethnic religions that were concerned to protect their identity in a hostile environment.

When ethnic religions were based on an outer orientation, had separation of sexes, and encountered a period of stress, especially the warfare surrounding the rise of kingdoms, they tended to develop strong male dominance and patriarchal structures. Accordingly, ethnic religions may be characterized by their patterns of inclusion and exclusion related to the separate worlds of men and women, and spatially expressed by the demarcation between inside the home and outside the home. These patterns, however, were asymmetrical with male dominance, unlike the symmetrical patterns of inclusion and exclusion in many tribal religions.

Denise Carmody speaks of the "covenantal monotheism" of ancient Israelite religion that was based on the conviction that the one true God "had made Israel his chosen people." The form of the relationship was the covenant, and continuity from the forefathers Abraham, Isaac, and Jacob was important. This convenantal monotheism, according to Carmody, explains much about Jewish ideas of ethnic self-consciousness, special identity, survival of the group, the importance of procreation and family life, and finally motherhood as the "raison d'être of the Jewish woman through history." Herein lies the clue to the Jewish woman's sacrifice for "her people's national survival." Patriarchal authority led to a regulation of all sexual behavior, including "strong effort to control women's sexuality," as well as elaborate designations of female impurity, and a refusal to allow women to initiate divorce. Exclusive male spheres developed in the religion, which had their antecedents in the pastoralism of the ancient Jews; the different periods of exile and migration such as to Egypt and Babylonia, which also involved control of marriage for the preservation of ethnic identity, no doubt contributed to male dominance and the separation of the spheres, which was portrayed in one creation account by characterizing the Fall as: men work, women bear children in pain. Moreover, in the biblical period women had a few religious roles such as prophecy, mourning, and temple singing, but they were excluded from the priesthood because they were deemed ritually impure on account of menstruation; by the second century C.E., the Mishnah excludes women from the temple, and they were not to "participate even in the cultic liturgy" just as later Rabbinic Judaism excluded women from the study of the Torah, which created an educational gap between boys and girls. A woman's sphere was the home. When the Temple was destroyed, the home became the spatial focus of Judaism, and the religious activities surrounding the preparation of food gave women a religious role beyond that of motherhood involving exceptionally strong power.

Similarly, in early Brahmanism in India there was an attempt to preserve the ethnic identity of the Indo-Europeans. The ancestors were worshiped and the family was directly linked to the deities, for they would visit only those homes where a husband and wife resided. A woman's role as wife and mother was praised, and she was to be the mother of sons. After the period of the Ṛg-Veda, which had witnessed an improvement in the status of women with the development of settlements and an agrarian economy, there once again developed great stress caused by the rise of kingdoms and constant warfare. This anxiety was accompanied by a concern with the pollution of women and virtually exclusive male spheres for education and asceticism.

In Confucianism, strong male dominance was expressed in the Five Cardinal Relationships, one of which insisted on the subordination of women to men. A woman was "'the treasure of the house,' responsible for the well-being of the family, loyal to her husband, persevering in her duties, nurturing toward her husband's ancestors and his children, frugal, and resigned to the guidance of the master of the house" (Guisso, 1981, 50). Predictably there developed strict separation of the sexes, related to a warrior society:

> To be sure, Chinese culture originated under the banner of pure militarism. Originally the *shih* is the "hero," later the official. The "hall of studies" (*Pi-yung kung)* where, according to ritual, the emperor in person interpreted the classics seems originally to have been a "bachelor house" such as prevailed among almost all warrior and hunting peoples. There the fraternity of young warriors were garrisoned by age group away from family life. After having proven themselves, they were armed and initiated through the 'capping' ceremony. . . . It is possible that ancestral spirits also gave advice there (Weber, 1951, 24).

Women, by contrast, had their world centered in the home and there was a strict demarcation between the men's world and the women's world. In the Li-Chi, which dates from the first century B.C.E. and is about ritual, we are told that "males had their proper work and females had their home"; according to the Book of Changes we find the most extreme expression of this separation of sexes: the good wife "perseveres, content to observe only so much of the world as she could see through the crack of her door" (Guisso, 1981, 49, 57). According to the Li-Chi, girls from the age of ten were not to leave the women's apartments; they were to be taught pleasing speech, manners, weaving, and to watch the sacrifices; boys, by contrast, learned reading, writing, mathematics, music, poetry, and martial arts in schools (Guisso, 1981, 58).

Another observation of Sagan's is found in Chinese patriarchal society, that is, the split between the chaste woman and the prostitute. For instance, there is great stress on the chastity of women in the roles of mother, wife, and daughter, but at the same time, Chinese society witnessed the institution of the courtesan. Men both feared and enjoyed what they perceived to be women's lust. The most famous woman on the model of courtesan was the Empress Wu, who had many husbands and male concubines along with her political and literary career, but was condemned as a "lustful woman" (*yin-tang*) by later scholars and historians (Sung, 1981, 72). While male dominance certainly contributed to Confucianism as a state cult and general order of society, it is important to note that the ancient Chinese view of harmony is also incorporated into Confucianism. Theresa Kelleher in her chapter on women in Confucianism in this volume understands the focus of Confucianism to be the cosmic order "comprised of the triad of heaven, earth, and the human," which was understood as "life-giving, relational, and harmonious in the interaction of its parts." Any interpretation of the perspective and role of women within the religion with reference to ancestor worship, filial piety, and the sacredness of the family thus had preservation of the cosmic order as its primary concern.

It is Kelleher's thesis that the role of women in Confucianism was to "mirror the cosmic order," that "women were identified in terms of their roles in the network of human relationships rather than as individuals," and that "their behavior was informed by the elaborate ritual code." Given this perspective, we can understand the source of the Confucian women's self-esteem and why they often "appeared more faithful in carrying out their Confucian duty than have the men." Kelleher's analysis is an important reminder that women played by the rules of the game, so to speak, but also exercised their freedom to relate to the religion in positive ways. Their concern for the harmony of the cosmos and their important role in maintaining it was perhaps more focal to their perception of the religion than the rules of decorum, with their stress on patriarchy, would lead us to believe.

From the above discussion, it may be concluded that ethnic religions were not uniformly fair to all women. Since it was through motherhood that women had the benefits of religion, a denial of motherhood obviously had catastrophic implications for a woman's positive spirituality and self-esteem. The "spinster," for lack of a better term, and the barren woman did not have direct access to these benefits and were more subject to negativity expressed by male and female alike, for such unfortunate women threatened identity and the concept of cosmic order. As Carmody remarks, "the greatest affliction an Israelite woman could suffer was barrenness. It made her pitiable, one judged harshly by God." While the spinster and the barren woman were usually supported and controlled by the family, the former represented the flaw of external factors or an independent spirit, while the latter bore a tragic flaw in female existence itself.

When women conformed to social rules and embodied the norms of sexual life, they fulfilled their role. Male control and responsibility were positively appreciated or were hardly an issue for them, for society and religion supported their biological role. But if, for whatever reason, they chose not to or could not follow the norm in an ethnic religion, they were often maltreated for their negative dependence on the family and their threat to the central concerns of the group. In ethnic religions, then, the religion and society functioned for the majority of women, but a minority suffered extremely, usually because there were no honourable roles outside the family. The woman who did not follow the norm was sometimes accused of sorcery, and in Judaism was "an abomination to the Lord."

Ethnic religions became vulnerable when their identity was threatened. Ethnic religions were based on particularism, but tension with universalism developed along with the rise of kingdoms which necessitated a religious symbolism and appeal to all groups within a kingdom in order to cultivate a sense of unity and loyalty. If the early definition was that one was born a Jew, the definition later came to include conversion to Judaism. Similarly, if birth as an Aryan (Indo-European) was important in the early phase of Brahmanical religion in India, the ethnic definition was gradually replaced by the conept of *dvija* ("twiceborn," that is, Aryan birth *and initiation*, which shifted the emphasis to superior knowledge and behavior), and finally by the idea of birth as a Hindu or birth into a particular caste. In short, ethnic religions began to take on a universal dimension as they sought to govern different groups in their territory or absorbed marginal or alien groups, as was often the case in China. While religion and culture became the critical criteria for belonging to the nation, kingdom, or empire, aspects of ethnicity remained, such as the importance of motherhood, purity and pollution, and a strict separation of the sexes. The Indian definition of caste as not marrying or eating with a person of another caste was a case in point.

Universal religions began with a reform that was so major that it was perceived in time as a new religion. The shift from ethnic identity to universal identity meant that doctrine and experience crystallized around a charismatic leader who initiated change to restore or fulfill an original order or to categorically transcend the social and cosmic order altogether. When the new group was formed, its identity was based initially on association rather than birth, and access to the soteriology was individual, though it often came to be mediated by the group.

Hence *experience* was focal, despite the fact that it was eventually ritualized. Because of women's participation in the initial reform and the universal dimensions of the new view, women not only belonged to the group but had direct access to the soteriology through their individual or group experiences. The corollary of the above is that the family had secondary importance compared to the group, though its value was by no means underestimated and marriage was sometimes sacramentalized.

The question arises: how did universalism affect male dominance? Initially it mitigated against it, for universalism by definition meant a religion for everyone. Universal religions, despite an emphasis on supreme male deities or extreme transcendence, which was related to the rise of kingdoms, stressed soteriological equality and placed emphasis on personal experience. For these reasons, women were included in the initial stage of the religion in activities that took them beyond the role of motherhood and the sphere of the home. This spirit of equality gave way in time to male dominance, legitimized either with reference to the male deity or the male founder of the religion, though the scriptural images of women as key figures periodically inspired women of later ages and occasionally challenged male dominance.

I begin this discussion of universal religions and women with Islam, for although Islam developed later than Christianity and Buddhism, I think that it has some structural similarities to the ethnic religions, because marriage is normative, and a woman's sphere, at least in the past, was in the home.

According to Jane Smith,[8] several centuries before the Prophet Muhammad there developed in the Arabian peninsula a patrilineal and patrilocal family structure, which viewed women as property and restricted their sphere of activity to the home. When Muhammad united the local tribes of the Arabian peninsula into a new Islamic identity, he found that women came on their own to give allegiance to him and they even participated in battle by inciting the warriors to victory through song and dance. The Prophet extended to them full and active participation in the new community. As Jane Smith remarks in this volume: "The earliest messages of the Qur'ān, and the twin themes that run through all of the chapters, are of the realities of the oneness of God and inevitability of the day of judgment. All persons, men and women, are called upon to testify to those realities. . . . Religiously speaking, then, men and women are fully equal in the eyes of God according to the Qur'ān." This equality included both responsibility to submit to God and the reward of salvation. Islam, like other universal religions, was predicated on reforms. Some of the reforms in Islam related to women. For instance, there was abolition of female infanticide, allowances for women to inherit, provision for them to keep their dowry, regulation of the number of wives a man was allowed to have, and an insistence on marriage along with a refusal to allow lax morals.

Despite its inclusive soteriology with reference to gender, the various reforms relating to women, and even to prominent position of the Prophet's wives such as the business woman Khadīja, Islam came to insist upon a clear separation of the roles of men and women. Even if it is argued that in the Prophet's own time this universal soteriology and the reforms he instituted resulted in ameliorating the position of women, it cannot be denied that according to the Qur'ān men are a step above women and are the protectors of women. The segregation of men and women became a hallmark of the *sharī'a* (Islamic law). Purdah expressed this separation of spheres visually, by interpreting the Qur'ānic injunction for women to be modest in public and a suggestion that the Prophet's wives were to be addressed from behind a curtain, to mean that all women should be veiled when outside the home. As Jane Smith notes: "Veiling and seclusion have been major factors in the lives of Muslim women, then, since the early days of the growth of the Muslim empire;" "early in the development of the community women began to find the mosque, the common place of worship, less and less accessible. As segregation became increasingly the pattern, it is not surprising to find them ... squeezed out of the more formal aspects of the Islamic faith." Given the analysis developed in this chapter regarding the rise of patriarchal religions, we can better appreciate how Islam fits the general pattern, for its antecedent conditions of a patrilineal and patriarchal family with women restricted to the home and later the development of the Muslim empire, which involved both wars and migration into newly conquered lands, contributed to a situation of great stress. Here are the factors necessary for strong male dominance. It is likely that when Arabs began to migrate to their new lands, some desired to protect their Arabian identity by strictly controlling their women in other to prevent miscegenation. The desire by some to preserve ethnic identity, despite the universal dimensions of Islam, may be one reason that Islam with its strict segregation seems to be closer to the ethnic religions. In any case, the custom of purdah helped men who were often away on military campaigns or for trade both to protect their women and to control them in their absence. In the final analysis, one also wonders whether the radical soteriological equality proposed by Islam that involved direct access to God without any intermediary, especially male intermediary, entailed at the societal level an especially sharp segregation of the roles of men and women. This observation is reminiscent of the strict spatial demarcation in periods of Confucianism, which also had marriage as mandatory.

In her chapter on women and Christianity, Rosemary Ruether finds a conflict between two views, "one affirming the equivalence of men and women as human persons and the other defining women as subordinate to men, socially and even ontologically ... through the whole of Christian history." The former had its base primarily in Jesus' appeal to "outcast groups," which were sometimes respresented by women. In the very early Christian community, women were included in major roles outside the home as teachers, prophets, martyrs, leaders of local churches, and traveling evangelists.

But this theology of inclusion with reference to leadership roles was quickly marginalized, perhaps as a response to Roman Catholicism's exclusion of Gnostic groups. The early Catholic Church continued some support of equality by allowing the monastic option for women. By and large, however, the Church became modeled on the patriarchal family in that generally monks had nominal control over nuns, just as husbands had control over their wives and the male papacy had control over both monastics and families.

The male papacy and male priesthood were both expressions of male exclusivity related to male dominance. Although celibacy was preferred, Roman Catholicism still viewed marriage as sacred and extolled the female role of motherhood much as in the ethnic religions, but perhaps for a different reason - to replenish the Church in the face of celibacy and to extend the church - rather than to preserve ethnic identity. But because of the simultaneous acceptance of female monasticism as an option for women in Roman Catholicism, necessitated by the soteriological equality in this universal religion and the initial involvement of women in the religion outside the home, it should not surprise us to find that the acceptance of female monasticism could be threatening to male domination. Men countered female power not only by male control but also by such rationalizations as that of Aquinas who builds on Aristotle and the early Church Fathers and argues that "A woman is inferior in her essential biological and psychological nature. She is weaker physically, lacking in moral self-control and inferior in reasoning powers" (see p. 218) in this volume). Accordingly, the initial equality of the religion, with its recognition of options for women, was situated firmly within the context of the male control of the sacraments and the ecclesiastical authorities, which was religiously sanctioned in no unmistakable terms by reference to biology.

One last point may be made with reference to Roman Catholicism. If independent female mystics and charismatics arose, a phenomenon which is to be expected in a religion that emphasized experience as a special gift of God, then their independence was also potentially threatening to male authority. Perhaps for this reason the Church found ways of institutionalizing such women, either by the founding of new religious orders in which male authority could be ultimately reestablished, or by officially recognizing such women as saints (with the implication that they were acceptable to the Church and its doctrine, which opened the way to regulating them).

On a similar note, Ruether says that new female religious communities were viewed by the Church as "hotbeds of dissent and heresy" which were "often modified and eventually suppressed in the struggle to win ecclesiastical approbation or avoid condemnation." Other independent women who could not be made to conform in practice or image to the Church as represented by male authority were then ignored if they posed no threat. If they did, as happened with the so-called witches, they were persecuted and burned, especially in times of social stress.

Protestant Christianity differed considerably from Roman Catholicism on the issue of women. When Protestants rejected monasticism, they eliminated the challenge to the status of the family. At the same time women had virtually no alternatives to marriage. But did this change mean that the role of the woman was once again akin to the role of motherhood? Though it was called a "God-given vocation," marriage for most Protestants was not a sacrament and motherhood did not have quite the religious significance it had in ethnic religions and Roman Catholicism. The churches did provide some roles for women outside the home, although most mainline denominations prevented women from having positions of power and authority in the roles of priest or minister.

The hierarchy in Protestantism remained Christ, man, woman. If there was simultaneously male domination in the home as well as in the Church, must this not have led to a strong subordination of women and perhaps be one of the reasons for the contemporary Protestant woman's deep concern with problems facing women in patriarchal religion? Ruether says: "The Reformation as a whole cannot be said to have had a liberating influence on women." Lutheranism, Calvinism and Anglicanism "inherited trends of both ecclesiastical and sociopolitical subordination of women," and, I would add, without the compensating sacrality of virginity and motherhood as focal to the religion. On this note, it is important to look at what happened to women in the main Protestant denominations who acted independently of male power and authority.

Despite the proliferation of orders in Catholicism, it was basically unicephalic because of the papacy. Such a massive aggregation of power and authority found it relatively easy to accommodate strong expressions of female religiosity through the institutionalization of female orders and the sanctification of charismatic and mystical women. In bypassing papal authority, Protestantism became polycephalic, with each of its various denominations representing individual aggregations of power. Hence it was more sensitive to the threat posed by female piety, which came in the wake of the Protestant emphasis on dissenting congregations, the renewed role of individual inspiration, and the appeal to the Gospels, in which women played an important role. In other words, when male power was localized, independent and powerful women were more threatening. Because their power could not be easily institutionalized, conflicts were often resolved by a trial (Anne Hutchinson) or hanging (Mary Dyer, the witches of puritan New England). As Sanday notes, when women no longer perceive male domination as real, men may kill a few women to reestablish their control. In short, there was patriarchal retaliation. To avoid such conflicts, many strong Protestant women were encouraged to become missionaries and to exercise their authority in far distant lands.

While retaliation or relocation occurred in the main Protestant groups, the Protestant emphasis on dissent, inspiration, and scripture also led to an alternate response: that of equal partnership with women as in the Society of Friends, or even leadership by women, as shown by Mary Baker Eddy's role in the establishment of Christian Science.

Thus Protestantism faced a deep dilemma. Jesus took women seriously, and they followed him; Protestantism took an independent conscience seriously, and so did Protestant women. Yet there was simultaneously strong male power, particularly at the local level, whether in congregations or in the home. The dilemma was resolved either by a severe subordination of women, albeit with appreciation of their domestic role, as in mainstream denominations, or by equality, as in a number of marginal groups. Because in the mainline Protestant denominations male domination was pronounced while in other denominations examples of female power were common, Protestant Christianity belongs to the middle range of the continuum.

For different reasons early Buddhism or Theravāda also belongs to the middle range of the continuum. Nancy Schuster argues that doctrinally Buddhism was always egalitarian: "the same teachings were given by the Buddha to his female and male disciples, the same spiritual path was opened to all, the same goal pointed out." Yet monks kept women out of positions of leadership and power. We may recall that like Christianity, Buddhism began as a reform but was perceived in time as a new religion. Here, too, the new group first formed its identity around a pivotal male figure and his teachings. Both men and women were among the early followers, but when the monastic order was established for women—which Buddha was initially reluctant to do until Ānanda convinced him that his own teachings had the premise that all human beings have the capacity for enlightenment—an additional eight rules were instituted for women to safeguard the authority and control of the monks. Thus there was male deference, though not male dominance in the early period.

Although asceticism became an option for women, it was kept under nominal male dominance. While both Roman Catholicism and

Buddhism preferred asceticism over family life, Buddhism unlike Catholicism did not bring the family into the limelight. This is not to say that Buddhism ignored the family or saw it as unimportant. A modified set of practices existed for the laity and a complementarity between monastic and lay persons developed in that the monastic person was to teach and the layperson was to give to the monastic. While woman as mother was obviously important to Buddhist society, marriage did not receive the sacramental importance it did in the ethnic religions and Catholicism, nor was motherhood glorified. Asceticism, by contrast, was emphasized because it was the avenue to salvation, even though the path could be postponed to another life. But although the cosmic or sacramental importance of motherhood was minor if not absent in early Buddhism, the laywoman's role as giver, symbolized in giving monks their daily food, had indirect salvific significance. She earned merit and enhanced her spiritual qualifications for the time when she would take up the proper path. Thus she too had access to salvation, albeit usually in some future birth.

The last two religions on my continuum are closer to female power and what Sanday calls the inner orientation. Along with kingdoms developed the need to govern them and to ensure their prosperity and harmony. At this stage, along with the variety that appeared in the imaging of the transcendent, there was a coming to terms with the variety of different groups within the kingdom. When the economic base of the kingdom involved agriculture, which was often the case, the king had to become more concerned with nature and rituals to ensure fertility or at least find substitutes to cater to these needs. As nature became important and the environment perceived as a partner rather than a hostile force, there was in Sanday's terms:

> a reciprocal flow between the power of nature and the power inherent in women. The control and manipulation of these forces [was] left to women and to sacred natural symbols; men [were] largely extraneous to this domain and must be careful lest they antagonize earthly representatives of nature's power (namely, women) (Sanday, 1981, 5).

When agriculture became important, the former outer orientation of the society adjusted to the inner orientation contributed by women. Related to the activities of the female world such as childbirth and food gathering, the religious symbolism projected power inward onto those aspects of nature and supernature that contribute to growth - the earth, the water, the female creator, nature deities (Sanday, 1981, 110).

Though in the patriarchal religions male dominance was never completely dislodged there was often a greater recognition of male-female reciprocity once the kingdom became stable, there was less warfare, and the economy was based on agriculture. At moments the strength of women made it appear as if they were simply playing the game and male dominance was more mythical than real. This situation comes close to what Sanday terms a dual-sex configuration. A clue to the presence and relative equality of the outer and inner orientations was the presence of both inner and outer religious symbols of power in the Weltanschauung.

The status of women improved because of the "permeability between the categories of female and nature" (Sanday, 1981, 5), unless, that is, men began to fear re-engulfment or became so fixated on the Great Goddess that they projected their fears onto women, which was occasionally the case with ascetics in Hinduism who were misogynists on the human plane despite their adoration of the Mother on the divine plane. A patriarchal religion such as that of ancient Israel, which existed alongside strong mother goddess cults in its formative period that constantly threatened to engulf ethnic identity, was more careful to sustain strong male images of creative power and define public religious roles with reference to men. Regarding the relationship to nature, there was great variety when we look at the spectrum of world religions. Tantra was a major movement in Hinduism and Buddhism after the seventh century C.E.; while it was not a "religion," neither was it a "sect." The often esoteric forms of Tantra attracted some women and allowed them to appropriate roles and religious activities generally reserved for men in the normative traditions of Hinduism and Buddhism. Nancy Schuster notes that Buddhist Tantra "counts large numbers of famous female practitioners and teachers in its ranks, and rises above other Buddhist schools in that respect." That laypeople could be *siddhas* (accomplished ones), no doubt helped make Tantra popular and especially attractive to women. Schuster observes that female Tantrics still faced much opposition from fathers and husbands but that "a woman siddha could really abandon all traditional female roles within society, even more radically than nuns did, for each siddha followed a unique path." In some ways, then, Tantra was a reversal of norms and accordingly was a complement to the normative forms of the religion; it provided alternatives, especially for women, that did not have to be officially recognized. But the radical stance or counterculture of Tantra, which may have had its popular base among the peasants engaged in agriculture, also made it more difficult for high status women to participate.

According to Barbara Reed in her chapter on women and Taoism, Taoism featured a great deal of feminine imagery. The Tao was unnamed but dark and mysterious like the female, and when it was manifested it was compared to the womb of creation. In Taoism, "traditional sex roles and biological differences were recognized but denied determinative status." Furthermore, there were no "sex restrictions for the immortal beings," and women served as models. While the overarching pattern of sacredness was the complementary dualism of yin and yang, the balance, says Barbara Reed, was grounded in yin. Similarly, it has been suggested that feminine symbolism such as the mother, river gorge, valley, and water "is highly suggestive of the concavity, openness, darkness and moistness of the female sexual organs and the generative vacuity of the womb;" these images act as a compensation to images of male dominance in the society as a way to restore the true complementarity of yin and yang and to emphasize the natural order as an alternative to extreme political control (Ames, 1981, 32–37). In religious Taoism, women attained the eight grades of perfection in a way parallel to men, though the path was only "male at the highest rank." Women were important alchemists, had their own monasteries, and served major roles as shamanistic mediums.

It would seem, then, that Taoism provided a powerful ideology and arena for women that competed with Confucianism. That religious Taoism was closer to the lower levels of society, however, meant that it was not always attractive to all. The control of women in the Confucian family was also an important constraint, though once the patriarchal norm was fulfilled, at least on a societal level, Taoism no doubt offered respite for some women. In this sense, then, Taoism was generally a complement to patriarchal Confucianism rather than a threat, except in those historical periods when Taoism had power. The same may be said of Buddhism in China, for the order for nuns was a refuge where a woman might find a home; it was also a place to exercise talents, especially scholarly ones; further, it was a place to practice religion in which the accomplishments of women were not considered inferior to those of men (Tsai, 1981, 19). Both Buddhism and Taosim provided alternatives to Confucian expectations, which resulted at times in intense rivalry between the two (Tsai, 1981, 19).

Now that we have understood how the religions may provide complements within the society and various opportunities for women despite the general patriarchal restrictions, we return to a discussion of stress as the hermeneutic clue for understanding why women's status changes in the history of a religion. If a situation of stress occurred and there was once more extreme male dominance and if the stress was not satisfactorily acted out with aggression toward the enemy, the anxiety was often projected onto women. Mary Douglas observes that concerns are projected onto women, who serve as a stage on which to control the dangerous forces they face, for the body is a symbol of society (Sanday, 1981, 92–93). If there were strong competing agricultural religions whose female symbolism and powerful women threatened identity, then female symbolism would continue to be anathema and women would continue to be carefully controlled.

It is impossible to go into all the details here, but my survey suggests that Neo-Confucianism, which followed a period of Taoist and Buddhist domination when women had alternate roles in monasteries, was particularly severe on women, as ancient Israelite religion was when its identity was threatened by the Canaanite goddess cults; according to Carmody, "Not only did the Goddess religion challenge Jewish monotheism, it also threatened the male dominion that patriarchal Israel assumed was necessary for good social order." Carmody also observes that when Jewish identity was threatened by the destruction of the temple and the diaspora into Babylon in the sixth century B. C. E., followed some centuries later by the destruction of the second temple (C.E. 70), fear of marriage with foreign women prompted misogyny against women in general. Following Mary Douglas, we can now understand that when men feel threatened yet cannot effectively remove the threat, they may project their fears onto women who become nymphomaniacs, temptresses, and categorically evil by nature. In a similar way, when Brahmanical religion was threatened by Buddhism and Jainism (not to mention Islam much later) and miscegenation with non-Aryans, it also reacted by curtailing women's activities. This relationship between stress in a society and strong male dominance is also found in Indian Buddhism. Although spiritual equality and a monastic order for women were established in the Buddha's lifetime, nuns gradually lost their status in India (and in some other Buddhist countries). Moreover, Buddhism itself eventually disappeared in India, the land of its birth. It is possible that as Buddhism began to lose ground in the land of its birth to Hinduism, this created anxiety in the monks who, in turn, blamed the nuns as responsible for the decline of Buddhism. The Pali Canon purportedly predicts the decline of Buddhism because of the Order for women. The idea that this passage is an interpolation by a later monk and attributed to the Buddha makes sense from the perspective that when men are under stress, they project their fears onto women and blame them for events beyond their control in the outer world. In all these situations, women, by demonstrating alternative roles or by threatening the ethnic identity through intermarriage, may have instigated male misogyny, which was then generalized to all women. This point is best illustrated by the neo-Confucian aphorism of Zhu Xi, which was used to oppose widow remarriage: "It is a small matter to starve to death, but a large matter to lose one's virtue" (Waltner, 1981, 130).

To conclude, this analysis of women in world religions suggests a particular understanding of the nature of patriarchal religion. At the beginning of this dicussion three meanings of the expression patriarchal religion were identified. How are they to be assessed in the light of this discussion?

The idea that religion itself is solely a creation or projection of male concerns seems to be excessively reductionistic given the varied images and concepts of transcendence and the encompassing soteriologies of the world religions that broadened their scope beyond the formative symbolism of supreme male deities. The danger of reducing religions to their origins is well-known. Since one enduring element of world religions is some form of male dominance in society, the expression patriarchal religion in the final analysis has reference to social structure, specifically to the family, which is structured by patrilineality, and by extension to other social and religious organizations that are controlled by men. That the world religions discussed in this volume continued throughout their histories to give religious legitimation to male dominance in the social structure justifies the use of the expression "patriarchal religion" beyond the correlation of male images of creative power and male dominance in a formative stage. Thus, despite their promise of soteriological equality and concern with the human condition, the world religions that grew out of an outer orientation, the separation of the sexes, and the rise of kingdoms supported patriarchy by generally sanctioning male control of women and by emphasizing exclusive religious domains for men as more important than the domestic sphere of women. The androcentrism of religious texts written by men reflects this state of affairs. At the same time, it is recognized that male dominance and spheres of exclusivity are not unrelated to women's concerns. Furthermore, the home as the woman's sphere of activity and concern was often a locus of female power despite male dominance in the outer world.

Thus I agree with Sanday that the expression "patriarchal religion" refers to a complex social and historical reality that has primary reference not only to the differentiation of the sexes but also factors of environment, human subsistence activities, and physical and emotional needs. Her analysis of male dominance in tribal societies was extremely helpful in understanding the antecedents of male dominance in patriarchal religion. The work of Eli Sagan provided another set of correlations that characterize the rise of kingdoms. These correlations helped me to determine the historical stage of development for the formation of patriarchal religions, which Sanday suggested occurred quite late in human history. Her analysis of factors for change in the scripts of sex-roles was valuable in studying the variety of sex-roles that appeared even within the patriarchal religions as responses to changing conditions.

In the final analysis, it may be argued that patriarchal religions are predicated on a stress syndrome. There is a correlation of stress points: historical, psychological, sociological, and biological. From the historical perspective, a pivotal or foundational epoch in the world religions grew out of the extreme stress involved in the rise of kingdoms. This historical stress was related to the psychological stress observed in the stage of child development called separation-individuation, which was fraught with anxiety and ambiguity regarding women. This historical stress was also related to the social stress of male tyranny over women and children in the family as a mirror of the king's omnipotence and male ambiguity regarding chastity and sexual license. If the world religions grew out of a situation of extreme stress and were, in part, formed by this milieu, they also responded to this stress syndrome by searching for a new order and vision of harmony. Focal to this order was a stable family structure and careful definition of gender roles, which reflected the male dominance of the age but also tried to tame it by ensuring economic and physical protection of women. In fact, underlying the androcentric religious texts of the world religions was a kind of reciprocity between the sexes, a reciprocity that must be phenomenologically appreciated as an improvement on the extremism posed by the rise of kingdoms yet nuanced by that very extremism.

All said and done, however, I am struck by that fact that even when women have real power as in a number of tribal societies, they still subscribe to what Susan Carol Rogers calls mythical male dominance, a game of deference (Sanday, 1980, 165). Occasionally in the world religions as well it seems that women are but playing a game. My favorite example from Hinduism is how women of a Hindu household in India—women, we must remember, who were to view their husbands as god and raise their sons with great service and devotion— gather at the time of the marriage of one of their male kin to chide him mercilessly on all his shortcomings that make him intolerable and undesirable, and that, too, in the presence of his prospective bride. The near universal occurrence of real or mythical male dominance makes me wonder whether the male perception of women relates in the ultimate analysis to male perception of female biology, which gives women a positive role in the life process and the privileged position of being protected to ensure the continuity of the group or even the species. I find myself asking the question whether real and mythical male dominance is not a way to render female biological power less threatening. For the female power to bear children, which is exclusive to women aside from the minor male act of impregnation, is potentially a power that can lead to female domination. That women can withdraw their services of reproduction, can dominate male offspring and consequently men through a radical form of matrilineality, and can choose who would father a child all have potential to threaten men. Could it be that the asymmetry created by women's biology in itself creates a situation of stress for men and this makes men want to redress this imbalance, which leads at the very minimum to an insistence on deference or mythical male dominance? If this is so, our religious and cultural expressions reveal not only a primary reference to the differentiation of the sexes in the various sex-role plans but also to the male perception of the same. Rita Gross observes in her study of the Australian Aborigines in this volume that there is:

a sort of fascination with women and women's biological functions, [for] the complex of men's religion also involves ritual duplication of childbirth and menstruation. The women serve as models for men ... 'many of the rites which men carry out themselves, away from women, imitate symbolically, physiological functions peculiar to women. The idea is that these are natural to women, but where men are concerned, they must be reproduced in ritual form' (Berndt and Berndt, 964, 221) ... A boy's initiation, marked by circumcision, signifies death to the world of women and children and rebirth into the male world. But the circumcizers behave like male mothers and the novices are thought of as their infants. Before the circumcision, but after the boys have been taken from their mothers, they are sometimes carried about by their fathers in the same way women carry babies (Warner, 257). After the operation, the pattern continues. The initiators imitate women in childbirth ... The newly circumcised boys learn from men how to behave in their new role, just as babies learn from women. The novices learn a totemic language unknown to women, which parallels their learning to talk when they were babies. Finally the boys are ceremonially exhibited as new beings by the men who have transformed them and seen them through rebirth, just as a girl is exhibited after her first menstrual seclusion.

It is a biological fact that women alone can bear children, but it is fallacious to deduce from this fact that the religious position of women is biologically rather than culturally determined. Their position in all its variety is not only related to the fact that they bear children, but by the male response to that fact. This response involves at the very minimum some nominal compensation such as deference.

Mythical male dominance arises when women seek to maintain their power base while leaving men room to maneuver. For example, women may react to the male attempt to seize control by "playing the game" of balancing formal male power against informal female power. Females seem to respond to stress in these instances by striking a conciliatory note. In other instances women fight for their rights. They succeed unless men kill a few token women to show that the battle for male domination is real. In these cases women acquiesce. They do not believe that "the trees that bear the fruit" or "the mothers of men" should die. If there is a basic difference between sexes, other than the differences associated with human reproductivity, it is that women as a group have not willingly faced death in violent conflict. This fact, perhaps more than any other, explains why men have sometimes become the dominating sex (Sanday, 1981, 210).

The truth of the matter is that women generally have not had to subject themselves to the possibility of death in conflict, because of the male role to protect women (although the phenomenon of the female warrior is not unknown). The serious problem lies, of course, with the restriction of female roles and male misogyny, which is sometimes found in the histories of the patriarchal religions. Although the world religions have had a special type of complementarity at their core and have functioned over long periods of time, they are no longer acceptable to many people, men and women alike, within many societies in the modern world. It would therefore be valuable to look again at all the negative factors that have resulted from the old models of complementarity operating in the world religions, lest we forget the extreme price that women in particular, but also men, have paid. We must be grateful for the researches of concerned women who have scrutinized the human damage that occurred when women were controlled and subordinated within or outside the home as a result of the male attempt to redress the asymmetrical powers of biology and come to terms with the environment and other needs.

In particular, though a religion's concern for a stable family structure may be appreciated, the great hardship that the single woman underwent because of the emphasis many world religions placed on motherhood should not be forgotten. Moreover, in the most extreme expressions of male exclusivity with reference to knowledge, cultural creativity, and action outside the home, we are shocked at the image of woman as ignorant and incapable by virtue of her biology. This perspective may lead to viewing woman as inhuman and to inhuman treatment.

This problem concerns men as much as it does women. A wife or female companion who is ignorant or insecure outside the circle of intimate relationships or who is so bored and frustrated by family routines or is even neurotic through male control and domestic confinement is neither a healthy person nor is able to relate well to others. Today's connotation of the expression patriarchal religion as male oppression of women stems from the feminist critique of such negative repercussions of patriarchal religions. In the light of these repercussions, such religious, cultural, and intellectual achievements as were made by women in the past call for even greater appreciation.

We are in the midst of a major change in religion and society. A number of factors are responsible for this change: concepts of equality that inform political consciousness, technological advances to prevent or plan motherhood, women's growing competition in traditionally male arenas and the confidence which that has engendered, as well as awareness of the negative dimensions of patriarchy.

We cannot move back in time to an old social order. It is my assessment that the world religions are flexible enough to absorb these changes, for their dominant soteriologies are already gender-inclusive and the histories of some of them demonstrate that images of the transcendent may change their gender or even move beyond gender as societies change. The real issue is what to do about the sociologies that they endorse. While it may be possible to develop a real harmony based on attitudes supportive of equivalence, we may be naive if we are not sensitive to certain male needs with references to identity and if we do not seek new deep structures to ensure a balance of power at the same time that we seek to expand the definition of female identity to include culture outside the home and positions of religious leadership. How to change the old sex role models in patriarchal religions that cling to extreme male dominance is the challenge of the future when we think about women and religion or, for that matter, just women and men.

There is also a complicating factor: the increasing secularization of modern life. The reader will have noticed that this introduction has looked at the position of women in world religions in terms of an intricate interplay between nature and culture. The modern secular world is characterized by the tendency of culture to be the dominant member of the dyad, as technology increasingly controls biology. What implications this general trend towards secularization has for the position of women in world religions remains to be seen.

I realize that I have gone far beyond the scope of the chapters of this book on women and world religions, just as I have gone beyond my own expertise.[9] The preceding analysis does not necessarily reflect the views of the individual contributors, though it may not be antithetical to their views. I should like to emphasize that although I have drawn freely on the work of the contributors to this volume[10] and interspersed my analysis with quotations from their chapters, I have built my own arguments with the help of Sanday and Sagan and may thereby have used some material out of context. This was a risk, and I hope a justifiable one.

Rita M. Gross

TRIBAL RELIGIONS: ABORIGINAL AUSTRALIA

T HE topic of women's participation in tribal religions is extremely vast and varied. Tribal societies have been found on every continent and have exhibited a great variety of economic and kinship systems. Thus no single description of women's religious lives in these various traditions could be accurate, and except for a few generalizations, this chapter will not attempt to discuss tribal traditions globally. Instead, it will focus on only one group of societies—that of Aboriginal Australia. Considerable attention will also be devoted to a general discussion of the methodology of studying women in tribal traditions. That part of this chapter is intended as a suggested guideline for studying the details and specifics of women's involvement in other traditions.

METHODOLOGICAL PROBLEMS AND GUIDELINES

For many years I have been convinced that methodological considerations about women in tribal traditions are both the most important questions on the topic and the only questions about which significant generalizations can be made. I am also convinced that unless one clearly knows *how to proceed* with one's investigation of women in any tribal tradition, one will end up with merely a jumble of incomprehensible details and with projections of familiar cultural values onto the situation being studied (Gross 1975, 1977, 1983; Falk and Gross 1980).

Significant methodological considerations can be grouped under three headings, the most important and basic of which involves the repudiation of androcentric methodologies, biases, and values in reporting, organizing, and interpreting the materials being studied. This repudiation represents a considerable challenge. Tribal traditions are often difficult to interpret not only because they are quite different from the more familiar religions, but also because much of the literature about them is highly androcentric. Thus someone investigating women in tribal traditions faces a double challenge. She must try to understand women's participation in a relatively unfamiliar religious context, and she must untangle the information about women and religion from its usual entanglement in androcentric scholarship.

Now that feminist scholars have worked with these materials for ten to fifteen years, there is more awareness of the existence of difficulties of androcentrism in scholarship and less defensive denial of its presence. Nevertheless, it is still valuable to define androcentrism and to discuss the methodological necessity to avoid it. Briefly stated, androcentrism is a tendency to think and write as if men represent the normal, ideal, and central kind of human, whereas women are somehow peripheral and marginal to that norm. Androcentrism pretends that humanity contains only one gender, so that one might readily speak of androcentrism as a "one-sex model of humanity" (C. Berndt 1974). Far more information is collected about men than about women, what men do is usually deemed more interesting and important than what women do, and society or religion is described as if it were solely the possession and creation of men. Typically, one may encounter statements such as, "The Egyptians (or whomever) allow women to ..." That kind of linguistic habit clearly reveals a perhaps largely unconscious thought pattern in which "the Egyptians" are the men of the society, while the women are not quite Egyptians but are objects about whom the real Egyptians make decisions. Thus most of the limited information about women found in an androcentric account is actually literally *about* women as they are viewed *by* men or *in* cultural stereotypes; we rarely find information concerning what women actually do, think, or feel. Views about women are important, but they certainly are not the complete information concerning women, and perhaps not even the most important information.

To anyone who self-consciously and deliberately holds the view that women, though perhaps different from men, are no less human than men, the inadequacies of an androcentric methodology are obvious and compelling. A basic paradigm shift that takes account of the fundamental humanity of women and of the fundamental two-sexed or androgynous character of humanity is mandatory. This paradigm shift involves a basic and thoroughgoing change in the model of humanity that guides the process of collecting, organizing, and interpreting the information that becomes one's description of a society, tradition, or religion. This transition is basic and somewhat difficult, as anyone who has experienced it will attest, but it is the only feasible corrective to the one-sided descriptions of, and theories about, religions and societies that have been so prevalent. Only with this corrective will we have accounts of societies and religions in which full information about women is integrated into all discussions. The special chapter or footnote *women and . . .* can then disappear. Until then we will need chapters and books, such as this chapter and book, that focus directly on information about women.

The second of the three basic methodological considerations involves determining the relevant information for studying women, not just in tribal religions, but in any religion. Three different kinds of information have generally been jumbled together in many androcentric accounts. Cultural stereotypes about women and men's views about women have probably been most consistently reported. Often goddesses and other mythic females are also reported and studied. But usually these two sets of information are thought to represent what women actually are or experience. The third, most important set of information—the actual lives, attitudes, and activities of women—is often overlooked, an omission which presents an obvious problem. This information should be of first priority for understanding women's participation in a tradition and also of first priority for understanding the totality of any tradition. When studying women in any tradition, it is important to disentangle these three sets of information and to pay some attention to all three, but especially to women's own lives and attitudes.

The final set of methodological guidelines has to do with recognizing the pervasive presence of sex roles in most or all religious traditions, especially in tribal traditions. It is important, first of all, simply to recognize how basic sex roles are in most traditions and how much they affect the aspects of a tradition that are available to the religious persons being studied. Once having recognized that to study a tradition one must study both women's and men's sex roles, not just some abstract situation, one may well wonder how best to set about that task. I would advocate studying the sex roles as complementary, by which I do not mean that men's and women's roles are equal or that women and men may not be antagonistic toward each other. What I mean is that however unequal or antagonistic the roles may be, they should be seen as together constituting the whole pattern of a tradition. I also feel that it is far more important to try to figure out what each sex role is and the pattern of complementarity than to try to assess the relative status of men and women. Frequently, assessments about women's high or low status are either culturally relative or an inaccurate projection of one's own cultural values onto the tradition being analyzed. In any case, whatever their status might be, women always have something to do with religion, and determining their contribution should be our primary concern. Even if we could establish beyond a doubt that a religion is extremely androcentric, it would not do to study it in an androcentric fashion.

TRIBAL RELIGIONS: SOME GENERALIZATIONS

To study women in tribal religions, it is useful to have some understanding of tribal religions themselves. Generally speaking, tribal religions are the widely varying religions of people at the tribal or small-scale level of social organization; usually these societies do not have a written script and rely on foraging or horticulture in their economy. Several characteristics that are common to the religions of these societies help to differentiate them from more widespread forms of religion. First, religion and society are immersed in each other and are often coextensive. Social identity and religious identity are barely separable dimensions of a single life-style. Second, religion is involved with the sense of the sacred and the inherent sacredness of the phenomenal world. Spirits or deities commingle with phenomena rather than being separate distinct entities. Therefore, phenomena are sacred. These two traits together mean that the primary concern of religion is world maintenance, the integration of the everyday or ordinary into the sacred cosmos. Ritual, sometimes inconspicuous, sometimes grandiose, is the primary method of realizing this goal.

In the light of these generalizations, we can expect that women's religious lives in tribal societies will probably involve both gender-specific and societywide ways of maintaining the cosmos and of connecting with a sense of the sacred, particularly through ritual. Probably we will also find cultural stereotypes about women which attest that women are responsible or partially responsible for world maintenance. Sometimes these stereotypes may be primarily part of the men's religion, and sometimes they may be part of a general religious outlook. One may also expect, if one examines the mythologies supporting the world-maintaining rituals, to find numerous female mythic figures of all kinds. Especially in tribal religions, however, the focus should first be directed towards women, not mythic figures, in our attempt to understand women's roles in those religions.

In general, women's (and men's) religious lives in tribal societies can profitably be studied as a *pattern of exclusion and participation.* By 'exclusion' is meant aspects of religion specific to one sex, and by 'participation' is meant aspects of religion available to both. This device allows us to see men's and women's religious roles as together contributing to the whole pattern of a tradition. It also allows us to focus on the specificity of each sex's religious roles as well as anything they might share in common. In a study devoted primarily to understanding women in tribal religions, one would focus first on women's religious lives in so far as they are unique and gender specific. Next, one would focus on the information about women revealed by those aspects of religion that are available only to men. Men's secret attitudes towards women, men's reasons for excluding women, and men's religious behaviors during men's rituals tell us a great deal about women. Finally, to study participation, one should investigate aspects of a religion in which both men and women participate. These aspects could involve almost the entire tradition or very little of it, and could be conspicuous or almost inconspicuous.

OVERVIEW OF ABORIGINAL SOCIETY AND SCHOLARSHIP ON ABORIGINAL RELIGION

The Australian Aborigines, the native inhabitants of Australia, were a foraging people with an exceedingly simple material culture and an exceedingly complex nonmaterial culture, especially in the realms of kinship and religion. Though fieldwork among them has been relatively late and scanty, interpretations of their religion and society have been widespread (C. Berndt 1981). These interpretations therefore constitute prime material for the study of methodology and preconceptions. Unfortunately, much of the literature is quite androcentric in content and also quite insistent on the interpretation that Aboriginal society is male centered, male dominated, and scornful of women. The most conspicuous example of this tendency is W. Lloyd Warner's *A Black Civilization,* which argued that men are sacred and women are profane and unclean (Warner 1958, 384). That interpretation of Aboriginal religion was challenged quite successfully in Phyllis Kaberry's classic, *Aboriginal Woman: Sacred and Profane* (1939), and by much of C. Berndt's work. More recently, others have begun to point out that the two-sex model is much more appropriate for studying all aspects of Aboriginal society. The simple portrait of a society in which men exchanged women as passive objects, men provided important foodstuffs, and men determined family residence in addition to dominating religion is somewhat inaccurate (Gale 1974). Finally, in 1983, the first book-length field study on Aboriginal women since Kaberry's work, Diane Bell's excellent *Daughters of the Dreaming*, appeared. It was not available to me when this paper was written, and so references to it do not appear in the body of the paper. However, the book, though very different in approach and in data discussed from my own work on Aboriginal Australia, does not change any of my claims or interpretations, but rather intensifies them.

THE PATTERN OF EXCLUSION:
WOMEN'S RELIGIOUS LIVES AND ROLES

In Aboriginal Australia, the women's ceremonies, like the men's, fall roughly into two classes: lifecrisis ceremonies occasioned by major physiological transitions, and periodic ceremonies unconnected with the life cycle and performed at various intervals for a variety of purposes, from enjoying the ceremony to promoting the overall health and wellbeing of the entire group. The dividing line between these two types of ceremony is not always sharp, though it is clearer in women's ceremonies than in men's. I will attempt to summarize many descriptions of women's ceremonies and to refute the older interpretation that sees them as "a pale imitation of masculine ceremonies playing little part in tribal life" (Abbie 1909, 125).

Women's life crisis ceremonies chiefly revolve around menstruation and childbirth, though some prepuberty rituals to enhance physiological maturation have been reported (Kaberry 1939, 98, 235). A woman's first menstruation is generally the most significant event in her ritual progression from the relatively insignificant religious status of childhood to the religiously significant status of womanhood. The reason for this importance lies in the significance of menstruation itself.

> Because menstruation was introduced by the mythical characters—as, so to speak, a rite performed more or less automatically by women (although imitated artificially in various religions, by men)—it has mythical sanction: it is ... not a mundane or or-

dinary state of affairs. . . . Menstrual blood is "sacred," declared to be so by the mythical Sisters themselves. (C. Berndt 1964, 274).

The details of first menstruation rituals vary considerably, but the pattern is always the same. The girl is secluded with other women of the group. During the seclusion men are avoided and various ritual practices are followed. After the seclusion the girl's return to the group involves a celebration and recognition of her new status. A description of the girl's return evokes the celebratory character of the event:

> When the period is over she is taken before sunrise down to the water, where all the women splash and duck her in noisy excitement. Then she is decorated, painted in red ochre and white clay, with a large painted dilly bag hanging empty in front of her. She is brought triumphantly into the main camp in formal procession, followed by an old woman who jokes and dances, clowning, stamping her feet, throwing her arms about, in contrast to the solemnity of the others: the girl's mother especially, is crying and wailing. . . . The girl steps ritually over a row of food . . . then sits down while more food is heaped beside her. Afterward she distributes this. (Berndt and Berndt 1964, 154)

This ritual pattern is identical to that found in men's rituals. A close study of both women's and men's initiations shows that innumerable details of ritual practice are also identical. Furthermore, before contact, first menstruation rituals possibly were much longer and more elaborate (Berndt and Berndt, 1951, 89–90) and probably included spiritual instruction (Gross 1975, 200–201). The evidence does not bear out an interpretation that women were "profane" creatures with only limited religious practices (Roheim 1933, 259) performing "pale imitations of masculine ceremonies."

Because menstruation is so significant, subsequent monthly periods are also ritualized to some degree. These ritual practices usually include seclusion or avoidance of men, as well as some dietary restrictions. Even today, though seclusion is impractical, some care is taken to ritualize menstruation periods (C. Berndt 1964, 274). While menstrual blood is to be avoided by men, it is considered valuable to women so long as they observe the rituals correctly. For example,

> at each menstruation until she is fully developed a young girl receives some of her own menstrual blood, which is rubbed

upon her shoulders by the older women. When she is mature, she may perform this duty for younger girls. (Piddington 1932, 83)

Those who have tried to see women as profane vis-à-vis the sacredness of men have imposed menstrual taboos on women because they find this aspect of womanhood the most profane of all. However, this interpretation does not seem to point to the true reason why men avoid menstrual blood. Menstrual blood is powerful and magical and therefore must be handled carefully and circumspectly, but it is not shameful or unclean. A menstruating woman is taboo, but she is not impure. This realization is extremely important for an adequate interpretation of the role that menstruation plays in women's and also in men's religious lives (Gross 1980).

Childbirth functions as a religious resource for women in much the same way. Pregnancy and childbirth are mythically grounded; female totemic ancestors underwent those experiences themselves and provide the models for women today (Mountford 1965, 49–50). In the relatively informal age-grading system that applies to native Australian women, pregnancy and childbirth mark another transition and another level of attainment (Kaberry 1939, 237). Childbirth ritual is secret. Children, younger women, and men are prohibited from the place where birth is occurring just as rigorously as the uninitiated are prohibited from the place where male sacred rituals are culminating. This prohibition is very widely reported. Even in those cases in which a medicine man attends some stages of labor, no man is permitted to see the actual birth (Mountford and Harvey 1941, 157–159).

Fortunately, the literature concerning childbirth rituals is richer than that dealing with menstruation. Phyllis Kaberry (1939, 242–45) and Ursala McConnell (1957, 135–43) have both provided extensive description, based on their field experience, of Aboriginal childbirth ceremonies.

Phyllis Kaberry's lengthy description is invaluable for its insights into the religious significance of these practices.

The old women and those who had children went apart with a pregnant woman and danced around her. . . . Songs were sung. The old woman examined her and then would sing. The women said it would make birth easier and charm the pelvis and the genital organs. . . .

As the moment of birth approached the pregnant woman left the camp with her mother and an old female relative, one of whom would act as midwife. During labor, songs were sung to facilitate delivery and prevent hemorrhage, the umbilical cord was cut and the placenta was buried secretly.... Mother and child were secluded from the men for about five days....

This ritual is characterized by features which would seem to be typical of that associated with most of the physiological crises of the individual:

(1) The observance of food taboos—this time by the mother on behalf of the child; (2) the spells and rites to safeguard them both during parturition.... (3) the remedial use of smoked con-kaberry bushes.... (4) the belief that the blood from the female genitals is dangerous to the men; hence the secret burial of the placenta and the refusal of the women to discuss it in the presence of men. (5) Finally, the segregation of the woman—a prohibition that is paralleled by the seclusion of a girl at her first menstruation and subincision. These two factors are so closely interlocked that they can scarcely be considered apart. On the one hand, the child itself may sicken if the placenta is found by the men or if the cord is lost; on the other hand, both mother and child, whether the latter is a boy or a girl, may be harmed if they have contact with the men until four or five days afterwards....

Now although the men know some of the details of chldbirth, such as the severing of the umbilical cord by the female relative ... still they are ignorant of those songs which are sacred ... songs which for all their simplicity are fraught with the power that they possess by virtue of their supernatural origin .... their efficacy is attributed to the fact that they are narungani; that they were first uttered by the female totemic ancestors. They have the same sanctions as the increase ceremonies, ... subincision and circumcision....

The whole of the ritual surrounding pregnancy, parturition, and lactation ... has its sacred and esoteric aspects, to the women, and which are associated specifically with female functions. They are believed to be a spiritual or supernatural guarantee from the Totemic Ancestors that a woman will be able to surmount the dangers of childbirth.... (Kaberry 1939, 242–45)

In addition to the physiologically based life crisis rituals, the Aborigines also engaged in women's *corroborees*, or secret ceremonies that were performed periodically for various reasons unconnected with women's biology. These secret ceremonies were only mentioned in passing by a few of the early ethnographers. They have been observed more systematically by Kaberry and C. Berndt and have been reported sketchily by others. The major sources give one the impression that while these ceremonies are expanding their range and are now practiced more widely than they were formerly, the general decline of the sacred life in the contact situation is adversely affecting the frequency, enthusiasm, and quality of their performance (Kaberry 1939, 253–68; C. Berndt 1950, 1964).

The general configuration of the ceremonies follows the same basic outlines of all Aboriginal secret and sacred activity, whether men's or women's. However, the ceremonies also involve some additional features that are typical of male secret and sacred activity, and that are not found in the life crisis rituals.

The ceremonies are held at some distance from the main camp, where the men are. Men, children, and girls who have not reached puberty are generally not allowed to attend. As in the men's rituals, a considerable portion of the time spent on the ceremonial ground is spent in various preliminaries which are essential to the overall experience. Women paint one another with various designs which have been discovered in dreams and which refer to various totemic ancestors. The patterns are sometimes painted with armblood (drawn from women) and down, a feature exceedingly familiar from the men's rituals. While painting, they sing songs, also discovered in dreams, which tell about the purposes and objectives of the rituals. After all the preparations have been made, some of the women dance, while others sing and provide rhythmic accompaniment. During the dances the women sometimes carry or dance around objects and emblems which the men never see and which thus correspond to the men's secret and sacred objects. They may erect screens to hide themselves from view, as men do. Sometimes food is brought to these ceremonies, which, being thereafter taboo to the men, is eaten only by women. Like all Aboriginal rituals, these ceremonies are performed for many reasons.

> The ceremonies include rites which can be used with other
> aims in view: healing the sick or wounded; stopping quarrels;
> "quieting" a man who is having too many extramarital affairs;
> or attempting to strengthen or restore a man's affection for his
> wife, or bring him ... safely home from a journey. In addition,
> some women—young as well as old ... stress the religious, or
> sacred, or Dreaming aspects of the ceremonies. Others again
> ... make much of the fact that the ceremonies are owned and
> controlled by women, not men. (C. Berndt 1964, 242–43)

THE PATTERN OF EXCLUSION: WOMEN IN MEN'S
RELIGIOUS LIVES

The Aborigine men's long and elaborate rituals, from which women are completely excluded, are almost the only data concerning women that made it into most accounts of Aboriginal religion. The fact that women are excluded from these rituals is the best-known fact about women's roles in Aboriginal religion. The vast feminine symbolism and mythology underlying the men's rituals are barely mentioned, and many of the subtleties about the exclusion of women are glossed over, resulting in a rather superficial but influential hypothesis that in Aboriginal religion men are sacred and women are profane (Warner 1958, 384).

In several contexts (Gross 1975, 1980), I have sought to replace that hypothesis with one that more coherently explains both men's exclusion of women and the attitudes about women that predominate in the men's religion. It is true that sexually mature women—those who menstruate and give birth—are rigorously excluded from men's rituals; however, in some rare cases older women past menopause are initiated into the men's rituals (Berndt and Berndt 1964, 181, 237; Elkin 1938/64, 88). Furthermore, outside the men's ritual context, women are not generally avoided unless they are going through menstruation or childbirth. When these subtle aspect of women's exclusion have been noted at all, they have been interpreted as evidence that menstruation and childbirth are considered negative symbols—the men's rationale for excluding women from their ceremonies. However, the avoidance of women's blood in both menstruation and childbirth is part of a very complex ritual and mythical pattern in which these same events also serve as potent and important metaphors in the religious lives of men.

Let us consider some of the men's myths first. (Many relevant myths are excluded because of lack of space.) The northern Australian epic of the Djanggawul brother and his two sisters illustrates one kind of response to women's physiological events (R. Berndt 1952). The sisters are perpetually pregnant and giving birth. During these childbearing activities the women are not kept separate from the man. Instead, the brother often helps his two sisters as they deliver their children. Although this myth dwells extensively on childbirth, there is no implication of danger and no ambiguity. It is also interesting that menstruation is not mentioned at all. Equally important is the fact that at this mythical time the sisters still carry the sacred emblems and perform the tribal ceremonies. Later, things change. The brother steals the religious paraphernalia and rituals from the women as part of a series of events that mark the transition from mythic to postmythic conditions. Only when the women perform the tribal rituals do the men participate in childbirth. Thus it seems that what was mythically an undifferentiated complementarity became in postmythic times two mutually exclusive, but still complementary, spheres.

The mythology of the Wawalik sisters, also from the north, contains other themes that can help us understand the men's attitude toward women (R. Berndt 1951, Warner 1958, 234–326). Few statements illustrate more clearly the ambivalent fascination with childbirth, menstruation, and women's blood than the central parts of this narrative. The two sisters are traveling, and the elder is pregnant. After she has her baby, she and her sister take to the road again while the afterbirth blood is still flowing. They camp near a sacred well, and the python residing in the well is attracted by the smell of blood. The snake causes a great storm as it emerges from the well, intent on swallowing the sisters. The younger one dances and is able to keep the python away, but she tires and asks the older sister to dance. She, however, cannot keep the snake away because the odor of her blood attracts it. Finally the intense dancing causes the younger sister to begin menstruating. At this point she, too, cannot fight the snake, and all three are swallowed by it. The sisters later revealed these events to the men in dreams, after which they became the mythic basis of the men's ritual cycle. Clearly the women and their blood are quite potent. Although the elder sister's mistake of traveling too soon after delivery had negative results, since that mistake is a mythic model often ritually repeated by the men, one cannot say that the menstruation, childbirth, and the attendant blood are evil, profane, or unclean—only that they are potent, fascinating, and ambiguous in their potential.

The men's rituals are even more interesting than their myths. It seems that, in addition to the avoidance of women and a sort of fascination with women and women's biological functions, the complex of men's religion also involves ritual duplication of childbirth and menstruation. The women serve as models for men and their rituals, a point that has been made by prominent anthropologists and students of Aboriginal culture: "Many of the rites which men carry out themselves, away from women, imitate, symbolically, physiological functions peculiar to women. The idea is that these are natural to women, but where men are concerned, they must be reproduced in ritual form" (Berndt and Berndt 1964, 221).

It is difficult to imagine an initiation that does not involve rebirth symbolism. Therefore, in an abstract way, any initiaton is a duplication of birth. Thus duplication of birth could be said to occur in almost every religious and cultural context, not just among the Australian Aborigines. However, one seldom finds such an explicit, self-conscious, and graphic duplication of birth as that practiced in Aboriginal men's secret rituals.

A boy's initiation, marked by circumcision, signifies death to the world of women and children and rebirth into the male world. But the circumcizers behave like male mothers, and the novices are thought of as their infants. Before the circumcision but after the boys have been taken from their mothers, they are sometimes carried about by their fathers in the same way women carry babies (Warner 1958, 257). After the operation, the pattern continues. The initiators imitate women in childbirth to the extent that sometimes "the old men build a stone fire and the men inhale the smoke and squat over the fire to allow the smoke to enter their anuses." The explanation given is that "'this is like the Wawalik women did when that baby was born'"(Warner 1958, 318). (Women who have just given birth go through this same healing and purification rite today.)

Novices and initiators are both secluded from women—a practice that parallels women's seclusion from men at childbirth or menstruation. The newly circumcized boys learn from men how to behave in their new role, just as babies learn from women. The novices learn a totemic language unknown to women, which parallels their learning to talk when they were babies. Fnally, the boys are ceremonially exhibited as new beings by the men who have transformed them and seen them through rebirth, just as a girl is exhibited after her first menstrual seclusion. No wonder circumcision "is said to symbolize the severing of the novice's ... umbilical connection. ... " (Berndt and Berndt 1964, 144).

Although not usually so graphic and explicit as in Aboriginal religion, the equation of birth and initiation is relatively common in religions around the world. However, male duplication of menstruation is much less common. In Aboriginal Australia men's menstruation is less widespread than men's childbirth but still occurs over a wide enough area to be germane to this analysis. Two methods are used to produce male menstruation. Subincision is an operation in which the underside of the penis is repeatedly cut until it is grooved from root to tip. The initial operation is far less significant than the subsequent re-openings of the wound, which can be done periodically, yielding large quantities of blood. The large amounts of blood are used as body decoration and glue for attaching down and feathers to the body, thereby transforming the man into a totemic dream-time ancestor.

Ashley-Montague contends that subincision is considered valuable because it allows men to menstruate, thereby getting rid of a collection of "bad blood" that results from sexual activity or dangerous tasks. Women lose this "bad blood" naturally, but men must take direct action to obtain the same result (Ashley-Montague 1937, 204–07).

Several authors who have written on the subject have made a further interesting observation concerning subincision. Not only does the male organ now produce blood periodically, but the operation transforms the penis so that it looks much more like the vulva. Thus the man can be said to possess symbolically the female as well as the male sex organs (Berndt and Berndt 1964, 146).

Groups which do not practice subincision also imitate menstruation. Among some groups, blood obtained from piercing the upper arm is used for the same purposes and interpreted in the same manner as subincision blood.

> The blood that runs from an incision and with which the dancers paint themselves and their emblems is something more than a man's blood—it is the menses of the old Wawalik women. I was told during a ceremony: "That blood we put all over those men is all the same as the blood that came from that old woman's vagina. It isn't blood any more because it has been sung over and made strong. The hole in the man's arm isn't that hole any more. It is all the same as the vagina of that old woman that had blood coming out of it. . . . When a man has got blood on him, he is all the same as those two old women when they had blood." (Warner 1958, 268)

Thus, the men's secret ritual life has a kind of double-edged quality. Men are introduced to a world that is closed to women, but myth and ritual proclaim that nevertheless this world is the province of women in important ways. Achieving the sacred status of maleness occurs through mythic and ritual appropriation and imitation of the female mode of being—even though women themselves are avoided. Then, once men are inside the realm of male sacredness—having made the transition by ritual imitation of childbirth and menstruation—the secrets that are now revealed to them can include myths about female totemic ancestors, rituals reenacting their adventures, and designs and emblems representing them. At a certain point, the male initiate in some groups learns of mythic times when men knew nothing about the sacred. One day, he is told, the men reversed that situation and stole religion from the women. The men's myth states that when the Djanggawul sisters discovered what had happened, they said: "We know everything. We have really lost nothing, for we remember it all,

and we can let them have that small part. For aren't we still our _uturi?_"
Contemporary Aborigines seem to agree with that mythic statement.

> But we really have been stealing what belongs to them (the
> women), for it is mostly all women's business; and since it con-
> cerns them, it belongs to them. Men have nothing to do really,
> except copulate, it belongs to the women. All that belonging to
> those Wauwalek, the baby, the blood, the yelling, their dancing,
> all that concerns the women; but everytime we have to trick
> them. Women can't see what men are doing, although it really
> is their own business, but we can see their side. This is because
> all the Dreaming business came out of women—everything;
> only men take "picture" for the Julunggul. In the beginning we
> had nothing because men had been doing nothing; we took
> these things from the women. (R. Berndt 1951, 55)

One could hardly find a more decisive statement that women's
unique experiences are potent metaphors in the men's religious lives.
Such a conclusion can be stated also in another form: it seems clear that
women's experiences provide men as well as women with access to the
sacred. By duplicating menstruation and childbirth and by identifying
men's blood with women's blood, men transcend the ordinary and
become sacred. They become the mythic models themselves.

Thus I would argue that when one carefully analyzes all the relevant data—the myths and rituals of the secret male sacred life and not
just men's ritual avoidance of women—a different interpretation of the
relationship between the men's sacred life and the exclusion of women
must emerge. Men's avoidance of women is only part of the total picture. It is one element of an ambiguous, ambivalent reaction to an incredibly potent and significant presence. Therefore, the exclusion of
women is part of a typical avoidance-attraction pattern relating to that
which is perceived as sacred and should not be interpreted as indicating
religious irrelevance or lack of value. Insofar as the term sacred is relevant, there is every reason to use it in interpreting men's ritual responses to women.

THE PATTERN OF WOMEN'S AND MEN'S
COPARTICIPATION IN MYTH AND RITUAL

Only a highly inaccurate study of Aboriginal religion would end
having discussed only men's and women's secret ceremonies. Though
coparticipation is a minor strand compared to exclusion, ritual and

mythical situations stressing a common ground between men and women do exist in Aboriginal religion and are of great significance in understanding the role of women. However, scholars have paid little attention to this dimension of Aboriginal religion. To be sure, the ethnographies contain countless descriptions of women participating peripherally in the men's secret and sacred ceremonies. But more subtle and significant kinds of coparticipation are noted much less often in scholarship on Aboriginal religion.

Two distinct kinds of coparticipation exist in the Aboriginal religious situation: ritualistic and ideological. Ritual coparticipation involves the visible, social dimensions of Aboriginal religion and situations in which women and men engage in the same rituals. Ideological coparticipation involves religious beliefs about the similarity of women and men and other aspects of the Aboriginal worldview.

Several important generalizations can be made regarding ritual and ideological coparticipation. First, ritual coparticipation does not necessarily involve equality or even men and women doing the same acts. Often women and men mutually occupy the same ritual space while performing different elements of the ritual. Second, despite the usual separation between men and women in ritual, in the belief structure surrounding these rituals one finds a remarkable insistence that men and women are identical in their mythic origins and destiny; that is to say, ideological coparticipation often emphasizes a kind of equality or sameness between women and men despite ritual exclusion in the same contexts. A final important generalization concerns religious situations on the borderline between visible social aspects of religion and the mythic world. These religious situations involve a fascinating exception to the usual pattern of exclusion and participation. Rituals of healing, death ceremonies, and the phenomenon of "clever men and women," the Aboriginal version of shamans, all involve situations of liminality, of actual or potential transition, between the ritual and social order, with its rituals for women only or for men only, and the mythic order, with its insistence that women and men have the same origin and destiny. These three rituals are also the only aspects of Aboriginal religion that break the usual pattern of ritual and social exclusion, demonstrating instead almost identical ritual practices for women and for men.

Ritual participation involves women and men performing different aspects of a ritual together at the same time and in the same ritual space. Such coparticipation is a relatively minor, but still important, aspect of Aboriginal religion, and quite important to understanding the totality of Aboriginal women's role in religion. This ritual coparticipation is quite varied. Almost every description of an Aboriginal ritual contains accounts of women dancing accompaniments to men's rituals. In some cases the women dance on the men's "sacred space," from which they are normally excluded, to consecrate it and prepare it for the men to use (Meggitt 1965, 289–305). Furthermore, women are actually involved to some extent in the most dramatic portions of the men's rituals. They participate in the separation rituals when the circumcision novices are taken to the men's camp, even engaging in ritual combat with the men (Elkin 1938/64, 179–81; Warner 1958, 251). They may dance at the edge of the group of men circumcizing the boy, fully aware of what is going on though unable to actually see (Berndt and Berndt 1964, 145). Dramatic fire-throwing combats between men and women sometimes accompany or precede circumcision (Gould 1969, 114–15). Women are also often called upon to observe or act in some parts of men's ceremonies or dramas. In one male ritual drama, several women dance the women's discovery of the bullroarer—that supreme symbol of the men's secret and sacred realm which no woman is ever supposed to see—"and the men hang their heads in fear" (R. Berndt 1951, 50–59). Finally, ritual sexual intercourse in the sacred space also occurs somewhat frequently in these ceremonies and obviously involves women's participation (Elkin 1938/64, 135; Kaberry 1939, 152; R. Berndt 1951, xx–xxi). This kind of list can be made quite extensive to prove the point.

Another widespread form of ritual coparticipation that cuts both ways should be mentioned. Often relatives of the person underdoing a life crisis ritual are expected to follow special observances in sympathy with their relative. Men follow this practice for women undergoing childbirth, and women do it for relatives being circumcized. The observances include food and speech taboos, scarification, and other ways of identifying with the initiate. For example, in one group, while her son is being circumcized, the mother lies in the same position in the women's camp as he does in the men's and keeps the same food taboos that he does. For several days before he is circumcized, she carries a lighted firestick which symbolizes her son's life. If she lets it go out, he will die. The night of the circumcision, she watches from afar, and when the men have decided the circumcision has been successful, they dash a burning pole to the gound and the mother puts out her firestick (Meggitt 1965, 289–305). Then she observes other practices to aid in her son's recovery.

What about these numberless examples of ritual coparticipation? First of all, Catherine Berndt, who knows as much as anyone about Aboriginal women's lives, says they are quite important to the women, who look forward to these ceremonies as well as their own secret ceremonies with "eager anticipation" (C. Berndt 1964, 261). Such a small detail adds much to a portrait of women's religious lives. It would be interesting to have a major ritual gathering described from a woman's point of view. It has never been done. Second, from the Aboriginal point of view, these practices are essential parts of the whole ceremony. They seem to represent ways that women can magically insure the success of the rituals. The total effect is a kind of collaboration in which both women and men are partners, using parallel and distinctly different modes of ritual behavior to foster a common result. Thus in some ways women's participation in these male rituals is not less important than the men's; it is only less spectacular. "All the men's 'work' may go for nothing if the women do not perform properly their part of the ritual" (Berndt and Berndt 1964, 221). Thus Elkin's statement that "we can . . . speak of sacred ritual proceeding simultaneously on two levels" (1938/64, 191) makes a great deal of sense.

Ideological coparticipation in Aboriginal religion also involves other concerns. For the most part, the Aboriginal ritualistic and social order seems to emphasize sexual distinctiveness and separateness; one might say that it emphasizes "male-izing" the males and "female-izing" the females. When this order is left behind for the mythic order, however, coparticipation seems to involve sameness and equality between the sexes much more than it emphasizes their differences. To understand this claim, it is necessary to understand certain aspects of the Aboriginal mythic worldview. Though space prohibits any detailed presentation of the phenomenon, it is important to note that Aboriginal mythology, like so many mythologies, is replete with the motif that women and men were more equal, or that women dominated religions, in the mythic "Dream Time" (Gross 1975, 117–37). This equality is also evident in Aboriginal views of the mythic origins and destinies of women and men. Before the beginning and after the end of each individual's ritualistic and social lifespan, everyone, whether male or female, resides as a spirit in the spirit centers found throughout the landscape. Furthermore, some groups that believe in the continued reincarnation of the spirit entities are also said to believe that those entities are incarnated alternately in male and female bodies. Upon birth, a person loses some dimensions of membership in the Eternal Dream Time and regains that membership only through initiations culminating with the death ceremonies, which are similar for women and men (Warner 1958, 5–6; Elkin 1938/64, 337). Even during life, this mythic disregard of gender has important implications. All of the most important elements of the male's secret and sacred life are subject to rules of inheritance that operate without regard to gender. Thus, though women may not know of them and cannot practice them, they can be owners or custodians of incredibly important male rituals or cult objects which are the most significant links with the Eternal Dream Time. More than that, the women do participate vicariously in all the ceremonies since, as embodied entities of the mythic Eternal Dream Time, they too have inherited and embody central representations of that true reality. The only difference is that they do not actively participate in the ritual expressions that go with their mythic status; instead, male relatives take on this task for them (Elkin 1938/64, 190).

Finally, the kind of coparticipation that occurs on the borderline between ritualistic and social dimensions of Aboriginal culture and its mythic, ideological dimensions are extremely important for understanding the overall pattern of exclusion and participation. The primary example of such a religious situation involves death and mourning. Healing rituals fall into much the same category, and closely connected with both death rituals and curing rituals is the work of the religious specialist, who both causes and cures illness and sometimes conducts a postmortem inquest. It is easy to see how borderline these situations are; therefore it follows that they would also exhibit transitional features between the ritualistic and social order and the mythic order.

The existence of women shamans in Aboriginal Australia is one of the more closely guarded bits of information in the ethnographic record. Yet practically every reliable major and or early source reports such people, without going into suitably extensive discussions (Kaberry 1939, 250–51; Spencer and Gillen 1968, 526; Howitt 1904, 393; Parker 1905). Since the religious specialist is at the heart of some important aspects of Aboriginal religion, it is disappointing to have the existence of women specialists so little recognized and commented on. Yet what literature does exist indicates that female and male shamans were no different, except that female shamans are alleged to be less effective at black magic and at killing people (Kaberry 1939, 212).

Healing rituals involve a different kind of deviation from normal patterns. In them, direct reversal is sometimes practiced. For example, in dire emergency, genital blood from a member of the opposite sex, normally a very dangerous entity, is used as a medicine. Thus a sick man will be rubbed with blood from a woman's genitals, while a sick woman will receive blood from a man's subincision (Spencer and Gillen, 464–65).

Death rituals are the most interesting and complex example of borderline ritual situations. On the one hand, they reflect the positions of both the deceased and the mourners in the ritualistic and social order; on the other hand, they affect the deceased's final transition from that order to the mythic order. Since practices vary greatly among groups and since the generic masculine habit of reporting has obscured some of the specifics about women's funerals, generalizations should not be overworked. But the available literature fosters the conclusions that, though women are mourned less and are expected to mourn more than men, nevertheless funeral ceremonies for men and women are far more similar than any other male and female ceremonies, and that female and male mourners engage in much more similar practices than do men and women at any other point in the life cycle (Elkin 1938/64, 331–33).

OVERARCHING AND PARALLEL MODES OF SACREDNESS: EXCLUSION AND PARTICIPATION IN PERSPECTIVE

Put most abstractly and succinctly, the pattern of exclusion and participation found in Aboriginal religion involves both overarching and parallel modes of sacredness, available to and expressed by both male and female ways of being. To understand the toal pattern of exclusion and participation, both modes must be recognized and understood, and their relationship with one another must be carefully delineated. On the one hand, both men and women participate in the religious life and are sacred; in that sense, the sacredness is overarching. However, at the same time, religious feeling is almost always expressed in parallel rituals for males and females.

It is crucial first to recognize the overarching sacredness, since if that point is missed, the parallel modes of expressing female or male sacredness will probably also be missed. In referring to an *overarching sacredness*, I mean that at a more abstract and general level there is a culturewide Aboriginal religious worldview into which the separate women's and men's religious lives fit as two members of a single class or as variants on a theme. Both myth and ritual demonstrate this overarching sacredness. Both men's and women's various activities and their very modes of being are referred to by the same Aboriginal worldview, which translates as "sacred." The uninitiated-initiated dichotomy, so important in the Aboriginal worldview, pervades the religious life of both. The basic concept of that worldview, the Dreaming, is the basis of both sets of religious activity, and women, like men, think of their ceremonies as given to them by the Dream Time beings and as fostering their reunion with the mythic Dream Time. The same overarching similarity is found in the rituals. Ritual practices are identical in their basic form for men and for women. For example, the same food taboos are imposed on women and men going through transition rituals or performing periodic ceremonies. In sum, if one simply discounts the physical separation and distinctiveness of women's and men's religious lives, it is absolutely clear that we are dealing with different manifestations of the same phenomenon.

However, in the same examples we also see parallel modes of access to the overarching sacredness. The religious life is characterized by rituals limited to one sex or the other. For example, although the same food taboos are kept by women and men at parallel life cycle ceremonies, those ceremonies also exclude the other sex. Yet though the ceremonies exclude one sex or the other, they accomplish the same basic purpose for each sex, thus illustrating the dense interplay between overarching and parallel modes of sacredness.

Aboriginal religion often demonstrates this complex pattern. Aboriginal ritual points in two directions at once. On the one hand, the rituals are based on Dream Time models and reintroduce the novices to the Dream Time. They are the vehicle for approaching the overarching sacredness so important in the Aboriginal worldview. Nevertheless, these rituals must also orient people to their parallel, proper modes of being in the ritualistic and social order; in other words, they must reinforce both male and female sexuality. They introduce persons to the specific sacredness of the male mode or the female mode of being, which is the only way an Aboriginal person can approach sacredness in the interlude between birth and death.

The full complexity of the rituals is clearer yet when we remember another feature. Despite the fact that sexual differentiation is dominant in the rituals of the interlude between birth and death, during which a person is oriented to his or her proper mode of sexuality, the parallel male and female rituals use *the same set of experiences-become-symbols*. That set expresses the female mode of being, especially it reproductive capacity as manifested in childbirth, menstruation, and women's blood.

This pattern appears to reflect a contradiction. One the one hand, men and women are both sacred. In that sense, the sacredness is overarching. On the other hand, a person can be sacred only in a male or a female fashion, but not in a mixed, intermediate fashion, at least not until old age or death. Despite an overarching sacredness, sexually differentiated expressions of sacredness are dominant in present-day empirical aspects of Aboriginal religion.

But the whole situation is even more complex. Both women's and men's religious lives move between two poles: the interlude between birth and death, otherwise known as "life"; and the prebirth and postdeath condition of full identification with the mythic Eternal Dream Time. This Eternal Dream Time is characterized by the overarching, nonsexually-differentiated mode of sacredness, while the interlude between birth and death is characterized by parallel, sexually-differentiated expressions of sacredness. Myth and symbol tend to be the characteristic modes of expression for the overarching kind of sacredness that is especially connected with the prebirth, postdeath, mythic Eternal Dream Time. Ritual, on the other hand, is the characteristic mode of expression for the parallel expressions of sacredness that dominate the life cycle between birth and death. Therefore, as we have seen over and over, in ritual sexual segregation predominates, while in myth and symbol, including every aspect of a person's life except for its ritualistic and social dimensions, there is little difference between male and female.

Since all the elements of this complex pattern of overarching and parallel sacredness occur simultaneously in most Aboriginal religious phenomena, great care must be taken to decipher each phenomenon, especially with reference to the role of women. Simple generalizations, especially those that depend on alleged differences in rank and status between men and women, are usually inadequate.

Katherine K. Young

HINDUISM

T HIS analysis of Hindu women is divided into three parts: the ancient period (ca. 1500 B.C.E.–500B.C.E.), the classical and medieval period (ca. 500B.C.E.–1800 C.E.), and the modern period (after 1800). Part I looks at the various strata of texts contained in the Vedic corpus, the *śruti* or scripture par excellence for most Hindus. It analyzes, in the context of historical dialectics, how Rg-Vedic values, Brahmanical education, and Upaniṣadic asceticism and "wisdom" contributed positively or negatively to the classical orientation of Hindu women. Part II focuses on ideals of femininity in classical Hinduism as represented by the *smṛti* texts, which are of secondary scriptural status. Here a phenomenological appreciation of women's domestic religiosity is attempted with reference to the concept of *strīdharma* (the ideal behavior of a Hindu woman); the influence of religious practices such as apotheosis, henotheism, sacrifice, *yoga*, and devotion on the lives of women; the ideal life cycle of the normative Hindu woman; and alternative images of the feminine. The so-called medieval period of Indian history has been subsumed under an extended classical period because the dominant medieval ideas and ideals affecting Hindu women were by and large an extension of the classical. Part III looks at criticisms of the feminine ideal at the beginning of the modern period, ensuing reforms and hermeneutics to advocate and rationalize change, the role of women in the Independence Movement, the position of women in the Constitution and the new secular state, and the critical assessment of development during International Women's Year. Questions of a strīdharma for the future are entertained as a conclusion.

The explicit limitation of this essay is that its exploration of images of Hindu women is based mainly on an analysis of Sanskrit texts that have a prevailing Brahman, masculine, and North Indian bias.[1] Yet to understand Hindu women, even today, one must gain access to the past primarily through available scriptural and literary sources, even though the absence of autobiographies and texts composed by women themselves makes reconstruction of the religious dimensions of women's lives tenuous at best. It is recognized that such an approach provides little access to understanding how women may have contravened, ignored, or redefined the ideals nor does it help us understand those lower-caste or tribal women who were not centrally influenced by Brahmanical values, thus making a largely "silent history" of women even more silent. Nevertheless, complementing the approach here undertaken, with its obvious Brahmanical bias necessitated by the largely textual treatment of the subject, is an increasing number of anthropological studies of the contemporary, albeit traditional, Hindu woman. With such contemporary recovery of the past being brought to bear on textual studies of Hindu ideals such as the present one, perhaps our understanding of Hindu women will grow.

EARLY BRAHMANICAL RELIGION: THE VEDIC INHERITANCE

The Vedas form the earliest and most authoritative scriptural corpus for Hindus. Consisting of the Saṁhitās (Ṛk, Yajur, Sāma, and Atharva Veda) and their appendages (Brāhmaṇas, Araṇyakas, and Upaniṣads), they are usually assigned the dates 1500-500 B.C.E.

The Saṁhitās

The Aryans who came to India in the second millenium B.C.E. brought with them the Indo-European tradition of the patrilineal and patrilocal family. Their religion, as reflected in the Ṛg-Veda, may be characterized as patriarchal, ethnic, family-oriented, and life-affirming. Preservation of male dominance and Aryan identity as well as desire for progeny, prosperity, and longevity were their goals of life, and the religious rituals to achieve those goals were based primarily on the family. Despite male dominance, woman as wife and mother was important to those goals; moreover, her role in the family and the rituals was related to the maintenance of social and cosmic order. Indeed, it may be argued that Vedic religion had an appreciation of both femininity and the complementarity between husband and wife, albeit within a patriarchal structure. This appreciation was probably an improvement on patriarchy in the prior Indo-European context. The semantic change of the term *dampati* best illustrates this point, for its former Indo-European meaning of "lord of the house" became in India "the couple," husband and wife (Shastri 1969, 18).

Much about the ideal role of a woman can be learned from the the images of the maiden and the bride. In the Ṛg-Veda the daughter (*duhitā*) and maiden (*kanyā*) were praised for their youthful beauty, radiance, appealing adornment, sweet odours, ample hips, and broad thighs. This description suggests an interest in feminine sensuality and the child-bearing capacity of the girl. At festival gatherings (*samana*) young virgins met eligible men; the flirtatious couple, after having initiated a relationship, turned to their parents for approval and the marriage arrangements. While there was some opportunity for romance unlike in later times, it may be surmised from the following description of the marriage ceremony that a girl was carefully watched and protected by her parents, for a bride was to be a virgin.

The marriage ceremony was elaborated in Ṛg-Veda X.85ff. (Sarasvati and Vidyalankar 1977, 37). Worthy of note is the prayer to Viśvāvasu, protector of virgins, to transfer his guardianship to another. The bride, who was called "fortunate" (*sumaṅgalī*) and "auspicious" (*śiva*), was decorated with ornaments. Prayers were made to the gods for the couple's good fortune (*saubhāgatva*), the attainment of old age together, prosperity, progeny, and the unification of hearts. In addition, practical advice was given to the bride. She was not to be angry or hostile to her husband; she was to be tender, amiable, glorious, the mother of males, devoted to the gods, the bestower of happiness, the bringer of prosperity to the animals, and a queen to the in-laws. The terms *jāyā* (a sharer of the husband's affections), *janī* (the mother of children), and *patnī* (the partner in the performance of the rituals or *yajña*) characterize the woman's role in the Ṛg-Veda (Shastri 1969, 16).

Because the religion, which catered to the well-being of the family, was centered in the home—that is, the gods were invited to visit and receive offerings there—the wife was present at these occasions and participated in the event through hymns of praise and gestures of hospitality. Both domestic and public rituals emphasized the copresence of husband and wife.

> The married couples, anxious to satisfy thee and presenting oblations together celebrate (thy worship), for the sake of (obtaining) herds of cattle. (Ṛg-Veda I. 131.3, Shastri 1969, 17)

The deities were receptive primarily to the family, whose minimal definition included husband and wife. In other words, the presence of a wife was necessary for the presence of gods, and a home was considered auspicious (śubha) only with the presence of both. Indeed, the fulfillment of life (happiness, wealth, well-being), the attainment of immortality (a paradisaical version of this life), and even the order of society and cosmos could not be had apart from this context. For example:

> For the sake of immortality, enjoying personal union, they (wife and husband) worship the gods. (Rg-Veda VIII.31. Sarasvati and Vidyalankar 1977, 42).

While woman as wife and mother was esteemed, the husband's role was dominant, for as the patriarchal head of the household, he was host of the guests, the gods, and was primarily responsible for pleasing them so that they would favor the family with gifts. It has been suggested that the Vedic woman was never more than a silent partner in the Vedic rituals. There is reason to think otherwise, however, for under no circumstances could the gods be left unattended and ignored. Thus if all men were absent from the home, it seems logical to suggest (though difficult to verify textually) that the wife assumed the ritual role of host. In addition to her usual job of tending the household fire (which was never allowed to go out and was understood as the god Agni, the "mouth" of the gods, which received libations, grains, and other offerings), she probably performed the necessary daily rituals when the men of the family were gone. Hence the wife most likely had a minimal amount of training in ritual, which, in any case, was relatively simple in this age. Moreover, there is evidence that the singing of hymns (Sāma Veda) was the special expertise of women who were trained in music (Upadhyaya 1974, 185; Basu 1969, 40). Then, too, later images of the brahmavādinī (a woman who discourses on the sacred texts), which associate women with Vedic fires and Vedic hymns, suggest continuity from the Vedic period.

The Hindu tradition has remembered some women in the Rg-Veda not just as reciters and singers of hymns but even as seers (rsis: the esteemed religious poets of the age, later understood as channels for Vedic revelation). The fact that there were at least a few female seers cannot be seriously doubted, but it is possible that the later tradition exaggerated the number by ascribing the status of rsikā to female figures merely mentioned by name in a hymn (Shastri 1969, 23-30).

While it is now commonly recognized that there is no necessary correlation between the status of women in a religion and the presence or absence of goddesses, it is still of interest how patriarchal religions relate to feminine imagery on the divine level and whether changes in the pantheon can be related to changes in the position of women in society.

The pantheon in the Saṃhitās included goddesses and semidivine *apsaras;* they were numerous but of relatively minor importance. Some were portrayed as (1) figures of great beauty such as Uśas, the personification of the dawn, a dancing maiden ornamented and robed, who revealed her bosom to human eyes and (2) figures of great eloquence such as Sarasvatī and Vāk. Goddesses such as Aditi, Sarasvatī, Rākā, and Sinīvālī were invoked to provide wealth, protection, progeny, and long life. Pṛthivī, Mother Earth, was requested to be tender to the dead, and Aditi was asked to grant release from sin.

While goddesses were related to the gods as mothers, sisters, daughters, and wives, the last-mentioned relationship was common. It developed from the metaphor of the couple as a pair of natural phenomena such as heaven and earth or moon and stars, as well as from the simple extension of the concept of the human couple into the divine: hence the divine couples Indra and Indrāṇī, Varuṇa and Varuṇānī, and Agni and Agnāyī. In fact, the human woman, not the goddess, was the usual standard of comparison in Vedic metaphor and simile. Even the apsaras, wives of the Gandharvas, who dwell in water, clouds, stars, and especially trees, were mentioned with reference to a human situation, for they were to make propitious music for a passing wedding party.

Goddesses rarely received offerings at the ritual (yajña), except as a group on new and full moon days. Male deities were dominant in the pantheon, which corresponded to the Indo-European patriarchal organization of society. Nevertheless, goddesses were generally viewed positively, like the positive evaluation of women in the society, though there were occasional glimpses of a darker side to their nature. For example, Uśas as dawn returned time and again and thereby wasted the lives of mortals; she was mighty and ferocious, a slayer of the enemy Vṛtra, and yet a protectress of her worshippers.

The contribution of the Saṃhitās to the religious psychology of Hindu women in later ages was significant; in fact, it is no exaggeration to say that many of the values and images elaborated above inhere yet today in the religious ideas of the traditional Hindu woman. The direct point of transmission was the marriage ceremony itself, which was based on Ṛg-Veda 10:85ff. Through the centuries, woman as maiden, wife, and mother was esteemed as fortunate (sumaṅgalī; subhagā) and auspicious (śivā). Her association with wealth, prosperity, beauty, grace, charm, and splendor became enshrined in a later age by the idea that she was Lakṣmī, goddess incarnate. Moreover, the visible expression of these qualities in the aesthetics of feminine form, clothing, jewelry, sweet-smelling unguents, and flowers continued to connote the well-being of the family as a whole, which in turn was a reflection of the fact that the deities had blessed the family.

In short, without the life-affirming religion of the Ṛg-Veda, the religious psychology and sociology of Hindu women would have been radically different. Aspects of this orientation became embedded in the three classical roles of worldly life (trivarga)—dharma, artha, and kāma—which inspired the life of the householder and situated mundane values in a religious framework akin to the spiritualized materialism of Vedic religion. Thus, by classical times, women contributed through their ideal behavior to dharma, the order of family, society, and the cosmos; through their essential role in producing sons, they contributed to artha, or material wealth in the patriarchal family; and through their aesthetics to kāma, desire and pleasure. Much of the positive self-image of Hindu women stemmed from the Ṛg-Vedic Age. In my estimation, it is important not to give undue importance to later Hindu asceticism if we wish to understand the Hindu woman's deep and positive identification with the religion. From one perspective, inherited from the Vedas, she remained central to its concerns, even if from another she became marginalized or excluded.

According to the Brāhmaṇa texts, Brahman specialists became teachers because the hymns had become so numerous and ritual had developed such procedural detail that to acquire the necessary expertise one had to undergo long training. The place for education no longer was the family home but rather the home of a teacher. By and large, it seems that sons, not daughters, went to stay with a teacher for this extensive and intensive period of study. According to Taittirīya Saṃhitā VI:3.10.5, every brāhmaṇa male when born had three debts which he must pay off during his life: to repay his debt to the sages, he must dwell and study with the teacher; for his debt to the gods, he must sacrifice; and for his debt to the manes, he must produce offspring (specifically sons).

A daughter generally remained in the parental home. If her father were a Vedic specialist, she might be educated by him (this situation may account for the later references to brahmavādinīs and ācāryās as educated women who discourse on the sacred texts and teachers respectively). More likely, she would be taught only a few hymns and ritual details to qualify her for her future role in the ritual (yajña) as wife and to endow her with the befitting level of culture. Accordingly, a mother would train her daughter for domestic activities, and then the parents would arrange the daughter's marriage to someone older who had finished his studies and was ready to repay his debts to the gods and manes. That Brahman boys were enjoined to study and provisions were made for their education by experts, while girls were optionally and only occasionally given extensive education, gradually led to great educational disparity between the sexes.

While it may be tempting to explain this development by reference to misogyny, since that was one outcome, it may be attributed to the pedagogical situation as analyzed above, which was necessitated by Brahmanical specialization and the desire of Brahman men for an exclusive domain. It may also be attributed to the biological reality that youthful fertility was necessary for a woman to begin to produce the desired ten children, for a long period of education would appear to decrease the time required to ensure adequate progeny. In any case, the result of this development in education was the increasing differentiation of sex roles. For marriage, a Brahman man was to have maturity and Vedic learning, which were the prerequisites for occupation; a woman was to have youthful fertility, domestic skills, service and devotion, and the aesthetics of pleasure.

The gulf between men and women on the educational level widened considerably, and although the idea of different but complementary roles served as a good rationale for role definitions, this "short change" would have serious consequences for women in the future. In the Brāhmaṇas, women gradually became silent partners in the yajña, except in those rituals to procure a son or bless the progeny. Their necessary presence at the yajña was debated. As the importance of a son increased—he was the boat that carried his father to heaven—rituals to prevent the birth of a girl came into vogue and daughters began to be disparaged. Moreover, as the polarity of pure (śauca) and impure (aśauca) became popular as a religious category, women came to be viewed increasingly as impure at times of menstruation and pregnancy (Kane 1974, 2:803). There were statements in the Brāhmaṇas that women were forbidden to go to the assembly, that they must take food after the husband, that they were powerless, that they had no inheritance, and that they spoke more humbly than even a bad man. Furthermore, as polygamy increased, women also had to contend with the insecurity and competition created by cowives (Shastri 1969, 74–85).

The issue of Vedic education for women became especially significant in later ages in view of the fact that knowledge of the Saṁhitā and the vedāṅgas (the auxiliary branches of learning, such as pronunciation, meter, grammar, etymology, astronomy, and ceremony) defined the status of the Brahmans, who claimed to be gods on earth (bhūdevatā) and the highest caste (varṇa) in the social order. Along with elaborate ritualism, knowledge (jñāna) became the religious idiom of the Brahmans and, by extension, of others who were dependent for religious leadership on the expertise of Brahman men as priests and exegetes. But although the Brahman caste prided itself on learning, yet Brahman women were by and large without extensive learning in the post-Brāhmaṇa age. Moreover, anyone without at least some Sanskrit learning was viewed as asaṃskṛ ta, that is, as positively uncultured. The extreme of being uncultured was represented by Śūdras, who were of non-Aryan or mixed origin and were generally thought to be avaidika (without knowledge of Veda and vedāṅga). As such, most Śūdras had no access to Vedic ritual. If Brahman women were not learned (paṇḍitā), were they not like Śūdras?

Indeed, by the first century B.C.E., one sees that this equation was made in the Dharmaśāstras (Kane 1974, 2:594–95). However, despite this development, with its negative overtones, Brahman men could not categorically deny their women status in the eyes of society, especially if they wished to maintain status in the society as family men. They compromised in part by (1) encouraging women to be saṃskṛta (cultured) in certain aesthetic dimensions in the home and (2) stating that the high-caste woman is positively defined by restraints of behavior or purity. Thus, since learning was not considered essential for a married women and since there were few learned wives to emulate, it is possible to conclude that an absence of learning positively defined high status for a wife. If one surveys the centuries, one arrives at precisely this conclusion: education in classical and medieval times was not an issue for the majority of Hindu women precisely because they were comfortable with the above definition of their status. Even the occasional equation of woman and Śūdra could not uproot their positive psychology, which was based on the Vedic appreciation of woman as wife and mother. This is not to say, however, that the concept of Brahmanical education was not pivotal to the ensuing dialectic of history with reference to women, especially since chastity and purity became a substitute for knowledge, and this substitute led, in turn, to a view that women were ignorant and incapable, even if chaste and honored.

> The development of a social hierarchy based on notions of relative purity has had a doubly unfortunate effect on the lives of Hindu women. On the one hand it has led to the belief that they are, especially during menstruation and childbirth, a source of pollution as great as that associated with untouchables, and hence of comparable social worth; on the other hand, it has led to their veneration as pure beings whose condition reflects on the honour and status of their menfolk. These two beliefs, though apparently resulting in quite contrary evaluations of women, share in common the social concomitant of male control. . . . Whereas the impure woman is believed to be dangerous, to have a destructive yet potentially creative, capability, the

pure woman is believed to be herself in danger and hence in
need of protection (male control). (Allen 1982, 5)

Allen argues further that when hierarchy was related to an ideology of
purity, as occurred in the development of the Indian caste system, institutions were also formed to control female sexuality. Female chastity
became a major issue, for a man's status was not unrelated to his
daughter's or wife's chastity:

> The valued though potentially dangerous sexual and reproduc-
> tive powers of women are rigorously controlled by men through
> such extreme institutions as child marriage, purdah, no divorce
> for women, a prohibition against widow remarriage, and either
> the social isolation through stigmatisation [sic] or the burning of
> widows. (Allen 1982, 8)

In short, the Brāhmaṇas greatly influenced the classical position of
women by their contribution to definitions of education and chastity.

The Āraṇyakas and Upaniṣads

The change of perspective towards asceticism, meditation, and enlightenment which began in the Āraṇyakas (forest treatises) and
culminated in the Upaniṣads had repercussions on the religious orientation of Hindu women. The influence of the critique of the family,
ritualism, and relevance of the Vedas cannot be understood apart from
the challenge posed by the Buddha, among others in the sixth century
B.C.E., who declared the Vedas superfluous, indeed an obstacle to enlightenment (mokṣa), and criticized Brahmanical ritualism for its un-
ethical killing of animals and its creation of psychological dependence
on the gods and their "middlemen," the Brahmans.

The Brahmans' reactions to these criticisms was divided. A few
already shared or accepted wholeheartedly the new perspective. The
majority quietly instituted internal reforms but tried to preserve their
Vedic inheritance by insisting that expertise in Veda and vedāṅga was
necessary, though concession was made by some that it was preliminary or lower, albeit a prerequisite to liberation (vedānta). Accordingly, the Vedas were enshrined by being termed "śruti (revealed),"
"satya (true)," and "nitya (eternal)." The resulting synthesis produced in
the emergent Hinduism of classical times an uneasy coexistence between the spiritualized materialism of the Saṁhitās and the orientation
of asceticism and enlightenment characteristic of the Āraṇyakas and
Upaniṣads.

Because most women had no extensive knowledge of Veda and

vedāṅga, thanks to the Brahmanical system of education, and because Brahman men had to insist upon Vedic knowledge as the necessary preparation for enlightenment (to secure their heritage, occupation, and status), the majority of women were automatically excluded from Brahmanical definitions of mokṣa, since they could not fulfill the prerequisites. Moreover, because saṁnyāsa (renunciation) involved wandering alone (unlike the communal wandering of Buddhist and Jain monks and nuns), it was probably unsafe for women to pursue this path (Young 1982a, 939–42). Given the male concern with female chastity and protection of women, an unprotected woman was doubly vulnerable: without male protection she was, by definition, unchaste.

History has shown that women in the Hindu tradition (except in certain Tantric orientations) rarely renounced their familiar ties on their own to pursue liberation. At best, they followed their husbands, when the husbands were willing, to the forest, ostensibly to initiate spiritual development by observing sexual chastity and a modified form of renunciation but more likely to express their strīdharma by following and serving their husbands. Even if one remembers the two famous women of the Upaniṣads, Maitreyī and Gārgī, who engaged in dialogue about the nature of the True Self (ātman), there is no evidence that they themselves desired or actively sought enlightenment through renunciation or solitary wandering.

Maitreyī, for instance, asked her husband, who was about to renounce his marital vows to become a saṁnyāsī (one who abandons worldly affairs, an ascetic) and was in the process of making a settlement for his two wives, whether she would be immortal if this whole earth filled with wealth were hers (Bṛhadāraṇyaka Upaniṣad 2.4.1). Vājñavalkya told her sweetly that there was no chance to gain immortality through wealth, and, when pressed, he discoursed on the nature of the True Self. Maitreyī then admitted that she was bewildered by his words, and Yājñavalkya offered one last exposition. A second account of this episode (Bṛhadāraṇyaka Upaniṣad 4.5.15), which was probably of later date, called Maitreyī a "brahmavādinī", which can either mean "one who discourses on sacred texts or the Vedas" or "one who asserts the identity of all things with Brahman, the Absolute." The second account also gave no evidence of her Vedic expertise or philosophical bent; it did add to the first account, however, by noting that, after his teaching, Yājñavalkya departed to become a wanderer (parivrājaka). No mention was made of Maitreyī's destiny.

As for Gārgī, she can be considered one of the learned individuals who assembled at a great sacrifice (yajña) and challenged Yājñavalkya's claims to preeminence in knowledge. But whether she personally pursued mokṣa (enlightenment) is not entirely clear from the textual accounts. Nonetheless, the fact that we find some women in the Upaniṣads discussing ātman (the True Self) seems to suggest that the position of women in that period may have improved somewhat from the excessive male sacerdotalism of the Brāhmaṇas.

Only a few references to women teachers, ascetics, and wanderers survived; for example, "the very fact that Kāśikā on Pāṇini IV.1.59 and III.3.21 teaches the formation of ācāryā and upādhyāyā as meaning a woman who is herself a teacher ... establishes that the ancient grammarians were familiar with women teachers" (Kane 1974, 2: 366). Moreover, the Mitākṣarā on Yājñavalkya's Dharmaśāstra III.58 quotes a sūtra or aphorism by Baudhāyana to the effect that according to some ācāryas even women could adopt the ascetic mode of life. Patañjali in his Mahābhāṣya mentions a female wanderer called Śaṅkarā; and Kālidāsa describes the paṇḍitā Kauśikī as dressed like an ascetic (Kane 1974, 2: 945).

The overt prohibitions against asceticism for women increased as evidence for women's education decreased. By the time of the Dharmasūtras (ca. 400–100 B. C. E.), women were classified into two types. There were the brahmavādinīs who underwent upanayana, or initiation into Vedic learning, which involved keeping fire and Vedic study and begging, all to be done at home under the parental roof. Far more common were the sadyovadhūs, for whom the upanayana was nominally performed and who straightway married (Basu 1969, 214). By the first century B.C.E. upanayana for a women was equated with marriage and serving the husband was equated with residing with a guru. This analysis reminds us one again of how women compared to Śūdras, an equation that occurred about this time.

The association of women and ignorance, combined with criticism leveled against the family and desire from the perspective of an ascetic, culminated in a common classical view that Hindu women were to be oriented toward rebirth. By contrast, the goal of renouncing the world and attaining mokṣa or liberation from rebirth, underlay Hindu masculine thinking, even the psychology of the man who decided to remain a householder during this lifetime and postponed active pursuit of mokṣa to another birth.

Thus, while the life of a woman henceforth was divided into three main phases—maidenhood (kaumārya), marriage (vivāha), and (should the husband die first) self-immolation in the funeral pyre of the husband (satī) or widowhood (vaidhavya). The ideal life-cycle of the Hindu man was divided into four stages (āśramas) studentship (brahmacarya), householdership (gṛhastha), forest dwelling (vānaprastha), and renunciation (saṁnyāsa). Only in the stage of gṛhastha was the Vedic complementarity of role and goal shared by husband and wife (and that too had its patriarchal penchant now exaggerated by androtheism). Always lurking in the background, however, was the threat posed by the new situation of man's desire for saṁnyāsa and mokṣa, which had power to create psychological and spiritual rifts in the relationship, for the complementarity sooner or later would be broken.

The Upaniṣads contributed to the later position of Hindu women in a number of ways. Desire (kāma) and control (yoga) emerged as two poles that structured the classical Hindu worldview, and much of subsequent religious history explored how this opposition may be mediated. For the ascetic, woman represented sexuality, reproduction, and the family, the very obstacles to liberation. This representation was mythologically portrayed in stories of celestial damsels or apsaras who attempted to seduce ascetics; it was sociologically expressed in the ascetics' denial of marital life and their concern to retain their semen as a source of yogic power. Many misogynist passages in the texts can be traced to the perspective of an ascetic-in-the-making who stereotyped women as temptresses before he had conquered his passions so that he was truly indifferent to the world.

Moreover, almost all darśanas (religious and philosophical systems) that stressed the path of knowledge (jñānayoga) viewed women either as ineligible or incompetent for higher and critical stages of religious discipline leading to mokṣa. After the eighth century c.e., the philosophical school of Advaita Vedānta formalized a trend that had originated in the Upaniṣads and is the famous case in point for the issue at hand. Śaṁkara, the key exponent of this school, never married and established his order for men only. So convinced was he that women were ignorant that he refused to acknowledge that the term paṇḍitā in Bṛhadāraṇyaka Upaniṣad 6.17 meant a "learned women;" rather, he felt compelled to give the gloss: "a woman skilled in household words" (Kane 1974, 2: 366). Moreover, the feminine principle occupied a low position in Advaita Vedānta, for at the cosmic level māyā was the feminine principle of ignorance, and at the level of the path women were a snare. While the majority of Hindu texts stressed that a man should pursue saṁnyāsa only when his sons were grown and his hair was turning grey, Śaṁnyakara advocated that the spiritually mature male bypass marriage altogether. Śaṁkara was soteriologically more accomodating of women in his commentary on the Gītā.

Conclusion

The Indo-Europeans contributed a patriarchal social structure which was patrilineal and patrilocal. Accordingly, there was male dominance and sons were important. This structure was complemented, in part, by the Ṛg- Vedic conception of woman as auspicious, vital to the well-being of the family, and necessary for the presence of the gods. The tension of hierarchy and complementarity was already posed. The Brāhmaṇas sowed the seeds of educational disparity and periodically viewed woman as impure, a perspective which increased the hierarchical distinction between men and women. The Āraṇyakas and Upaniṣads added the ascetic perspective, which made woman a symbol of rebirth and also tied her to rebirth by such a radical definition of renunciation that she was discouraged from wandering alone. Moreover, because women generally did not have Vedic education and Brahmanical asceticism inisited on knowledge of Veda as a prerequisite, women's spiritual horizon became rebirth, not mokṣa, that is, until the way of devotion (bhakti) and and later Tantra offered some alternatives in classical and medieval time.

Finally, it is possible to argue that the existence of Buddhist and Jain orders of nuns also influenced the psychology of Hindu women. For, faced with an example of independent women in the society, Brahman families may have guarded their women lest they leave the family to join those groups. This situation had the disadvantage of limiting a woman's horizon to the domestic sphere, but it had the advantage of unifying her perspective. Although it is generally felt that Buddhism improved the position of women in India, some reservations may be expressed in this respect (Paul 1979, 303-4).

It may be said that the Hindu woman, in contrast to the Buddhist woman, was free from ideological ambivalence regarding her domestic role. For the Buddhist woman, like for the Hindu man, the option of renouncing the world existed, at least in principle. Observing the competition that existed among different religious groups at the time, we may surmise that part of the Brahman criticism against the Buddhists and Jains would consist of commenting on any shortcoming or misdemeanour committed by their nuns. Consequently, Hindus would be less likely to encourage saṁnyāsa by their own women. At the same time, the dialectic with Buddhism and Jainism regarding ᵗhe status of women may well have led to an early apologetic for the religous status of Brahman women. Thus we have the curious suggestion that any feminine name in the Ṛg-Veda points to a ṛṣikā or female sage, or a goddess and the interpolation in Bṛhadāṇyaka Upaniṣad that defines Maitreyī as a brahmavādinī.

That Hindu reformers from the nineteenth century on have looked to the Vedas as the "Golden Age" for Hindu women may be based, consequently, not only on an appreciation of the values of this early society, but also on an early apologetic already structured into the texts. What the reformers often overlooked, however, was how the Vedic Age, especially the periods of the Brāhmaṇas and Upaniṣads, also gave rise to many of the features of classical and medieval Hinduism that would eventually be criticised. Hence my concern has been to trace not only those elements that contributed positively to the later religion of Hindu women, but also the transition from male dominance carefully situated in an ideology of complementarity (Ṛg-Veda) to spheres of male exclusivity, which gradually developed with reference to sacerdotalism, education, and asceticism, and made the question of the status of women more complex. This change in orientation cannot be understood apart from the new multiplicity posed by the heterodox religions on the one hand, and by the gradual Brahmanical adjustment to incorporate the religion of non-Aryan communities on the other hand. In the process ethnic identity dissolved and gave way to caste and hierarchy; Aryan, mixed, and non-Aryan components were brought into one structure, while a new ideology stressed universalism. How models of hierarchy and complementarity as well as inclusiveness and exclusiveness contributed to the structure of classical and medieval society with reference to women is my concern in the next section.

FEMININE IDEALS IN THE SMṚTI TEXTS

Smṛti is a vast category of scripture in Sanskrit whose authority in theory is secondary to śruti, the Vedic corpus. It consists of works on proper behavior (dharmasūtra and dharmaśāstra); epics (itihāsa) such as the Mahābhārata and Rāmāyaṇa; accounts relating to the activities of the gods (purāṇa, tantra, and āgama); and philosophy (darśana).

It may be argued that the religiosity of Hindu women had become a special category by classical times. A slight digression into Indian logic will help clarify the point. The concept of an "exception" in Indian logic may involve either a special privilege or an exclusion in the sense of, or with the effect of, discrimination (Hejib 1980). Strīdharma, the ideal behavior of a Hindu woman, entailed special privilege at the same time that it involved exclusion from aspects of men's religion.

But even this analysis may seem unduly androcentric, for anthropologists warn that woman's religion is by no means always derivative.

Rather, it may stem from woman's unique experiences, especially pregnancy and childbirth. As Doranne Jacobson has written of North India:

> Childbirth rituals are unique in the degee to which they are the domain of women in a culture where men often seem to dominate. The contrast is seen, for example, in a Hindu wedding; when the bride is given to the groom and his family, a male Brahman priest chants Sanskrit verses and directs the rites, while veiled women sing on the sidelines. In childbirth rituals, however, men play only minimal supporting roles. Giving birth is a skill in which no man can claim expertise. This is the heart of the domestic sphere, the women's domain par excellence. In dramatizing one of women's most vital roles, the rituals contribute to harmonious cooperation among women brought together to live in the patrilineal joint family, the key social unit in rural India. (Jacobson 1980, 76)

Similarly, another anthropologist, Susan S. Wadley, in her study of the calendrical cycle of rituals practiced by women in a North Indian village comments: "Whereas men's rituals are aimed primarily at general prosperity or good crops and at the world outside the house itself, women's rituals focus more specifically on family welfare and prosperity within the walls of their homes" (Wadley 1980a, 95).

Our texts, however, tell us little about women's exclusive rituals, for these belong to an oral tradition passed down from woman to woman. Rather, what we discern in the texts are the normative, and often male-inspired, models for women's religion which women internalized, lived by, and supported through their own integrity, if not self-interest. More specifically, we are interested here in how Hindu religious practices such as henotheism, apotheosis, sacrifice, yoga, and bhakti were transformed and transfigured to fit the domestic religiosity of women.

Put simply, the Hindu woman was to focus on her husband; he was to be her "god." One should not regard the apotheosis of the husband as simply an exaggeration of androcentrism. Rather, it is necessary to understand how this feminine focus was a part of Hinduism. Just as the R̥g-Vedic worshipper addressed each deity in turn as supreme (a practice called "henotheism;" Max Müller 1878, 254–309), in the same way, later Hindus honored individuals on ritual and festival occasions by viewing them not only as divine but supreme at that particular moment. It is as if the religious henotheism of the Vedas reincarnated itself as sociological henotheism. Moreover, "extended" apotheosis was not uncommon in Hinduism; Brahmans considered themselves gods on earth (bhūdevatā) and so did gurus and kings upon occasion. It may be argued that as Hindu theism became increasingly monotheistic in the sense of involving a primary if not exclusive devotion to either Viṣṇu or Śiva as supreme deities, a similar tendency may have developed in the domestic sphere so that the husband too became the "supreme and only" one. This tendency helps us account for the ideal woman's "exclusive" devotion to her husband. Thus, the semantics of *pati* may be bifurcated to mean either "god" or "husband," or unified to mean husband-god. An alternative explanation is based on the insights of psychoanalysis.

> According to Brahmanic norms the wife is expected to treat her husband as a god. This Brahmanic injunction is not simply a product of the sexism of the Purāṇas and Dharmaśāstras; it is also, I believe, importantly related to the fantasy life of Hindu women. The husband as god is based on the *model* of the man that the woman possesses in her own unconscious, and this in turn is based on her perception of her own father. The extreme idealization of the father occurs at practically every level of Hindu society and extends to Buddhist Sri Lanka. For the Hindu woman her father is *the* model of a man; this model is itself influenced by (and also influences) nonfamilial models of idealized male figure, the guru and the god. It is likely that she would want her husband to fit that model, to be an idealized and loving figure, almost a god . . . it is very likely that in a large number of instances the husband can never match his wife's ideal of the male, and often enough the real flesh-and-blood husband is a complete letdown. Hence sensitive females must search elsewhere for loving surrogate male figures, which in Hindu society are the guru and the idealized god . . . toward whom a woman can direct her life, her *bhakti* a combination of eroticism and devotionalism. (Obeyesekere 1984, 434).

Now, we know that a woman was also apotheosized in that she was viewed as Lakṣmī, the goddess of wealth and prosperity, in the home. Similarly, a daughter, wife, and mother were periodically the focus of supreme honor in certain ritualistic contexts. Does this fact mean, then, that the apotheoses of husband and wife were parallel? The complexity of this issue returns us to the existing tension in Hinduism between models of complementarity and hierarchy and how they operated differently for men and women. In brief, the apparent similarity between god and goddess incarnate may disclose a hierarchy when other factors are taken into consideration; for example, the patriarchal organization of the family and a woman's rebirth orientation led her to desire to be with her husband for lives to come. In other words, a woman's appreciation of her husband as pati or god was more central to her daily religious life and spiritual values than wife as goddess was to her husband's orientation. They shared a certain concept, it is true, but they appropriated it differently. Nonetheless, the nominal identification of women with a goddess and their periodic elevation to supremacy at ritual times gave Hindu women respite from patriarchal and other hierarchical structures. Such experiences of supremacy, temporary though they were, psychologically confirmed a woman's worth and spiritually elevated her existence.

A similar analysis may be made of the concept of feminine self-sacrifice in Hinduism. While self-sacrifice has been a feminine mode of religiosity in most patriarchal religions, a mode which is related to the psychology of female subservience and male dominance, its expression in Hinduism may also be understood to derive from the history of sacrificial religion or Brahmanical sacerdotalism. Sacrifice itself involved a hierarchy of "superior" and "inferior": the concept of *yajña* or 'worshipping by means of offering' implied a pair of the offerer and the recipient of the offering. It is obvious that the recipient god was offered a substance, which was disowned by the offerer and his act of disowning was rewarded by the god (Hejib 1980).

The "barter" of sacrifice had its parallel in the "barter" of marriage. A woman offered her service, her care, her well-cooked food, her aesthetics of pleasure, and her capacity for children as an offering to her *pati* in exchange for his protection, that is, his economic support and promise of marital security. While this sacrificial barter system was implicitly understood by the couple, it was never discussed directly. Euphemism allowed an individual to spiritualize the mundane (Hejib and Young, 1978a). Hence the self-sacrifice of a woman was understood by both a man and woman as a religious offering, like that to the gods, to be reciprocated.

The most explicit form of feminine self-sacrifice was in the form of a *vrata* (vow). The making of a vow was a kind of contract between a god and a woman, in which a woman voluntarily denied something to herself; for example, she fasted (*upavāsa*) in exchange for a favor for her husband (such as health or a son). Whereas in the usual religious sacrifice an individual requested a middleman (a Brahman priest) to make an offering to obtain a result from a god, in this context a god became a middleman who bestowed a favor on a husband, the "supreme" god, as it were. It is as if, out of devotion to their husbands, Hindu wives succeeded in making priests out of gods.

Self-sacrifice, which may involve some form of self-suffering, was related to another Hindu religious concept: yoga. Self-denial or asceticism (tapas) was thought to create a positive energy or power which could be transferred to another individual for his or her welfare. A woman performed tapas for the sake of her husband (and her children). She appropriated the yogic principles of restraint (yama), purification (niyama), concentration on a single point (ekāgratā), equanimity (kṣamā), and desirelessness (niṣkāmakarmayoga) in order to achieve her goal of union with her husband-god. Hence a woman's religiosity may be characterized as patiyoga, where the term yoga signifies both the discipline for, as well as the union with, the pati (Hejib and Young, 1978b). In this way yoga was integrated into the domestic religion of women, even though women rarely viewed themselves as yoginīs (female ascetics).

If sacrifice was primarily focused on action (karma) and yoga on the mind (manas), devotion incorporated human emotion and gave it spiritual direction. Love, according to normative Hinduism, was never simply physical desire or romantic attraction (that was left to the followers of the Kāmasūtra), for it was colored by the constraints of dharma, especially chastity, and the concept of bhakti. Because action, mind, and emotion converged in the final analysis, bhakti synthesized a variegated emotionality with yogic concentration and acts of selfless service. Needless to say, bhakti was directed to a husband, just as a devotee worshipped his or her chosen deity with love.

It is in the context of bhakti that the woman's private and public religion intersected. In the smṛti texts (which were recited for everyone to hear and therefore could be known by all, including women and Śūdras), worship of images in temples and home shrines was encouraged. By classical times, this shrine complex, despite its overlay of Brahmanical ritualism, allowed for more feminine participation than did the Vedic yajña, for the chosen or family deities could be worshipped by women with offerings of fruit and flowers, hymns of praise (often in the vernacular, bhajan), and spontaneous prayers from the heart. Being female was generally no bar to bhakti. It may be argued that worship of the image of a god as pati in his home (shrine in the house) was analogous to the bhakti expressed to a husband as pati. (In fact, so pervasive is the attribution of divine characteristics to a human, and human traits to a deity, that one wonders whether the religious psychology of a Hindu wife did not approximate that of the polyandrous woman, that is, one woman with two patis: she cooked for both, she served both, she entertained both, she was devoted to both.)

Marriage mysticism was common in bhakti literature. The lady devotee (*bhakta*) was none other than the woman in love who lamented any separation from her beloved, her chosen deity (*iṣṭ adevatā*), and ecstatically rejoiced in union with him. It is striking that most lady *bhaktas* who were remembered as saints, for example, Āṇṭāḷ (ninth century C.E.) in South India, refused to marry (or renounced devotion to a human husband) in order to be totally devoted to God. Curiously, their defiance of marriage, which was mandatory for women according to Brahmanical norms, was so extraordinary that they were recognized as saints by men and women alike. Thus, concentration on the pati for a female saint meant exclusive devotion to the deity understood as supreme husband, whereas for an ordinary woman devotion was expressed both to her human husband as pati and to the deity as pati (assuming the chosen deity was male). Therefore the *two foci* of her devotion and her normative household role made her ordinary; the *exclusive focus* of the saint and her denial of marriage or patriarchal control made her extraordinary. It is striking that Hinduism labored to instill and enforce social norms but then recognized and even rewarded the independent woman who dared to break those norms.

Because of the male-female attraction, we find, at least for some of the bhakti traditions, that a woman was paradigmatic as devotee when the supreme deity was male. Thus, for a *male* devotee to enter into "marriage mysticism" with a *male* god, he had to assume the psychology of a woman in love. Here again, through reversal symbolisms and psychological appropriations, Hinduism, at least contextually and temporarily, allowed for transcendence of sexual hierarchy. If a man were to feel and act like a woman in the context of his devotion, he must be able to understand and appreciate feminine psychology just as God himself does (Young 1983b, 186; Nikhilananda 1942, 444–49).

Now we are in a position to understand how the path of bhakti gave a universal soteriology to Hinduism just at the moment when Brahmanical sacerdotalism and asceticism encouraged extreme androcentrism. Furthermore, the ensuring popularity of bhakti yoga (it became the most widespread form of Hinduism) resulted in no small measure from its inclusion of such marginalized groups as women and Śūdras and its support of such social norms as marriage. In many ways, it was a Hindu middle path between the extremes of world renunciation and Tantric incorporation including reversal of all taboos, though the spectrum of bhakti ideologies eventually came to include the extreme poles.

Before we leave this topic of bhakti and its relation to women, let us consider, for a moment, how the concept of 'heaven' became a bridge between the rebirth and soteriological orientations of Hindu women.

While 'heaven' was often understood as *svarga*, a paradise that could be enjoyed as a *temporary* reward for good deeds (and therefore was a woman's reward, so to speak, for her good service to her husband), 'heaven' from the bhakti perspective usually signified Supreme Heaven, such as the Vaiṣṇava Vaikuṇṭha, and going to heaven meant no paradisaical "vacation" *within rebirth* but salvation itself. The ambiguity or swing between notions of 'lower heaven' and 'supreme heaven' gave women a way to operate within yet bridge the universes of discourse associated with rebirth and mokṣa.

A woman's devotion to her husband as pati was informed and inspired by the metaphor of the divine couple, which became increasingly important in the smṛti texts. The various epic episodes of mythological accounts of the relationship of husband and wife stressed the feminine orientation of strīdharma with its emphasis on loyalty, chastity, docility, and humility, but also strength, which arose out of tapas. The image of Sītā in the epic Rāmāyaṇa was the very embodiment of this concept of ideal womanhood. The gist of Vālmīki's Rāmāyaṇa is as follows:

> Rāma, the oldest son and heir to the throne, is banished to the forest as a result of King Daśaratha's fulfillment of a boon to his second wife that her son Bharata be king. Sītā follows her husband Rāma to the forest and endures the hardships of forest life. Sītā is abducted by the demon Ring Rāvaṇa and is imprisoned by him on the island of Laṅkā until she is rescued by Rāma. When her fidelity is doubted by the citizens, Rāma, in accordance with sacred law, repudiates her. Sītā proves her chastity by a fire ordeal. After Rāma and Sītā are reunited, they return to Ayodhyā. Bharata renounces the throne and Rāma becomes king (Dutt 1969).

An alternative and probably later ending to the story referred to further gossip by the citizens regarding Sītā's purity; Rāma's banishment of his now pregnant wife to the forest; Rāma's sight of his twin sons years later and ackowledgment of them; Sītā's final act to prove her innocence by calling on her mother, the Earth, to swallow her up; and the fulfillment of this request. This epic is certainly more a statement of feminine loyalty than it is of marital bliss, and the pivotal episodes provide occasion to expound on the virtues of strīdharma. For example, when Sītā insisted that she accompany Rāma to the forest, she argued that a woman's place was with her husband, that a wife shared her husband's fortunes and karma, that the shade of his feet was greater than all palaces, and furthermore, that she had trained her mind for the hardships of the forest. Her mother-in-law Kausalyā praised this decision, noted that she had overcome the fickleness, instability, and weakness of women, and proclaimed that she will preserve the dignity of the family and will aid the spiritual welfare of Rāma.

The epic (Ayodhyākāṇḍa 39:29, 30) endorsed androtheism with the words *strīṇām bhartā hi daivatam* (indeed, the husband constitutes divinity for woman). Furthermore, it illustrated how a woman resorted to austerities such as vows (vratas) and fasting (upavāsa), for spiritual strength in order to overcome severe obstacles and tests such as banishment to the forest, feminine competition over a man, capture, and the mental torture of having one's integrity questioned after such heroic attempts to protect the feminine ideal. Feminine strength did not triumph in Vālmīki's epic, but then every character in this epic faced tragedy ultimately. The chastity of a wife was given due recognition in the statement that nations perish for a righteous woman's woe (see also the Tamil epic Cilappatikāram). In short, she was the pillar of strength in the family and the kingdom; her feminine behavior (strīdharma) even supported the cosmos, according to the classical view.

Another exemplar of Hindu womanhood was the princess Sāvitrī. She chose to marry Satyavat, a prince living in exile with his blind parents, even though she knew that he was destined to die shortly after marriage. When this foreordained event came to pass, Sāvitrī followed Yama, the god of death, so persistently that he tried to get rid of her by granting her any boon except the restoration of her husband. When she requested one hundred sons, however, Yama was trapped, for how could a chaste wife have sons? Consequently, through her perseverence and cleverness, Sāvitrī accomplished her goal of returning her husband to life. This epic tale made the name Sāvitrī one of the most auspicious appellations for a girl; moreover, it was the name of an especially arduous vow performed by married women to prevent widowhood (Mukherjee 1978, 51).

One last illustration of ideal womanhood was Satī, who gave up her life rather than hear her father berate her husband Śiva. In her next life as Pārvatī, she was instructed by her father to care for a god in meditation. This god was none other than Śiva who had retreated to the Himālayas after the death of his wife Satī. Destined to be reunited with her husband, Pārvatī attempted to charm the ascetic but to no avail. As a last resort, she became a yoginī and through her tapas finally attracted the attention of Śiva, which occasioned their reunion.

The art of medieval India depicted the feminine ideal boldly. Lakṣmī tenderly caressed the feet of her reclining Lord, and Pārvatī sat demurely and radiantly by Śiva, who tenderly embraced her shoulders, his fingers impishly touching her breast. The "one couple" —Viṣṇu and Lakṣmī or Śiva and Pārvatī—signified the appreciation of the polarity (dvandva) of male and female, but the religously powerful concept of onenesss raised the polarity to a higher unity. Nowhere was this concept more clearly portrayed than in the image of Śiva as half male and half female (ardhanārīśvara). In the great sculptures, so organic was the unity of the two halves that the dividing line was almost imperceptible, yet the curved eyebrow, full bosom, and delicate ankles of the one contrasted with the vigorous brow, strong torso, and stalwart ankles of the other. And yet, despite the powerful portrayals of the "one couple," the hierarchy of male over female was often apparent. Lakṣmī caressing the feet of her Lord is a case in point.

Having looked at ideological features of domestic religion, it is time to return to a more detailed analysis of the normative life cycle. Maidenhood, especially the innocence that was so often likened to a gentle but skittish doe, fascinated Sanskrit poets. While poets delighted in the portrayal of maidenly innocence, its charms, and romantic love, parents became obsessive in protecting the innocence and purity of their daughters. In the literature, we encounter maidens making vows for securing a husband. Their training in single-minded concentration on a husband as the sine qua non of their existence had already begun, and by means of epic and mythic models described by the older women of the family, the ideal of femininity was instilled. Youth, after all, was the training ground for strīdharma. "Since females' emotional commitment to these ideals must be established, it can be presumed further that they [were] taught in very early childhood, as part of the socialization of the female child" (Obeyesekere 1984, 431). Consequently the women of the family were the disciplinarians for female children, which left the father free to express affection for his daughters. Because part of this female socialization process involved extreme control of sex and aggression, this led to segregation of girls from boys with the result that the "female grew up in an almost exclusive world of females, which usually [resulted] in positive identification with the mother and acceptance of the female role" (Obeyesekere 1984, 432).

Chaste daughters, in fact, had very high status in Hindu families and were worshiped as the virgin goddess (for example, during the festival of Durgā Pūjā, even today). The great importance of chastity led parents to arrange the marriage of their daughters as early as possible. While lack of education and desire for children contributed to the early marriage of Hindu girls, more reasons must be provided to explain the development of child marriage, which appeared with the proliferation of caste in classical Hindu society. It may partly be attributed to the increasing rigidity of the caste system and the desire to ensure purity of caste and stability of the social order. When there was early marriage, there was no chance for romance and individual choices regarding the marriage partner. The tradition of arranged marriage also allowed the family to make political and economic alliances with another family. Puberty was the point in the biological cycle that signified a change in status and made possible the bearing of children. It is understandable why it would be perceived as an opportune moment for a rite of passage, that is, marriage. Moreover, marriage at the time of puberty would absolve the parents of responsibility for protecting the girl's chastity. Then, too, a girl was destined to leave home and live with her husband's family; this was reason not to want to support her longer than necessary.

Why the age of marriage became even much lower than puberty (at least for Brahman girls) is harder to explain. Perhaps it absolutely guaranteed purity by avoiding menstrual blood altogether and was a way to ensure that there would be a husband if there was a dearth of eligible men. Or perhaps the concept of single-minded concentration on the husband could be instilled more easily in the early years. It certainly enabled the parents to discharge their responsibility with regard to the arrangement of marriage before accidents, personality developments, and other complications made the girl a less attractive candidate. Perhaps, too, the girl's marriage was performed at this age because marriage was termed the upanayana for women and the upanayana for Brahman boys occurred about eight. Moreover, the argument that without marriage a girl could not go to heaven was an incentive for an early marriage.

The sacrament of marriage performed by Brahman priests for the higher castes was generally a traumatic experience for a young girl. From the moment of marriage she was uprooted from her home where she had grown up in an atmosphere of affection. Once a girl married, she moved to her husband's family and was strictly controlled by his kin. Although she was auspicious, by virtue of her marital status according to the religious treatises, folk tales (and more recently anthropological studies) reveal that the husband's family often looked on her as a dangerous figure, a temptress, until she bore her first child, preferably a son, after which she was safe. Consequently, despite the high praise given to motherhood in Brahmanical texts and the high status a woman enjoyed among her own kin when she returned to her native place during festivals and times of illness and childbirth, a married woman had to cope with low feminine status when she entered her husband's home. Moreover, as we have already noted, a young wife who looked for the image of her loving father in her husband was often disappointed. Hence the birth of her first son was doubly important, for a son both improved her status in the family and gave her an outlet for her emotions.

> The mother-child relationship is a powerful symbiotic bond in Hindu India. On the level of personality this implies that the child will develop strong dependency and nurturant needs; these needs continue to be satisfied in adult life, since the mother is a continuing presence in the joint household. The relationship between a woman's husband and his mother is a continuous one, whereas the husband and wife are strangers recently united in marriage. The mother's continued physical presence in the household implies that she remains the dominant person to her married son. Furthermore, her (jealous) presence thwarts the development of affective and nurturant bonds between the son and his wife. It is the mother, not the wife, who continues to give nurture and love to the son. The wife for her part is sentimentally attached to her own family of orientation and practically tied to her child, who—rather than the husband—becomes her object of nurturance and affection. (Obeyesekere 1984, 450).

Now we can better appreciate the Hindu woman's fear of barrenness and especially lack of a male child.

The upper-caste woman's sphere was exclusively the home. While her focus was her husband and eventually her eldest male son, with whom she forged the strongest emotional ties, her reality was not limited to those interests. For, in a large extended family, women related primarily to other women. The relationship of mother-in-law to daughter-in-law was pivotal to this female world; also important were relationships to sisters-in-law. Status based on kinship, age of the husband, male children, and other factors defined the hierarchy of the women of the household, whose daily cooperation was necessary to ensure its efficient running. Indeed, much of the psychological strength of Hindu women has been attributed to their ability to cope with the complex reality of an extended family living under one roof. In point of fact, a woman found her support and friendship here too. Domestic space was the prescribed sphere of feminine interaction, all the more significant in Hinduism in view of the absence of alternative spaces provided by educational institutions, monastic orders (saṁgha), and even the broader concept of community.

Over the years a wife's status increased as long as she had borne at least one son; by the time of menopause, when she had become once again asexual like the ascetic, both her purity and domestic power combined to give her high status. James M. Freeman has noticed in his study, "The Ladies of Lord Krishna: Rituals of Middle-Aged Women in Eastern India," that vows performed by women in Orissa to prevent the death of their husbands are generally done by menopausal women, for a number of reasons. They no longer menstruate, and so can undertake a month-long vow in a state of purity. They have greater freedom because of their age and asexuality, and hence can leave domestic responsibilities to others as well as sing and dance publicly. They may be motivated by fear of widowhood. In short, says Freeman, they "enjoy the highest degree of domestic, social, and ritual freedom than any adult Hindu woman ever knows" (Freeman 1980, 126).

In classical times, if her husband died before her, a woman theoretically had the extreme option either to perform satī,[2] self-immolation on the funeral pyre of her husband, or, more commonly, to undergo the rite of passage to widowhood. The contrast in the status of the satī and the widow is striking: that satī (which literally means "good woman;" for example, *satī pārvatī* means the "good woman Pārvatī") was viewed as auspiciousness par excellence, whereas the *vidhavā* (literally, "the one whose husband is gone," that is, dead) was considered not only unfortunate but positively inauspicious, an "ogress who ate her husband with her karmic jaws" (Hejib and Young 1978b). These two embodiments of good (dharma) and evil (*adharma*) are exemplified in the following descriptions.
The sati:

> For the woman who opts for *sati, sati* is like the performance of an especially solemn religious ceremony. Ideally her decision is immediate and without deliberation. She herself calmly orders the preliminaries of the *sati* rite and dons her bridal sari. Though others may implore her to reconsider her decision, especially for the sake of her children, she does not seem to hear them. She benevolently blesses them. She sheds not a tear, even though great lamentation may surround her, for she looks upon this moment as the most auspicious of her life. This is the supreme opportunity for self-sacrifice that consummates her life of dedication to her husband. As if departing on a joyous journey she prostrates herself before the elders and asks for their blessings. They then generously bless her and, reversing the usual norms of respect, prostrate themselves to her in return: they look upon her as the goddess incarnate. As she leads the procession to the cremation ground, where the corpse of her

husband is awaiting cremation, she is joined by the people of
the village, who come to witness this awesome moment. After
the performance of the preliminary rites, she bids final farewell
with folded hands (pranāmāñjali). With perfect tranquillity, she
climbs the ladder, sits down on the pyre and tenderly takes her
husband's head on her lap. Optionally she may recline beside
him. Even when the flames reach her, she maintains her com-
posure. The crowd acclaims her as a good wife, a true satī, one
who has brought immense dignity and honour to herself, her
family, and the community ... they also express gratitude that
they themselves had a chance to witness this noble sacrifice.
(Hejib and Young, 1978b).

The widow:

It is said that the "lines of misfortune" are written on her
"white forehead" because it does not have the red dot (tilaka)
any more. Her tonsured head or flowing hair unadorned with
flowers bespeaks her miserable status. No jewels adorn her nose
and ears, no chains her neck, no bangles her wrists, no rings her
toes. Clad simply in a cotton sari of prescribed colour, often
without a blouse, she as a rule goes about barefoot. Not only is
she denied such enjoyments, but every other opportunity for
pleasure (bhoga), such as participation in social gatherings, festivals, the partaking of rich food, indeed, entertainment or pleasures of any sort. So complete is the redefinition of her status
and role from wife to widow that she bemoans the loss of her
husband every moment. (Hejib and Young, 1978b)

A widow felt guilty because she had failed in her sacrifice, yoga, and
bhakti to ensure the husband's prosperity and longevity. In brief, she
failed as a woman in her religious acts and goal, or so it seemed initially.
Given the presupposition of rebirth, however, even a widow had something to look forward to: reunion with her husband in the next life. To
purify herself of her bad karma, which caused her husband's death, and
to produce good karma for the next life, a widow practiced austerities
(tapas) in the time intervening between her husband's death and her
own. As such, she became like a tapasvinī, that is, a female ascetic or
yoginī, for she practiced perfect chastity in speech, mind, and deed
(brahmacarya); she had virtually no possessions (aparigraha), she became without desire (niṣkāma), she developed endurance, and finally
she became indifferent to all polarities, thereby achieving perfect
equanimity. Although the tapas of a widow may have been viewed by
society more as a punishment for a bad deed, yet such tapas earned the

widow, who emerged from her ordeals serene and radiating benevolence, positive albeit unspoken admiration. Her own death, unlike
that of her husband, was viewed positively, for it heralded the moment
of reunion between husband and wife.

When the widow is compared with the satī, many similarities
become apparent. The satī expressed yogic-like discipline and control
in the act of sati. By entering the fire, she burned away her bad karma,
thereby purifying herself and producing good karma for the next life.
Her equanimity expressed in her decision to perform sati and her
courage at the moment of sati revealed her yogic fortitude. And her act
was said to radiate benevolence, not only on the family and those present, but on the generations to come. Thus both the widow and the
satī were said to perform tapas. The striking difference between them,
which made one inauspicious and the other auspicious, lay in the reaction to a moment. Upon knowledge of her husband's death, the satī immediately announced her intentions of instant reunion with him. The
widow, by contrast, thought of herself and her own life; hence she had
to use the hiatus between his death and hers for the metamorphosis
back to being a good wife (satī). Moreover, the act of sati ensured that
the couple would be reunited in heaven, while widowhood left open the
destination (earth, heaven, or hell?). In other words, while clarity regarding the result of her actions graced the satī, ambiguity tormented
the widow.

So it is that the term patiyoga offers a plausible interpretation for
understanding the concepts of Hindu widowhood and satī from a
religious perspective. This is not to suggest, however, that there is not a
concomitant sociological perspective. Because of the tradition of marrying girls young, even as children, to older men, it was very possible that
the husband would die first. Moreover, it was not uncommon that a girl
would be widowed while yet a child. With marriage, a girl was guaranteed protection and support by her husband's family for the remainder
of her life. Thus, the framework of a widow's tapas conveniently
reduced her needs to a minimum on economic, social, and physical
levels. Moreover, the enforcement of physical chastity and unattractive
appearance (such as a shaved head) on a young widow removed her as a
sexual threat to the family. The act of sati ended a family's responsibility altogether, for a widow who was still capable of reproduction
was obviously a threat to the purity of a family, both by her "unproduc-
tive" menstrual blood and the possibility of her misdemeanor. As such,
it has been argued that sati was predicated on the purity ideal (Allen
1982, 8), a point which returns us to the issue of male control. It is
significant that sati became common in regions where a wife could in-

herit her husband's property. Bengal is a case in point. Perhaps too, some acts of sati were more suicidal than religious, especially since widowhood, with its severe norm, was the only alternative.

Finally, although sati and widowhood must be phenomenologically understood within the broader framework of Hinduism and not simply reduced to adharmic abuses of the ideology such as forced sati, yet there remained an obvious difference between woman as yoginī and man as yogī. A man had total freedom of choice whether to become a yogī or not. A woman, on the contrary, could only choose between being a satī or a widow (no remarriage was possible); moreover, her yogic-like spirituality was rarely recognized, for people were unaware of deep structures and remained content to view women's domestic religion as lower (albeit appreciated) than the male's ultimate goal of renunciation of the family and liberation from the cycles of rebirth.

This discussion returns us to the point of friction between the classical Hinduism of men and women. Alaka Hejib, in her article "Wife or Widow? The Ambiguity and the Problems Regarding the Marital Status of the Renounced Wife of a Samnyāsī" (1982), exposes the full tension between the perspectives of domestic religiosity and asceticism-knowledge, although this tension, technically speaking, was experienced only by the renounced wife, whether she was totally abandoned or only sexually renounced. Hejib analyzes the identity crisis of a renounced wife as follows:

> Since it is the wife who is 'renounced,' she does not technically and truly belong to the husband in any capacity subsequent to the point of his *samnyāsa*. However, the husband is not 'renounced' by her at all. So she may rightly [be inclined to] claim him to be still 'hers'. Thus, although she does not belong to him, he is still hers. (Hejib 82, 2).

> The *samnyāsī* presumes himself to be 'dead' through the ritual death. However, a Hindu woman has difficulty in accepting the 'ritual widowhood' imposed on her (Hejib 82, 2)

> The crowning ambiguity she confronts is thus: She loses *her* 'God' and the opportunity to fulfill her *pativratya* [devotedness to her husband] if she permits his *samnyāsa*. On the other hand, she becomes destructive toward him if she restrains his *samnyāsa* for the purpose of her *pativratya*. The question here is: how should she resolve this dilemma and the ambiguity of her wifely duties and emerge as a 'good wife'? (Hejib 82, 7)

One solution was that she herself might become, her husband willing, a vānaprastha (forest-dweller) and live her with ascetic "husband," observing the vow of chastity yet carrying out all other aspects of domestic religiosity as she tenderly cared for the one whom she had presumably renounced: her husband.

Thus, through classical Hinduism and into modern times, we have the following situation: "The wife's consent to saṃnyāsa was either taken for granted or forced on her. . . . Consequently the women underwent tremendous psychological trauma" (Hejib 1982, 14). In a society where divorce was not allowed, husbands could become saṃnyāsīs, not for religious reasons but primarily to escape marriage or a wife. Then, too, it may be argued that a man's prerogative to allow his wife to follow him into saṃnyāsa and his enjoyment of female service and devotion, even in the forest, continued the androcentric orientation of the religion.

This tension between the householder and the ascetic, which could create tension between wives and husbands, was alleviated officially in some bhakti traditions such as Vīraśaivism, which encouraged women to take saṃnyāsa in their own right, and Śrīvaisnavism, which discouraged saṃnyāsa as the norm for Hindu men and offered a universal means to salvation for all householders, male and female alike. Although it was not officially sanctioned, some women, even upper-caste women, became ascetics when widowed and went to live at an ashram. Especially if a woman had passed through menopause, she had the requisite purity for asceticism. Because she removed herself from the family and there was no need to support her, a widow's asceticism was a convenient solution to the ordeals of widowhood. In any case, anthropologists have noted that it is mainly Brahman women who have taken the above role of a widow seriously, and even Brahman women are changing rapidly today. The women of other castes have a variety of responses to widowhood and manipulate their environment to their advantage when they can.

To the above analysis of the domestic religiosity of the traditional Hindu woman one last point may be added. The segregation of the sexes became more severe after the twelfth century C.E. in those areas of the subcontinent that were under Muslim rule, especially the North, where Hindu women, already carefully controlled by or segregated from men, imitated the *purdah* of Muslim women. The consequence was that many upper caste Hindu women, already bound to the home, were further restricted so that they rarely left their residence; when they did, they covered their faces and traveled by closed carriage or palanquin.

This study of women in Hinduism has focused thus far on Brahmanical texts that contributed to normative Hinduism and thereby influenced the wider society. Lest I do real injustice to my topic, I must point out, however briefly, alternatives to the norms described above, even though they were not universally available to women.

I mentioned previously the presence of Buddhist and Jain monastic orders for women which existed in the society and provided an option, honorable at least in heterodox circles, for those women who joined. Moreover, we have seen how bhakti saints, by their spiritual heroism, ignored or bypassed the norms and accordingly were honored as saints in Hindu society. But there were others as well who were marginal to, if not outside, these norms altogether.

> A number of authors ... have noted that the position of women vis-a-vis men, both in terms of status and autonomy, improves the lower one descends the social hierarchy. This is, I suggest, an inevitable consequence of the hierarchy of evaluative ideologies. The Brahman, by reference to his dominant ideology of purity maintenance, feels obliged to subject his women, because of their recurrent and natural propensity to be impure, to extreme forms of control. The Ksatriya and Vaisya, by reference to their worldly desire for large and prosperous lineages, give an exaggerated value to women as mothers, with correspondingly negative implications for other female types. The Śūdra or untouchable, by reference to his sensual and materialistic criteria, has no option but to grant his women substantial autonomy and high regard. The Hindu woman is therefore in the unfortunate position of either experiencing a degree of autonomy, but at the cost of lowly position on the prestigious caste hierarchy, or high-caste status but at the cost of submission to rigorous male control. (Allen 1982, 16–17)

Thus, from our modern perspective, which perceives female independence as an indicator of high status, the Śūdra woman should be the high-status Hindu woman, whereas according to traditional Hindu norms, just the opposite is true. Since Śūdras far outnumbered Brahmans, relatively independent women were common in classical Indian society.

Moreover, independent women were important in the Tantra movement which developed around the seventh century C.E. This movement was sometimes esoteric and underground, for Tantrics delighted in reversing all Brahmanical norms; they consumed wine, meat, fish, and parched grain and meditated on or actually harnessed sexual energy to attain mokṣa. Tantric men, who were often high caste despite the possible origins of the movement among the lower castes, used low-caste women, prostitutes, and possibly temple dancers (*devadā sīs*) or their own wives to experience union (albeit still without the loss of semen), which was considered to be of a higher order than the union established by the Vedic marriage ceremony. Despite much Tantric feminine imagery, the woman herself was sometimes incidental to the ritual, except for her consecration and the final copulation.

If Tantra was primarily an avenue for male liberation among upper caste men, it did have some ameliorating influence on the negative status for women, for the occasional Tantric text prescribed that a man should cherish his wife and never punish her or be unpleasant. Furthermore, rudeness to women should be expiated, rape was punishable by death, daughters should not be given in marriage for money, and killing female animals was prohibited in the sacrifice. Consequently, the idea that every woman was an image of the goddess was not only appreciated by Tantrics but led some individuals to desire to improve the social position of women. Significantly, in some areas such as Bengal and the Himālayas, Tantric women were not only "used" but were also religious teachers of men, instructing them in esoteric lore and techniques. In certain areas the broad popular base of Tantra provided a religious option for women in the society who were either outside Brahmanical circles or who desired to escape the Brahmanical norms for whatever reason. Consequently, we find considerable female initiative and leadership in some areas under Tantric influence.

Another category of "independent woman" deserves mention: the courtesan (*veśyā*). Courtesans provided expertise in music and dance; in this capacity they were known as) *gaṇikās*. Whereas Allen associates the Kṣatriyas and the Vaiśyas with an emphasis on the motherhood of women, since those castes were interested in gaining power through large families and lineages, I think that the veśyā and ganikā represented their interests as well. Not only was a king made famous by the beautiful women in his harem, but his function to ensure the prosperity of the kingdom was enhanced by the presence of auspicious prostitutes, just as his reputation as a patron of the arts was established through the artistic renown of the gaṇikās in drama, dance, and music. The devadāsī, who served God through song and dance, was the preeminent member of this class, for not only did she enhance the prostitute's and artist's image through direct connection with the deity, but she also linked the fame and functions of the king with the temple. There is also a psychoanalytic perspective on the prominence of the prostitute in classical Indian society:

The child's erotic fixation on the mother, reaching well into puberty, may result later on in a polarization of the affect-tenderness and sensuality, these two being kept apart and expressed in social relationships with two types of female love objects—the "good" woman and the "bad" woman. Both are desirable females, but for different reasons. The first image of the mother is the idealized one: she is pure and undefiled, and therefore virgin. The unconscious equation "wife-mother" can in this case also be consciously recognized, since this female (wife cum mother) is idealized in myth and reverentially treated. It is commonplace for young men and adolescents to state explicitly that they want their prospective wives to be like their mothers, since the latter are idealized. By contrast, the idea of the degraded woman as mother, and to a much less extent as wife, cannot be brought into conscious awareness without producing extreme anxiety and undermining the values of the society. . . . In the projective system this leads to a very important "paradox": since the idealized mother is wife and virgin, she cannot bear children and is therefore barren, whereas the harlot (the degraded mistress-mother) is fertile. (Obeyesekere 1984, 454)

Obeyesekere argues that a male may be inhibited in his sexual relations with his wife because of the equation "wife-mother" and the incest taboo, and so he turns to the harlot to satisfy his sensuality. If this is the underlying psychology, then one may surmise that association with harlots and their impurity because of lack of chastity may have instilled a sense of anxiety on the part of the upper caste male but the association of the harlot with the arts, the temple, and Tantra which, in turn, gave the harlot a higher, if not divine, status helped to eliminate the ambiguity.

In sum, bhakta saints, devadāsīs and Tantric adepts all figured as independent women in the religious spectrum of Hinduism. Consequently, images of the feminine that were ostensibly antithetical to the prevailing norms of society became an acceptable part of the mosaic.

Just as normative, Brahmanical marriage had its divine prototype in the concept of the divine couple, so also the independent woman could look to a divine prototype in the Hindu pantheon. The Great Goddess, like the great gods Śiva and Viṣṇu, enjoyed a reputation as a supreme deity who creates, preserves, and destroys as well as defends dharma by battling the demons to preserve the order of society and cosmos. Nowhere is the image of the goddess as the Great Deity better expressed than in the Sanskrit text the Devī Māhātmyam, which synthesized every aspect of divine femininity with cosmic wonder and social concern to create a composite figure worthy of the description "great and supreme." Along with a gradual change in the pantheon to include more goddesses, worship of the goddess as supreme became popular throughout India, not only with individuals and families, but also with Tantrics and *śāktas,* that is, those who worshipped Śakti or divine energy as a goddess. Indeed, in some regions, such as Bengal, the goddess dominated, and even Brahman men and ascetics looked on her as supreme, though on the human level they continued to encourage strīdharma, ignored women altogether, or became misogynists. As for the so-called independent women of the society, they often worshipped the male supreme deities. This is not to say that the presence of the Great Goddess was without effect on female psychology. She may have been in a separate category from her human sister, but *she was there,* viewed by many, male and female alike, as absolutely or temporarily supreme. In fact, sometimes women's worship of the Goddess was carefully regulated by men, for fear that women would identify too closely with the Supreme Woman. To preserve the patriarchal social structure, goddesses, queens (and prime ministers) were considered to be in a special category and only when isolated as such from domestic norms could they be accepted as rulers by Hindus, who have had long experience with feminine supremacy in the cosmic realm and with apotheosis and sociological henotheism in the human arena.

The Hindu goddesses may also be subject to a psychoanalytic analysis. While one image is benevolent, the model of the Hindu wife such as Pārvatī, the other image expresses the paradox of grace and fury, such as Kālī. Obeyesekere thinks that the second image "represents the cruel, unpredictable, smothering, or castrating aspect of the mother, based primarily on the unpredictable (hysterical) nature of maternal rage as perceived by the infant" (Obeyesekere 1984, 440). Because the attachment of mother and child was extremely intense and the mother was often repressed in the family, she took out her frustration in the family on her child. The child both expected love and rage from the human mother and projected this emotional extremism onto goddesses who were unpredictable and a cultural channel to alleviate the tensions of such a family structure (Obeyesekere 1984, 427–440).

To conclude, in view of these images of the feminine in the classical and medieval periods, we are in a position to appreciate the complexity surrounding the question of the status of women, which itself is a nebulous concept and involves a number of factors.

> The "status of women" is an admittedly vague term. Status may refer to legal status, including inheritance rules and control of property, the physical quality of life both in absolute terms

and relative to men, the cultural attitudes towards women as expressed in religious beliefs and practices, status within the family (decision making, respect and esteem between men and women), access to material and social resources, and/or participation and influence in extra-domestic spheres—political, economic, and religious roles. (Lalonde 1985, 5)

Surely no single stereotype of status is possible, even in classical Hinduism, and the categories of *pure* and *impure*, which have been used by many interpreters of the society to organize the various images of the feminine, hardly do justice to the topic of women and Hinduism. In the final analysis, if Indian poets delighted in the variety of images of the feminine, Brahmanical law-givers turned their attention to the normative ordering of these images but remained sensitive to caste differences (so that each caste had its own ideal type, so to speak) as well as to processual differences through different stages of life, or, for that matter, days of the month.

But even normative order could be overthrown temporarily by divinization (apotheosis or what we have called "sociological henotheism"), gender reversals, or conscious cultivation of low status. For these reasons, it was difficult for Hindus to always appreciate the negative assessments of the status of Hindu women made by the heterodox or those foreign to the culture. This is not to say, however, that Hindus too did not perceive the need for reform by the late medieval and early modern period. The Brahmanical ideal for women which insisted on virginity in a bride, chastity in a wife, and continence in a widow all too often led to extreme repression in women and had such side effects as "sexual frigidity, somatization of conflicts, propensity to hysteria and masochistic tendencies owing to the internalization of aggression" (Obeyesekere 1984, 431). For these reasons reform became the prevailing issue of the following period.

III: THE MODERN AGE: LIBERATION, PUBLIC AND PRIVATE

Beginning in the nineteenth century, Hinduism came under severe attack, by both the Christian missions and the British Raj. A pivotal topic of Western concern was the position of Hindu women. Issues such as sati, the institution of temple prostitution, child marriage, exorbitant dowry, as well as lack of inheritance, divorce, and remarriage all aroused pity or horror. If the call for reform was instigated by those foreign to the culture who had a tendency to focus primarily on the abuses of the social system, for which they blamed the religion, impetus for reform came from within the tradition. Ram Mohan Roy, for instance, condemned polygamy and campaigned so vigorously against sati that the Raj under Lord Bentinck found a climate of public opinion favorable to reform. Sati was legally prohibited in 1829. The crusade against female infanticide began. Hindu schools were opened for girls, following the lead of mission schools. Marriage of Hindu widows was legalized under the Government Act of 1856. From 1870 on Mankar, Ranade, and Visnu Sastri Pandit agitated in the region of Bombay for the remarriage of widows. Dayānanda, founder of the reform movement called the Ārya Samāj, furthered the cause of women's education and opposed child marriage. Homes for widows were opened, and the custom of child marriage was so criticized that in 1891 the government passed the Age of Consent Act, which prohibited cohabitation with a wife under twelve (in the following decades this age was gradually raised). Thus, by the late nineteenth century, issues regarding women were addressed. Hindu leaders overcame centuries of custom and found ways to correct the situation.

Rationale for change was often sought in the authority of the Vedas; if a custom such as chid marriage or sati was not found in the Ṛg-Veda, it was argued that it was a later accretion and should be cast out for not belonging to true or revealed Hinduism. Another hermeneutical tactic was to argue that this custom was not to be practiced in the Kali Yuga, the present age. Yet another tactic was to suggest that the norm of behavior (dharma,) which varied from place to place, was to be established by the good people *(sādhus).* Exegetical and dialectical agility to foster change became more important than custom. Hinduism, as a crossroad of religions, had learned to survive through borrowing, integrating, and refining alternative views. Nonetheless, Western criticism was perhaps the most severe challenge that Hinduism had faced throughout its long history, for it came at a moment of extreme social rigidity, political and economic decay, and colonial demoraliztion.

The British Raj went so far as to add the reason of social concern for Hindu women to its rationale for ruling India. Hindu leaders appropriated this criticism of Hindu women on political and domestic fronts and sought reforms. Hence, it is no surprise to find that the cause of Indian Independence was simultaneously the cause for women's liberation from the more oppressive aspects of the domestic situation. Significantly, it was a cause that both Hindu men and women joined. Gandhi forwarded the reforms of the nineteenth century by encouraging and training women to participate in the national movement. It is no exaggeration to say that much of Gandhi's ideology was derived from Hindu women's psychology and behavior.[3]

When Gandhi invented the term *satyāgraha* (which he translated as "soul force" and which became known in the West as "nonviolence"), he became innovative with the conventional meanings of its components. *Āgraha*, in popular parlance, connoted "grabbing," in the sense of insisting on having something (as in the haughty insistence of an unbending person). *Āgraha* also positively signified "pleading" or "urging" (as when a hostess urged a guest to eat more and more). Thus, to a non-English-speaking North Indian, the compound *satyāgraha* included connotations of psychological force, both a haughty and a gracious insistence on having one's truth (satya) or, in Gandhi's understanding, one's "soul," one's identity, one's country.

This admixture of unbending strength and noble benevolence toward an aggressor, an integrity which circumvented violence as a way to power, was much like the concept of *abalā*, the feminine power of the meek. As we have seen, Hindu women were trained not to show hostility or aggression. Their vratas (vows) and tapas (austerity) nonetheless gave them a determination and strength to overcome obstacles. Gandhi recognized in this potency, derived from self-denial, discipline and suffering bravely borne, a force that was Indian and could provide an alternative to the debilitating weakness induced by the British Raj. Although it was primarily based on women's training and psychology, it was a concept known to men as well through the domestic context and the broader context of *ahiṁsā* (noninjury), which was a religious tenet shared to varying degrees by Jainism, Buddhism, and Hinduism.

Because the concepts of strīdharma and satyāgraha were similar, women were attracted, unconsciously or spontaneously, to satyāgraha. Women knew well the language of self-denial, suffering, self-control, and patience, and could redirect that orientation from the domestic arena to the national front. When their traditional religious psychology became a tool for changing a situation rather than coping with it, they experienced a new freedom.

> In South Africa Hindu women quickly grasped the new idiom. They joined Gandhi's marches as they or their ancestors had traditionally walked for miles during pilgrimage (*tīrthayātrā*) in India. They made vows that they would not break their march or fast as they had made *vratas* before. They endured suffering with positive thoughts toward the exploiter, as they had been *tapasvinīs* (women who performed austerities) in the past. When the court invalidated all Hindu marriages, they decried it as an affront to Indian womanhood and motherland, and used the tac-

tic of *satyāgraha* for change. They formed novel shock troops known as the Tolstoy Sisters and Phoenix Sisters. With their babies in their arms they heroically crossed forbidden state lines. (Young 1983a, 92)

There was acknowledgement of the importance of women in the struggle for independence. According to Annie Besant,

> the strength of the Home Rule movement was rendered tenfold great . . . by the adhesion to it of a number of women who brought to its helping the uncalculating heroism, the endurance, the self-sacrifice of the feminine nature. Our league's best recruits and recruiters are amongst the Women of India. (Vasudev 1974, 21)

Vijaya Lakshmi Pandit, Nehru's sister and the first woman delegate to the United Nations, said the following:

> We have never had or needed a suffragette movement in India, and there was no antagonism between sexes. Thanks to the wise leadership of Gandhiji, the Indian woman stepped out of the home into social and political life without opposition from men and functioned as a comrade with great efficiency. (Pandit, 1979, 313)

While the political situation gave the basic impetus to this development, Gandhi knew that daily life itself had to be substantially altered for the transformation to be complete. Individuals had to learn how to change and to develop a new universal level of awareness without denying their individuality. The experimental cocoon for the transformation of daily life was Gandhi's ashram (spiritual retreat). Women were at the center of these ashram experiments, which engendered a new awakening through practical training and what today we term "consciousness-raising" techniques that foster confidence, fearlessness, and independence. Kakasaheb Kalelkar notes that at the ashram the problems of women were discussed and lectures on women were given. The theme of those talks was freedom for women:

> Woman is in fact not weak . . . there is no reason why she should be dependent on man; there is no eternal rule that leadership in society should always remain in the hands of men . . . woman can shape and develop herself, and thus only can she help in achieving human progress. (Kalelkar 1960, xii)

The gist of Gandhi's contribution to the evolution of female psychology appears in the following extracts from his letters to the ashram sisters (Kalelkar):

> Regard the Ashram as one family, and through it cultivate the sense of the whole world as one family . . . women hold the key to Swaraj. Become experts in your work, lead pure lives, and spread yourselves through India. (xv)

> Devotion means faith, faith as much in one's self as in God. (xviii)

> In the end, of course, she who is devoted to Dharma will sacrifice herself for the whole world. But one's country does not run counter to the interests of the world, service in the cause of one's country does take one toward salvation. (6)

> Woman is the embodiment of self-sacrifice. But at present her self-sacrifice is restricted to her family. Why should she not make for the nation even greater sacrifices than those she has been making for her family? (6)

> The ancient laws were made by men. Though these men were sages and seers, they show a lack of real knowledge of women. (98)

> I feel if Mirabai cannot get salvation, no man would ever get it. (103)

Hence Gandhi helped women break out of their domestic prisons by redirecting their traditional self-sacrifice and service from husband to nation. He helped women break into new jobs by divorcing occupation from roles defined by sex and caste and by advocating the dignity of all labor. He helped lessen women's rigid conservatism by promoting women's solidarity. Gandhi constantly encouraged the ashram sisters to travel to different regions of India and to initiate a new awakening among women. When he himself traveled, he provided inspiration to women by reporting on the activities of the woman's movement in other parts of the country. Thus women's solidarity advanced by crossing caste, religious, and regional lines. Finally, Gandhi put women on an equal traditional footing with men by acknowledging women's capacity for salvation. As we have seen, Hindu women were often oriented toward rebirth, while Hindu men had liberation (mokṣa) as their ultimate goal. By definitively stating that women have the capacity for liberation, Gandhi took steps to eliminate any possible misogyny on the religious level. Gandhi, who imbibed his mother's religiosity and had to confront his own personal cowardice, identified with women. According to one source, "it is not the slightest exaggeration to say that for the purpose of improving the conditions of women, he became a woman himself" (Kalelkar, xix).

With Independence (1947), the rights of women were enshrined in the Constitution (III:15; IV:39). There was to be no discrimination on the basis of sex with reference to social, political, and economic acts. At the same time, the state reserved the right to make special provision for women so that it could continue special plans to improve their status. When India became a secular state, certain areas of social law were redefined and relegated by the state. Thus, for Hindus, general issues regarding women such as health and education became the concerns of the state and central governments, while issues such as those relating to marriage, divorce, and inheritance fell to the jurisdiction of the Hindu Code Bill.

Optimism for the future of Indian women was often endorsed publicly, especially by those who participated in the Freedom Movement. Indira Gandhi, herself a product of this liberating period of history, wrote:

> What is remarkable about India is not the number of women who have risen to prominent positions at one time or another, but that women of character have been able to break through all barriers and prejudices and, once they have done so, they have been accepted without question by the public. (Gandhi 1981, 187).

While Indira worked for the woman's cause, as have other prominent Hindu women, the most recent assessment of the overall picture of women in India, which was stimulated by the International Women's Year, paints a pessimistic picture with reference to such women's issues as illiteracy, life expectancy, political positions, number of women in the work force, and dowry. Not only is women's status lower than men's, but the gap between the two is now widening.[4]

However, these issues are no longer perceived as specifically Hindu concerns. Rather they are Indian concerns. It is readily acknowledged that the legal and social advancements during the Independence Movement primarily affected upper- and middle-class Hindu women and only a small group of them. These women were the first to face the polarization between tradition and modernity, a cultural gulf in the domestic arena created by the husband who sought Westernization and the wife who, precisely because of this challenge to her security, became defensively conservative and obsessive in her protection of household ritual and custom. Since the honor of a woman was traditionally attributed to the preservation of family custom, any change of life-style was threatening to her self-image as a Hindu woman. The conflict was increased by the tendency for the husband to learn English and to have a Western education, while the wife spoke only her mother tongue and was often illiterate.

It is apparent that this polarization, which affected a minority of the previous generation, is becoming more prevalent throughout the society. Now, however, there is no common cause, such as the Independence Movement, to unify the interests of husband and wife. Moreover, while there are new programs today for social reconstruction and women's development, they are too often ineffective on a mass basis.

In the midst of all this, the Hindu woman faces the issue of what her strīdharma of the future is to be. She still remains, by and large, more conservative than male members of the family; for example, if men in a traditionally vegetarian family break the taboo of eating meat, women most often hold to dietary purity, and if men adopt Western dress, women usually continue to wear traditional dress such as the sari. Underlying this feminine conservatism is the issue of marriage. Especially for the middle classes, many old norms of strīdharma are prevalent in the choice of a wife. Furthermore, marriage remains the raison d'être of most Hindu women's lives, although the combination of education and earning power are now normally expected credentials for a middle-class bride. Domestic and public arenas increasingly overlap for Hindu women.

There are other changes that deserve comment when one thinks of women and modern Hinduism. Women who stay at home often perform the morning worship (pūjā) to the deity in the home shrine, especially in the urban areas, for the hours of the modern work day do not permit men time for traditional ritualism. The temple rituals and the rites of passage (saṁskāra), however, are still performed by male priests, and the question of women priests has not yet arisen. The reason is no longer a traditional denial of women's eligibility or competence (adhikā ra) regarding knowledge of Veda and vedāṅga (the auxiliary branches of learning) for Sanskrit became part of the curriculum with the advent of modern education. While many men and women turn to careers in medicine, science, technology, and business, those who pursue traditional subjects in the university most often now are women. Thus, more women are developing expertise in Sanskrit, which may include Veda and vedāṅga, although it is only fair to say that outside the university there may still be obstacles in the way of women's obtaining traditional knowledge. For instance, some paṇḍitas (traditional teachers), wary of the menstrual impurity of women, do not proffer their practical training in ritualism to women. Then, too, women almost never request this training, for the status of the Brahman *purohita* (priest) is low among Brahmans themselves, who find it often difficult to make their living by this traditional means. In other words, the status of priest, minister, and rabbi as "leader of the community" in Western religions is different from the status of the Hindu priest. Hence, priesthood probably will remain a nonissue for Hindu women, and if it ever is formally practiced by them, it will probably occur more as a gradual takeover of a ritualism that men no longer desire nor have traditional training for, much as is occurring with domestic worship.

A related question is the issue of mokṣa for women. While the availability of Sanskrit learning for women has removed technical disqualifications for eligibility to the higher stages of the spiritual path, prognosis for the future orientation of Hindu women is difficult to determine. Some women may fulfill the prerequisite knowledge of Veda and vedāṅga. The possession of this knowledge, however, is no longer an issue, since scriptural knowledge is commonly ignored in the Hindu male spirituality of today in favor of the immediate and experiential accessibility of yoga and bhakti. In other words, the elitism of the Brahmanical tradition is being democratized. The effect of this change is visible in the presence of more women at the ashrams or spiritual retreats which developed out of the forest hermitages where male students lived with their teachers prior to modern education

The question arises: are there female gurus in modern Hinduism? A few modern gurus have emerged whose reputations were first established as the spiritual wives of husbands who had become ascetics. After the death of their husbands, these women took over the leadership of the ashram. For example, Śāradādevī, the "spiritual wife" of Ramakrishna, gave her leadership to the ashram, as did Mirra Alfassa, a french woman later known simply as the "Mother," who took over leadership of Aurobindo's ashram after his death. Finally, there are several examples of independent leadership. Ānandamayī Mā, after deciding to dedicate her life to the spiritual quest, gained national recognition as a contemporary guru. Jñānānanda, a guru and saṁnyāsinī, according to Charles S.J. White, was the "only woman ever allowed to take *sannyasa* vows by the present Shankaracharya of Kanchipuram" (White 1980, 23).

Nonetheless, these examples of women's religious leadership remain the exception rather than the rule for Hindu women. Now it is more an issue of women's preference than of eligibility. The future may well see more Hindu women who prefer the spiritual path, at least in the last stage of their life or if they are widowed.

CONCLUSION

The rich variety within the long history of Hinduism has been appreciated. I shall conclude this discussion of women in Hinduism by reflecting on the changing status of women in the light of the analysis I made in the introduction to this volume.

While the antecendents to early Brahmanism were outside my purview, let it suffice to say that the direction of Hinduism as a patriarchal religion had already been set by the time of the R̥g-Veda, the earliest text of the Indo-Europeans in India. The seeds of this patriarchy were related to the fact that the ancient Indo-Europeans were pastoralists. Men were central to this subsistence activity which, in turn, introduced a sexual division of labor, systems of meaning, and a program of behavior for the male and female worlds. Since men were important in the pastoral economy as they were in the subsequent migrations from the southern steppes of Russia, which involved constant warfare, it comes as no surprise to find the Indo-European pantheon predominantly masculine and the importance of women defined primarily by their production of male children to preserve the ethnic identity. It is only fair to say that survival rather than oppression was the primary modality of male domination in the early Indo-European context.

The portrayal of life in the R̥g-Veda suggested that with settlement in India came improvement in the status of women; the term dampati changed its meaning from "lord of the house" to the "couple." With settlement came agriculture, which, in turn, may have given women some vital stake in the economy and transformed the perception of the environment from one of hostility to one of partnership. This development helps to explain why in the R̥g-Veda male domination was modified with a new appreciation of the importance of women as partners and why a wife had to be present at all rituals for the gods to be present. The complementarity of male and female roles for the well-being of the family, society, and cosmos was perceived and reflected in the religious symbols through the idea of the divine couple. I suspect that separate female rituals for fertility, which later were to become a hallmark of the exclusive sphere of female religion in Hinduism, may date from this period and were continued in the oral Hinduism of women through the ages. Although male dominance may have been muted in the Ṛg-Veda by a new respect for complementarity, this did not occur to the extent of true balance of the sexes, where women had equal economic and political powers.

After the time of the Ṛg-Veda, the status of women began to decline. We traced this development through the separation of the sexes with reference to the development of specialized education as a virtually exclusive male sphere in the Brāhmaṇas and the development of asceticism in the Upaniṣads, which not only became another virtually exclusive male sphere, but also contributed to the eventual restriction of the higher stages of the path of knowledge and salvation itself to men only. The idea of enlightenment as extreme transcendence beyond the cycles of existence produced, in turn, symbols of women as not only categorically different from men but lower if not positively evil. Sagan's analysis of separation-individuation helps one to understand why ascetics sometimes had a great fear or hatred of women. Because the Hindu ascetic was to renounce society and family and wander alone, he pushed the idea of separation to the extreme, and this extreme made him particularly vulnerable to the desire to return to the security of home as represented by the mother. But because women symbolized bondage for the ascetic, he also projected his own fears onto them and called women in general temptresses.

These developments, which accompanied the rise of kingdoms, also affected man's position in the family. Men became more authoritarian. A number of rules in the smṛti texts emphasized the subordination of women; for instance, they were always to walk behind their husband, they were to eat after him, and, according to Manu, they were to be protected in youth by their fathers, in married life by their husbands, and in old age by their sons. While the smṛti literature incorporated features of male dominance developed during the rise of kingdoms into the norms of behavior, they also ameliorated the harshness of such dominance. In fact, classical India gradually restored some balance to the sex-role plans as it tried to integrate the family-based religion of the Ṛg-Veda and the asceticism of the Upaniṣads. Moreover, women themselves creatively adjusted many features of male religion to their own domestic worlds. Sacrifice (yajña), asceticism (yoga) and devotion (bhakti) were incorporated by women. Because the economic base of the kingdoms was agriculture and the king had to consolidate his realm by including and praising all constituencies, he now paid tribute, so to speak, to the chaste domestic woman and the courtesan as contributing to the welfare and prosperity of the land. As nature once again became a partner and her forces sacralized, there was, in Sanday's terms, a reciprocal flow between the power of nature and the power inherent in women. I think that the status of women did improve in classical India because of this permeability between the categories of women and nature. The Hindu woman knew this and took pride in her powerful religious role, for despite its limitation to the domestic sphere for the upper caste women, it maintained the cosmos, a no small feat. In this way the former outer orientation of the society was adjusted to the inner orientation contributed by agriculture and women. Recognition of the importance if not the power of women had its expression in moments of female henotheism such as honor to the mother, wife, or Tantric partner as goddess. Women themselves expressed their importance through oral traditions and female rituals surrounding birth.

Female power, however, never dislodged male dominance completely, in part because the upper caste woman did not have access to economic resources because of her confinement to the domestic sphere. When we compare Sagan's analysis of male authoritarianism with reference to the family during the time of the rise of kingdoms and Obeyesekere's reflections, we also see greater balance in the latter. The father may discipline his son whom he must continue to dominate through his life, but he may express great affection toward his daughter who will leave home at the time of marriage. Obeyesekere, from anthropological and psychoanalytic perspectives, however, still finds some ambiguity regarding women which, I have argued, is partially a product of the phenomenon of the rise of kingdoms. One wonders whether men offset their feelings of powerlessness in front of their mothers by extreme domination over their wives. Perhaps the stronger the mother-in-law, the more the wife will be dominated by her husband, and the more, in turn, that woman will dominate her son, who, in turn, will perpetuate the cycle and express his deep ambiguity to women by turning to the mother goddess or the prostitute?

Following Sanday and Sagan, we should expect to find changes in the status of women correlated with changes in the divine images. This is indeed the case, for we found that the Vedic pantheon began to include divine couples as the society recognized the importance of the complementarity of the human couple. With the rise of kingdoms from about the age of the Brahmans, male deities such as Viṣṇu and Śiva became supreme, which expressed on the divine level the omnipotence of the king on the human level. Later, as attention once again turned to agriculture in the society, we find renewed interest in the image of the divine couple, with an emphasis on the "oneness of the two," possibly on account of the Upaniṣadic stress on the oneness of Brahman, the Absolute. At the same time, there was a careful modeling of the goddess to parallel the normative view of the human wife as subordinate to the husband. Obeyesekere drew our attention to the fact that because of the extreme attachment of the mother to her eldest son and her general repression within the family, her omnipotence, so to speak, gave rise to a bifurcation between grace and fury, which was projected as a supreme independent goddess. This projection may be related to the ambiguity regarding re-engulfment, which was discussed in the introduction with reference to Sagan's views. Thus the attempt in the classical and medieval periods to seek complementarity did not completely eliminate male ambiguity regarding women.

The arrival of Islam and then Christianity, two more patriarchal religions which used violence to dominate the subcontinent, led once more to an increase in Hindu male dominance. This dominance, however, was not the reflection of male dominance in the outer world, as was the case before, but rather a reflection of the subjugation of the Hindu male, who redirected his frustration and hostility arising from powerlessness in the outer world toward his wife. Hence extreme male domination in the domestic sphere was compensation for powerlessness in the political realm. This extremely low point in Indian history led to the recognition by Hindu men themselves that reform regarding women was necessary. From the reforms of the nineteenth century through the independence movement to the constitution and the discussions during the International Women's Year, attempts were made to improve the status of women.

It is Sagan's thesis that massive changes in society beget great anxiety. A radical change in the status of women with new scripts for society and sex-role plans is precisely one of those massive changes, especially in a long-standing patriarchal religion and society such as India. Sanday's theory of stress and Sagan's saga of kingdom-building, which may have some relevance to the new nation of modern India, may be important interpretive clues for the future. The question for the future is whether male dominance will be real or mythical or disappear altogether. Certainly from a historical perspective it is too soon to tell.

Nancy Schuster Barnes

BUDDHISM

INTRODUCTION

Gotama the Buddha lived about 2,500 years ago, and the religion he founded has long since spread far beyond the boundaries of its original homeland in northern India and Nepal to embrace most of Asia. A religion which has had such a long history and has established itself over an enormous geographical area and within a great variety of cultures can obviously not be encompassed in one chapter. It is necessary to be selective. Therefore, I shall concentrate mostly on information found in the canonical literature of Buddhism produced in India, that is, on the normative Buddhist literary tradition which was transmitted to other Buddhist countries. Some interpretations made of those scriptural materials in China, Japan, and Tibet will also be described.

WOMEN IN EARLY INDIAN BUDDHISM (ca. 525-100 B.C.E.)

Doctrines versus Institutions

Doctrinally, Buddhism has been egalitarian from its beginnings. The same teachings were given by the Buddha to his female and male disciples, the same spiritual path was opened to all, the same goal pointed out.

Whoever has such a vehicle, whether a woman or a man,
Shall indeed, by means of that vehicle,
Come to *nirvāṇa*. (S.I. 33)

The Buddha taught a method for attaining liberation from the unhappiness and pain inherent in worldly existence. Unhappiness is caused by the uncontrolled desire people feel for every possible pleasure and satisfaction. One desires because one is extremely fond of oneself. A person normally believes that he or she is unique and that somewhere within is a special essence, a soul or a self, which is precious and different from every other individual in the world and which is well worth providing for in every way. The Buddha taught that this notion is mistaken, for everything that exists is ephemeral, and there is no personal, enduring self in anyone. If one can get rid of this false belief in a special self, self-centered desire can be abandoned, a detached attitude toward things and people can be cultivated, and unhappiness can be thereby destroyed. Destruction of self-centered desire and the pain which results from it is nirvāṇa.

To eradicate the false belief in the self and in the permanence of things, the Buddhist follows a path of meditation and moral discipline which leads to a powerful, liberating insight into the true nature of existence, by which one's mind is opened and changed. The early Buddhists felt that the quickest way to reach this liberating insight was to leave ordinary home life and become a wandering religious mendicant, living simply and without attachments. The Buddha therefore founded an order of monks *(bhikṣu-saṃgha)* and an order of nuns *(bhikṣuṇī-saṃgha)* to foster the life fully devoted to the pursuit of nirvāṇa. The Buddhist orders of male and female ascetics were among the first to be established in the world. An order of lay disciples was also founded; laymen and women often practiced a modified religious discipline while maintaining their normal occupations.

The Buddha wanted to show people the best and quickest way to liberation. Speculation on other matters, including any possible differences between the sexes, was considered not conducive to the goal. And since Buddhism is an atheistic religion, there was no reason to speculate either on the maleness or femaleness of a divinity. But when the monks' and nuns' orders (saṃgha) were founded, it was necessary to establish rules to regulate the daily lives of the ascetics; and in the heart of a religion which was free of any doctrines which fostered inequality, a patriarchal structure arose.

Nuns in the Early Saṃgha

The Vinaya, or Book of the Discipline, preserves an ancient account of the founding of the nuns' order (Davids and Oldenberg 1881, 3:320-26; Horner 1930, 95ff.; Paul 1979, 82-86). Details of this account vary in the Vinaya recensions of the various early Buddhist schools, but the basic elements of the story remain the same. Soon after the Buddha's own enlightenment he formed an order of monks, male renunciants of ordinary worldly life, and a few years after that he was asked by his foster mother and aunt, Mahāprajāpatī, to establish a similar order for women. But he refused her request three times, and only upon the intervention of Ānanda, his kinsman and constant attendant, did he agree to let an order be founded. This he did, however, only with the proviso that the women must agree to live according to eight rules which would place them in a position subordinated to the monks.

The Buddha acknowledged, according to the Vinaya of the Theravā da school, that women are quite capable of becoming *arhants*, that is, persons who have attained nirvāṇa. But he also declared that the saṃgha would be weakened by the presence of women within it, and for this reason they must be controlled by special regulations; moreover, because the saṃgha would be weakened, the true Buddhist teaching (*dharma*), which would have endured for 1,000 years, would only last 500.

Needless to say, the historicity of this account has been looked upon with skepticism by some modern researchers because its misogyny is uncharacteristic of the main body of early Buddhist scriptural writing. In fact, in some early *sūtras* (scriptural writings believed by the faithful to be the words of the Buddha) one finds hints about the founding of the nuns' order which suggest quite another attitude on the part of the founder. The Mahāparinibbānasuttanta records that the Buddha vowed, just after his own enlightenment, to go on living until the saṃgha of monks, nuns, male and female lay disciples had been established and had proven successful. Success would be proved when *all* members of the saṃgha had thoroughly learned the doctrine, were fully practicing the discipline, and were able to teach it all to others (D. II. 104-5, 113; A.IV.308ff.; S.V. 259; Horner 1930, 284). According to this story, then, the Buddha intended from the first to establish a saṃgha of men and women, and expected all saṃgha members to do the same things and achieve the same successes. The Vinaya story of the founding of the nuns' order is an old one, however, and certainly reflects the beliefs of early monk historians about the course of events.

A whole corpus of regulations for both monks and nuns gradually evolved, but there were also special rules which applied only to nuns. Of these, the Eight Chief Rules, said to have been instituted by the Buddha when he founded the nuns' order, were the most notable and the most stifling. The Eight Chief Rules require each nun to treat every monk as her senior and superior, they forbid her ever to revile or admonish any monk, and they direct that all the sisters' formal ceremonies be carried out under the guidance or in the presence of the monks' saṃgha, including the setting of penances for erring nuns. A rule was also promulgated which allowed nuns to receive dharma instruction from monks but did not permit nuns to teach monks (Falk 1980, 214). Whether any of these rules were actually established by the Buddha or whether they were added later by monks who were resentful of women's presence in the saṃgha, the end result for the nuns was the same: they were effectively relegated to a subordinate position within the saṃgha and had little hope of ever assuming leadership roles there.

Although monks were quite capable of real misogynist outbursts,[1] such passages are not common in the scriptures of any Buddhist school I know, for the monks seem to have been well aware that the main hindrance to their own enlightenment was not women, but their own mental attitudes.[2] However, it appears that the monks did want to keep power in their own hands in the saṃgha and this concern seems to be the motivation for the Vinaya story of the founding of the nuns' order and for some related statements in the early scriptures.[3] Monks and nuns had both renounced ordinary life in the world and had gone forth to follow the Way of the Buddha. On the spiritual path, monks and nuns do the same things, follow the same daily routines, live the same sort of disciplined lives, and practice the same meditation techniques. They even look alike, for they shave their heads and wear the same robes. In every way, monks and nuns appear to be a single group of renunciants, among whom distinctions based on gender no longer apply (Falk 1980, 213, 221). However, by imposing rules on nuns which would place them in a permanently inferior position in all their interactions with monks, the monks reserved for themselves the control and leadership of the entire saṃgha. Undoubtedly such a desire to exercise authority over nuns rather than to accept complete assimilation with them came from traditional ideas about the proper relative positions of men and women prevailing in India at the time. The monks could not, even had they wished it, inhibit the spiritual advancement of women once they were part of the saṃgha, but they were able to keep them at a comfortable distance within that institution and to clearly distinguish themselves from the nuns in the eyes of the laity on the basis of their own status as leaders (Horner 1930, 267; Falk 1980, 208).

The monks dominated the saṃgha, there were apparently more of them, and they were more in the public eye than were the nuns.[4]. Of course, outstanding female arhants did exist in the early Buddhist communities. The Therīgāthā, or Psalms of the Sisters (Davids 1909), preserves the enlightenment poems and other verses of seventy-some women traditionally believed to have been the Buddha's contemporaries. Some of the nuns to whom these poems are ascribed, especially those who were renowned for their learning and their skill in teaching the dharma, also appear in other early Buddhist scriptures (Horner 1930, 199ff., 251ff.). A few scriptures in the Theravāda canon were preached by women, and the most notable is the one preached by the nun Dhammadinnā to her former husband, the Buddhist lay disciple Visākha (M.I. 299-305). She explains the basic doctrines and practices of Buddhism, from the Four Noble Truths to the subtle details of meditative experience; afterward the Buddha himself praises her as very learned, possessed of great understanding. But not even Dhammadinnā's fame, nor that of other women teachers, could match that of the more renowned and more visible monk disciples of the Buddha.

Overlooked by the donors and patrons on whom the entire saṃgha depended for its existence, the nuns' order was not so well supported as the monks', and the women eventually faded into social, economic, and intellectual obscurity (Falk 1980, 216). This is, as we shall see, the pattern of women's participation in Buddhism throughout much of the history of the religion, including its dissemination to other countries in Asia. Women were there, are there, but most often seem to remain on the shadowy fringes of the religious life, not at the creative, influential center of religious activity.

The Laity

Nuns were not the only women in the early Buddhist communities, however; there were laywomen as well, and these women may have been, as Falk argues (1980, 220–22), more respected and better accepted by the monks than the nuns were. These women, who remained in lay life but were dedicated to the dharma and gave generously for the support of the saṃgha, were absolutely vital to the existence of the religious community. They, along with the generous laymen, were its economic foundation. The laity did not compete with the monks for prestige and influence within the religious community, for their role was to attend to the well-being of the saṃgha in the world and to remain the spiritual followers of the clergy. In return for their gifts, the monks taught them the dharma.

No distinction was made in the teaching offered to laywomen as opposed to laymen, except when someone on occasion asked a question specifically about women, concerning, for example, the duties of a wife. In general, when the advice offered to women is compared with that offered in other sūtras to men, one finds the same general conduct and attitudes urged on both: cleverness, diligence, prudence and economy to preserve the well-being of the household; respect and responsibility toward family members and dependents; generosity toward wandering religious; and, in all affairs, avoidance of jealousy, ill temper, vengefulness, and lust.[5] Although details of conduct varied for men and women, because their social roles differed in the secular world, all were expected to adhere to the same general code of behavior for the sake of the cohesiveness and prosperity of the entire community. In fact, the Buddhist laity lived and were expected to live much as their non-Buddhist neighbors did. The Buddha tried to nurture religious freedom, not social reform.

World Renunciation versus World Hatred

At its heart and from its inception, Buddhism has always been a religion for renunciants, for people willing to abandon ordinary worldly life with its conventional roles for men and women and to strive for personal liberation in the solitude of the forest. Some modern writers have assumed that world renunciation means world rejection and hatred of life. Some have asserted that Indian Buddhists identified the renounced world, *saṃsāra*, with the feminine (Falk 1974, 77–79; Paul 1979, 5–6, 9–10). Others have gone further and charged that the founder and the leaders of this ascetics' religion have felt contempt for women because they would not distinguish women from the worldliness they feared and fled. Altekar (1956), for one, believes that such contempt for women "is almost universal among the advocates of the ascetic ideal" (208).

Faced with such asseverations, anyone wishing to discover how Buddhists felt and feel about women must look into this matter of world renunciation and ask some questions: What do Buddhists renounce, and why? How do they perceive the relationship between women and the world? Is an ascetic religion really more likely to take antifeminine attitudes than a family-centered religion?

Why does a Buddhist nun or monk renounce ordinary worldly life and go forth with few belongings into the forest? To reach enlightenment-liberation as quickly as possible. Why is the homeless life most suitable for the rapid pursuit of nirvāṇa? Because the renunciant has left behind all possessions except for the mendicant's robe and alms-bowl, has abandoned all attachments to people, places, and things, and has severed all ties with her or his past life. Living simply and without distractions, the renunciant can progress rapidly in the practice of meditation. One who remains in the world with all its attractions is surrounded by every possible temptation, every conceivable hindrance to the attainment of the final goal (Schuster 1985a).

It is the complexities of worldly life which the renunciant leaves, then, because they interfere with spiritual striving. But must this imply that the world is something which must be repudiated by any genuinely religious person? I think the weight of evidence in Buddhist scriptures argues against that interpretation. The Buddhist ascetic was not taught to hate the world, worldly life, or worldly persons. Buddhist renunciants never lived cloistered lives. They remained in close contact with society, exchanging the teaching of dharma for gifts of food and clothing. Renunciants needed the world, and were not expected, could not afford, to hate it. No doubt many Buddhist ascetics feared worldliness, and, in some of them who were never able to overcome that fear through liberating insight, fear hardened into hatred. The aim, however, of the Buddhist ascetic was to understand the nature of existence and, by thus changing his or her attitude, to lose attachment to it. No one was intended to reject life out of terror. Fear and hatred were known to paralyze, not to contribute to spiritual progress.

Knowing that bodily appetites were the first and most seductive foe to vanquish, the Buddhist renunciant sought to control them by cultivating loathing for physical pleasures. But this loathing was induced so that one could press beyond it to the recognition of the body's impermanence, which would enable one to become detached from it and its needs:

> [A monk,] just as if he had seen a body abandoned in the charnel-field, dead for one, two or three days, swollen, turning black and blue, and decomposed, applies that perception to this very body (of his own), reflecting: "This body, too, is even so constituted, is even of such a nature, has not got beyond that."
> ...He keeps on considering how the body is something that comes to be...[and] passes away...and he abides independent, grasping after nothing in the world whatever. (D.II. 295; Dial. II. 331)

Lust is attachment to sensual pleasures, and lust for sexual gratification is one of the most powerful forms of bondage the renunciant must combat. But since lust is an attitude of the mind, it is the mind which must be controlled.

> I shall restrain you, mind,
> Like an elephant at the gate.

I shall not urge you to evil
You net of lust: bodyborn....
(Theragāthā, Songs of the Elders, Beyer 1974, 242)

Control of the mind is the Buddhist goal, and it is that which brings ultimate detachment and peace.

I do not long for death
I do not long for life
But I await my time
Mindful and attentive.
(ibid., 246)

It may be the sight of a woman's body which incites a man's lustful
feelings, but these feelings will not arise in a mind which is under control. Out of control, the mind proliferates notions and fancies about
what is perceived, and desires these fancies fabricated by itself. The
mind in control is focused on the present moment only; it does not raise
fancies, and does not fly out after things to possess them.[6]
    Worldly people are always confusing the objects of perception with
their own mental fantasies about them. The renunciant strives to win
out over that confusion, but it is not easy. In the midst of the struggle to
overcome lust, the monk's fury against his own mind sometimes slides
over into a hatred of the woman he lusts after, and then images of the
devil woman, the temptress, are conjured.

I see no other single form so enticing, so desirable, so intoxicat-
ing, so binding, so distracting, such a hindrance to winning the
unsurpassed peace from effort ... as a woman's form....

Go parley with a man with sword in hand;
Use question with a goblin; sit ye close
Beside th'envenomed snake, whose bite is death;
But never alone with a lone female talk!
(A. III. 67-68; GS. III. 56-57)

Women are like fishermen.
Their flattery is a net.
Men are like fish
Caught by the net.

The sharp knife of the killer
Is to be feared.

The woman's knife is to be feared
Even more so.
(Udayanavatsarājaparivarta, Paul 1979, 43)

But the monk should eventually get things straight, and in fact he usually does, for attacks like the above are rare in Buddhist scriptures. Most of the time the texts correctly direct their denunciation against a man's or woman's mental attitudes (Schuster 1984, 1985a).

Can one say, then, on the basis of the relative scarcity of frankly antifeminine statements found in Buddhist texts, that Buddhist ascetics were contemptuous of women? Did they regard women as evil? At most, I think one can say that Indian Buddhists believed women were by nature more deeply involved with worldly existence than were men because women produce and nurture life (Falk 1974, 77-79; Paul 1979, 5-6, 9-10). "Women's thoughts" (itthicittam) were presumed to be of life in the family and of the continuation of life, while "men's thoughts" (purisacittam) were of intellectual and spiritual matters (D. II. 271-73). That association suggests that men were imagined to be naturally disposed to turn from the world toward spiritual goals, while women were assumed to be less willing to do so.[7] But I do not find convincing evidence that women's lives in the world, or that fertility itself, were despised. Worldly life and procreation were renounced by nuns and monks for themselves, but not, I think, hated. It was the round of rebirths, continued becoming after this life is over, from which the Buddhist ascetic sought freedom. And this cycle of becoming was identified by Buddhists not with women but with Māra, the god of love and death, the male personification of human attachment to life in this world (S.I. 103-35: Māra-samyutta, Bhikkhunīsamyutta). Women are called "Māra's snares," and in some texts Māra send his daughters, personifications of Lust, Aversion, and Craving, to tempt the Buddha just before his enlightenment. (In the literature, Māra himself often tries to tempt female ascetics.) It is Māra who is the most prominent symbol of worldliness in Buddhist literature, and when female symbols of passion and attachment are made to accompany him, they are subordinated to him. Māra manipulates his female minions; these female symbols of passion and attachment are his tools and do not act independently of him. Worldliness is, and is imaged as, both male and female in Buddhist literature; but even in the Buddhist mythology of evil the masculine symbol prevails over the feminine.

According to the theory of the five ranks, which will be discussed later in this chapter, women cannot be Māra-gods any more than they can be auspicious Śakra- or Brahmā-gods, or universal monarchs or Buddhas. The Buddhists who upheld this theory excluded women from leadership in wordliness (Māra's realm) as surely as from other kinds of leadership. This is the real issue for the status of women in Buddhism, I think: it is not that Buddhist monks roundly despised women—they simply wanted to keep women out of all positions of authority, in theory and in practice.

I seriously question whether an ascetic religion like Buddhism should be regarded as antifeminine just because it places a high value on asceticism. Religions which are more oriented toward the family, like Judaism and Hinduism, have reason to attempt to control the power of female fertility and may construct theories about women's character which justify keeping them subservient to men. When there is a patriarchal god at the head of a religious system, the matter of women's character and women's place in the religion becomes even more problematic. Buddhist literature has shown relatively little interest in theories of women's character, largely because monks in early times were not thinking of controlling female fertility and moreover had no supreme male deity to be concerned about. What has always been important, however, in Buddhism as in other religions, is who keeps authority in their hands.

EARLY MAHĀYĀNA BUDDHISM (CA. 100 B. C. E. -400 C. E.)

Originally no Buddhist doctrines asserted any difference between women's and men's religious capacities, aspirations, and accomplishments. But some time after the death of the Buddha, his followers began to speculate about the implications of his teachings. Then, some time after about 300 B.C.E. and before 200 C.E., a doctrinal crisis erupted wherein the spiritual capacities of women were challenged and a real effort was made to prove theologically that women are inferior to men. It was during this period that Mahāyāna Buddhism arose, and it was some early Mahāyānists who became champions of equality against the adherents of some of the older Buddhist schools.

Mahāyāna Buddhist Thought

Mahāyāna, the "Great Vehicle" to liberation which has room for all beings, was a major Buddhist movement which evolved gradually out of

ideas and practices of the older Buddhist schools. By about 100 B.C.E. it
had emerged with its own interpretations of the Buddha's teachings
fully articulated in its earliest scripture, the Aṣṭasāhasrikāprajñāpāramitāsūtra, the Sūtra on the Perfection of Wisdom in 8,000 lines.

Basically, the Aṣṭasāhasrikāprajñāpāramitāsūtra and other early
Mahāyāna scriptures teach that every Buddhist should aspire to become a fully enlightened being, that is, a Buddha. Such an aspirant is
called a bodhisattva, which means a heroic being (sattva) utterly committed to attaining full and perfect enlightenment (bodhi) at some future time. The bodhisattva first aspires to attain Buddhahood (anut-
tarasamyaksambodhicittotpāda), and then makes a formal resolve
(praṇidhāna) to do it. Laypeople might be bodhisattvas just as well as
clerics so long as the commitment is there; but the same practical impediments to the layperson's success were still acknowledged, just as in
the earlier literature.

A bodhisattva aspires to become a Buddha not for her or his own
sake; after all, if personal liberation were the only issue, one could be
content with the arhant's eightfold path to nirvāṇa, a tried and true
method. Rather, the bodhisattva recognizes that the universe is full of
suffering beings in bondage and unable to help themselves, and she or
he wishes ardently to help them become free. Only by gradually acquir-
ing the Buddha's complete and perfect understanding can one truly
help all beings, and so the bodhisattva, motivated by profound compassion, is willing to exert the most strenuous effort during however many
lifetimes are required to bring about the liberation of all beings and to
reach perfect enlightenment. This, it was held, was what the historical
Buddha had done, and his life must be emulated completely by one as-
piring to his attainment.

In addition to the ethical dimensions of the Budhisattva's commitment, there is a philosophical explanation for this concern for the destiny of all beings which bears all-important implications for Mahāyāna
attitudes toward women. The bodhisattva seeks to perfect her or his understanding by realizing that not only does no person have an individual, unique essence which comes into being and endures at a
unique time in a unique place, but there is no such essence in anything
whatever. Instead, each phenomenon is dependent on other phenomena, its whole existence is conditioned by the influences of other
things. Therefore what we perceive around us can only be known relative to other things; nothing can be grasped in and of itself only. This is
the doctrine of emptiness, śūnyatā, which the bodhisattva's perfected
understanding accepts.

Stories of Buddhas and Bodhisattvas

No complete biographies of Gotama the historical Buddha were written during his lifetime, for interest was directed at the dharma which he taught and not at his person. But at least about 300 B.C.E., after the Buddha himself had been dead for several generations, some Buddhists did turn their attention to the person of the founder, and biographies of the Buddha began to be composed. One of the earliest was not really a biography of the historical Buddha but an account of the life of an earlier Buddha who had supposedly lived in the remote past; this is the Mahāpadānasuttanta (D.II.1–54; Mahāvadānasūtra in its Sanskrit version). This Buddha is presented as an ideal type, a model to which every Buddha's life will conform in every detail. This is because every Buddha-to-be must have reached the same level of spiritual perfection by the time of his final birth, for his *karma* (accumulated actions from the past and their results) is the same as that of all other bodhisattvas at this stage, and the fruits of that karma must be the same during the final existence in which Buddhahood is attained. The historical Buddha was a male, and the Mahāpadānasuttanta and other Buddha biographies assume that every Buddha will always be a male, and his body will conform to a canon of male perfection, the thirty-two major and eighty minor characteristics of the *mahāpuruṣa*, the Great Man.

In addition to the biographies of the Buddha, enormous numbers of old folk tales and fables were adopted into the canons of the Buddhist schools, tales which were retold as though they were about the many, many previous existences of Gotama the Buddha; these are the Jāaka tales. In fact, it is in the story literature of some Buddhist schools that some of the fiercest misogynist attacks are to be found (Falk 1974, 76). These stories reveal a changing attitude toward women within the Buddhist tradition which was closely connected with the concentration of theological speculation on the person of the historical Buddha himself. In the corpus of Jātakas adopted by the Theravādins, the Elders, into their Pali canon, the Buddha-to-be is reborn in many forms, including a variety of animals, but never appears as a female. Texts belonging to some other early Buddhist schools, such as the Mahāvastu of the Lokottaravādin school, also lack any references to previous female births of the Buddha. The Pali Introduction to the Jātaka goes so far as to say, in fact, that one who was to be a Buddha in the distant future could *never* be born as a woman after consciously setting out on the budhisattva path (Sharma 1978, 73; Warren 1972, 14, 33–34). The Theravādins seemed to see individuals as very nearly permanently fixed in one gender or the other. In the Therīgāthā Commentary, which recounts several previous existences of Theravāda nuns, the women's earlier lives do not seem to include any as males (Davids 1909).

Not all Buddhist schools shared the view that a Buddha could only have been a male during countless previous existences, however. In a Chinese collection of Jātakas, translated from an Indian language in the middle of the third century C.E. and published in French translation by Chavannes (1962 vol. 1, nos. 19, 71–73), there are three tales of previous female existences of Gotama (two as a woman, one as a mother swan) and one of a female existence of the next Buddha-to-be of our world system, Maitreya Bodhisattva. The Divyāvadāna (probably belonging to the Sarvāstivādin school and dating from around the third century C.E.) and Kṣemendra's Bodhisattvāvadānakalpalatā (a much later collection of stories from the eleventh century) both contain the tale of the compassionate woman Rupāvatī (or Rukmavatī) who cuts off her own breast to feed a starving mother about to cannibalize her infant.[8] Rūpā vatī was a previous incarnation of Gotama, according to these texts. Thus, although some Buddhist sects reveal a growing promale attitude shadowed by increasingly antifeminine assertions, other Buddhist schools maintained a far more balanced point of view, and the new Mahāyāna movement sided with the latter.

In the story literature of some Buddhist schools, families of stories seem to have been developed around the personalities of some women known from the early scriptures; then Mahāyāna sūtras took up these same characters and developed them further into idealized feminine bodhisattva figures (for example, the daughter(s) of King Prasenajit of Kośala, Gopikā the Śakya maiden, and the daughter or daughter-in-law of Ugra the generous layman). There are several Mahāyāna sūtras which have female bodhisattvas as heroines (Paul 1979; Schuster 1981). In these scriptures the female figures are used to argue for a more equitable attitude toward the sexes based upon an accurate understanding of the Mahāyāna doctrine of emptiness.

The Buddha as Mahāpursṇa, the Great Man

A bodhisattva is a Buddha-to-be. By about the first century C.E., there were Buddhists who contended that a woman could not be a Buddha, among them the later Theravādins (Sharma 1978) and some Mahāyānists (Paul 1979, 169–76). They asserted that there are five ranks of existence in the world for which a woman's body absolutely disqualifies her: she cannot be a Śakra-god, Brahmā-god or Māra-god, she cannot be a universal monarch (rājā-cakravartin), and she cannot be a Buddha (Schuster 1981, 27; Kajiyama 1982, 54ff.). These five inaccessible ranks had already been proclaimed in the Pali Nikāyas (M.III. 65–66; A.I. 28) and the Chinese Āgamas (T. vol. I, no. 26, p. 607.b.10–15; T. vol. II, no. 125, p. 757.c.24–29). They are also mentioned in the great Mahāyāna sūtra, the Saddharmapuṇḍarīka (Lotus Sūtra, Hurvitz 1976, 201; T. vol. IX, no. 262, p. 35. c.9–11, and no.263, p. 106.a.14–16); but the Lotus Sūtra then "proves" in a dramatic sequence of events that a woman can indeed become a Buddha. This feat is accomplished using the dramatic narrative theme of "changing the female body," which was first used in this way in the Lotus Sūtra and was then reused and refined in several other Mahāyāna scriptures soon afterward (ca. 100–250 C.E.).

Some treatises belonging to the older Buddhist schools (the Theravāda school's Aṭṭhasālinī and the Sautrāntika school's Abhidharmakośa; see Paul 1979, 171–73) and some belonging to the Mahāyāna (the Yogācāra school's Bodhisattvabhūmi; Har Dayal 1932, 224) argue that when beings are born female, it is the result of past karma (actions in previous existences) which cause them to be reborn in an inferior position. Females are females because they have not advanced as far, spiritually, as males. Being born male is the visible demonstration of one's moral and spiritual superiority. A Buddha is the best, most perfect of human beings and has reached ultimate spiritual and moral perfection; naturally he has the appearance of a male: that is the karmic reward for his unexcelled attainment. His body is the epitome of male bodies, bearing all the physical marks (lakṣaṇa) of manly perfection, the thirty-two major and eighty minor marks of the mahāpuruṣa, the Great Man. One of these is the mark of having the penis covered with a sheath (Schuster 1981, 27–28).

The most fundamental and most influential of all Mahāyāna sūtras, however, the Perfection of Wisdom (Prajñāpāramitā) Sūtras, assert that all apparent characteristics of beings are illusory, for everything is in and of itself empty of characteristics. It is therefore wrong to assume that there is a real distinction between female and male; only unenlightened beings believe that this distinction exists. A Buddha, then, cannot be distinguished by "his marks," and a Buddha is therefore not really "male" (Vajracchedikāprajñāpāramitāsūtra, Diamond Sūtra; Schuster 1981, 28; Paul 1979, 217–19).

To aver, as some Buddhists did, that a Buddha, the greatest of all beings, can only be male, was analogous to the profession in a theistic religion that the true deity is a masculine high god. This pronouncement revealed a genuine theological crisis in Buddhism, for it was an attempt to declare a male person to be the ultimate being, even though

Buddhists did not conceive of the Buddha as a creator-god or lord of all the universe in quite the style of genuinely theistic religions. Undoubtedly theological ideas appearing among Hindus at just this time had some influence on Buddhists. It was during this period (ca. 300 B.C.E.-200 C.E.) that the great Hindu epics, the Mahābhārata and the Rāmayaṇa, were taking form; in them, tales of the worldly manifestations of great masculine all-gods are told, and devotion to those gods is called the "true religion." I believe the Buddhist biographies of the founder were a response to this powerful Hindu devotionalism; and, most especially, so are Buddhist efforts to establish the Buddha as an exalted male supreme being. Before the personalities of the great gods Viṣṇu and Śiva emerged so awesomely in Hindu myth and literature, there was evidently no inclination among Buddhists to place men doctrinally in a higher status. But theological developments among their neighbors probably inspired some Buddhists to do just that, while others struggled to preserve the essential egalitarian instincts of mainstream Buddhism.

Changing the Female Body

In the Lotus Sūtra and several other Mahāyāna sūtras, the dramatic narrative theme of changing the female body is used to "prove" that a woman can become a Buddha. In the Lotus Sūtra, the 8-year-old daughter of the Dragon King is said to be superior in knowledge and understanding, to have made far-reaching resolves, and to practice the dharma faultlessly. The monk Śāriputra, spokesman for the conservative elders, the non-Mahāyānists, charges that even if she has accomplished so much, the girl cannot become a Buddha because her female body prohibits her from attaining Buddhahood or any of the other four special ranks of existence. Undismayed, the girl presents the Buddha with a precious jewel and says, "Now I shall achieve supreme enlightenment even more quickly than the Buddha accepted my jewel." With these words she changes into a male bodhisattva and then at once becomes a Buddha (Schuster 1981, 43; Paul 1979, 187-90).

The sequence of events in most of the other texts containing the changing-the-female-body theme is more complex, more dramatic, and also more explicit in intent. In the Vimaladattāsūtra, for example (T.vol.XI, no. 310, pp. 556-64; T.vol.XII, nos. 338 and 339, pp. 89-107; Schuster 1981, 31-35), Vimaladattā, the heroine, is the 12-year-old daughter of King Prasenajit of Kośala (in India). She had accumulated great merit in previous existences and now engages all the major male bodhisattvas and disciples of the Buddha in extremely subtle debate on dharma. She bests them all, thus demonstrating her profound comprehension of emptiness, śūnyatā. Nonetheless, a spokesman for the views of the conservative elders (this time it is Mahāmaudgalyāyana) accuses the princess of not having understood the bodhisattva way because it is known that no one can attain perfect enlightenment with a female body. She says, "If I shall truly become a Buddha in the future, let my body change into that of a young boy." This change occurs, and the Buddha announces that Vimaladattā had long ago aspired to attain perfect Buddhahood and she will do it. Still disgruntled, Mahāmaud-galyāyana asks Vimaladattā why she hadn't changed her female body to male long ago, if she was so wise. She replies that true enlightenment cannot be attained with either a female body or a male body; that is, such distinction-making has nothing to do with the perfect enlighten-ment of the Buddhas, and those who have truly embarked upon the path to that goal must leave all identification with gender and with sex-based roles behind.[9]

The change-of-sex theme is used in the Vimaladattāsūtra and most others to dramatically demonstrate what the Diamond Sūtra and other Prajñāpāramitā Sūtras assert, that all distinctions of sex, age (the pro-tagonists in many of these sūtras are children), social class, vocation, etc., are irrelevant to the life in religion. Anyone who sincerely aspires to be a bodhisattva can be one. The magical sex transformation of Vimaladattā and the others is accomplished by the performance of a ritual act of truth ("If I am truly x, let y occur"), and here magic is a metaphor for the free and unencumbered understanding of an en-lightened being. The change of sex is itself only illusion: as Vimaladattā says, there is no attaining enlightenment as a woman or as a man; so far as she is concerned, she had long since abandoned any attachment to the conventional role of woman or of man, and was merely a bodhi-sattva, a mode of being which is genderless.[10]

It is true that commitment to the spiritual path was anthropomor-phically symbolized in Indian literature by the male body; in Buddhist literature the preferred symbol seems to have been a young male *as-cetic's* body, a body which still resembles an ordinary male's but one which has abandoned traditional male roles, including procreation. A common Buddhist interpretation of the sheathed penis of the Buddha as mahāpuruṣa is just that: his penis is covered because he has aban-doned sexuality completely.[11] (Sometimes the body of a prepubescent male child is used as symbol; in that case, the boy has not yet stepped into a traditional male role.) This idea certainly plays a role in the sexual transformation sequences of the Mayāyāna sūtras discussed. There, too, the young girls' bodies are, at one level, surely symbolic of a woman's potential commitment to the traditional female roles of wife and mother and thus to the world of becoming, saṃsāra. Before reaching puberty, however, the girls opt for the spiritual life. Female bodies are not, according to this view, inherently impure. A female can choose a life of producing and nurturing life (saṃsāra), but she is not by her nature bound to it: she can also choose a spiritual life.[12] A male can make the same choices.

To make possible the liberating insight which frees the Buddhist practitioner from unhappiness caused by ignorance, it is necessary to rid oneself of all attachment to the concepts "this is myself, this is mine." In Mahāyāna changing-the-female-body sūtras, the inclination to cling to one's sexual identity is broken by the enlightened woman who transforms herself. Even more important—for the transforming woman is a teacher—her action challenges the sexual identities to which the less insightful males who dispute with her cling so tenaciously. The Mahāyāna sūtras demonstrate dramatically that the man who clings to his maleness is not an enlightened being, and the woman who does not worry about changing her sex is genuinely enlightened. This is a dramatic demonstration of the meaning of emptiness.

Female Bodhisattvas, Female Buddhas

Unfortunately, the astute employment of the changing-the-female-body narrative theme did not quell the debate, even within Mahāyāna Buddhism, about the spiritual status of women. The dispute raged on, and was never fully resolved. On the one hand, those who insited that women were not the full equals of men in spiritual attainment produced texts which argue that women can indeed be bodhisattvas, but only up to a certain level of advancement on the bodhisattva path; after that, the bodhisattva will never be reborn as a female (Paul 1979, 169–70; Har Dayal 1932, 224). The Daśabhūmikasūtra (which is now a part of the massive Avataṃsakasūtra) was perhaps the most important of those texts which attempted to fix the progress of the bodhisattva's career in a series of identifiable stages. Once this arrangement had been made, it was easier to argue that a woman's body does not fit the definition of the bodhisattva who has reached the highest stages of the path: the eighth, ninth and tenth of the ten stages.[13]

Opposing such a rigid view were texts like the Gaṇḍavyūhasūtra (also part of the very influential Avataṃsakasūtra) and Śrīmālādevīsūtra which matter-of-factly introduce women as great teachers of the bodhisattva path or as imminent Buddhas (Gomez 1977; Paul 1979; Schuster 1981). Queen Śrīmālā, who speaks with the authority of a

Buddha in the sūtra named for her, is the best-known great female bodhisattva (Paul 1980a; Wayman 1974). She is supremely wise and is thereby closely associated with *prajñā*, wisdom, as are all female bodhisattvas in Mahāyāna literature.

There were ideas and images from the very beginnings of Mahāyāna scripture writing which solidly supported the notion of bodhisattva and Buddha as feminine. In the Aṣṭasāhasrikāprajñāpāramitāsūtra, the earliest known Prajñāpāramitā Sūtra, and its versified rendering, Ratnaguṇasaṃcayagāthā, Prajñāpāramitā (a word which in Sanskrit is grammatically feminine) is presented as the female personification of liberating wisdom. She is barely personalized in the sūtra and is no deity, but the perfect understanding which liberates is clearly imaged as feminine (Macy 1977, 315). Prajñāpāramitā is the mother of the Buddhas and the bodhisattvas, their instructress in this world, genetrix, and nurse (Macy 1977, 319). Without perfect wisdom there would be no perfectly enlightened beings, and so, as teacher and as what is taught, Prajñāpāramitā is the mother who bears and nurtures the enlightened ones. She is the source of light which reveals the truth; she is the eye which perceives it (Macy 1977, 320).

Every bit as important as the symbolizing of perfect wisdom as female is the imaging of the bodhisattva as both masculine and feminine. A bodhisattva is generally thought of as masculine: the word in Sanskrit is grammatically masculine, and some authors have explicitly claimed that all bodhisattvas are actually male, even if they appear in the form of a woman (Tsai 1981, p.1, n.1). This interpretation is found in some later Mahāyāna sūtras and in some Chinese commentaries on scriptures (Yamamoto 1973, 1:10–11; Paul 1980a, 23–24). But the bodhisattva in the Aṣṭasāhasrikāprajñāpāramitāsūtra and Ratnaguṇasaṃcayagāthā incorporates aspects of both male and female, thus demonstrating a "peculiar and sometimes bizarre fluidity of sexual identification" (Paul 1979, 170). By imaging the bodhisattva as both masculine and feminine, he/she is presented as the ideal to be emulated by both women and men; and since the bodhisattva incorporates within its androgynous self aspects of both sexes, any attempt to insist that the bodhisattva is only masculine is misguided. The bodhisattva in this literature reflects the most intense experiences of both sexes. The bodhisattva on the verge of enlightenment is like a pregnant woman about to give birth; the bodhisattva who does not let go of the perfection of wisdom is like a cow who does not abandon her young calf; the bodhisattva pondering on Prajñāpāramitā and striving after her for many aeons is like a lover preoccupied with thought of the woman he is to meet who has been delayed (Macy 1977, 319–20; Conze 1973, 28, 41, 64–65, 184, 209–10).

MAHĀYĀNA AND VAJRAYĀNA BUDDHISM OUTSIDE INDIA (AFTER ca.400 C.E.)

Buddhism began to be carried by missionaries beyond India's borders already in the third century B.C.E. with the sanction of the powerful Emperor Aśoka. By the beginning of the common era it had been transported across central Asia and into China. By the seventh century it had penetrated nearly every corner of Asia. Mahāyāna Buddhism has dominated east Asia for the past 1,900 years, and the offshoot of Mahāyāna, Vajrayāna (the Diamond Vehicle), has long been well entrenched in Tibet and the Himalayan area. Theravāda Buddhism, the only one of the pre-Mahāyāna sects to survive into modern times, is the major form of Buddhism practiced in southeast Asia and Śri Laṅkā today. In China and in Tibet, the Buddhist religion has developed in some especially interesting directions.

China: Women as Nuns; Women in the Chinese Buddhist Schools

The nuns' order was established in China in the fourth century C.E., and unlike nuns' orders in most other Buddhist countries, it has survived as an unbroken tradition until the present. There are still active communities of nuns in Taiwan and in the People's Republic of China. Chinese nuns were obliged to live according to the same disciplinary rules as the first Indian bhikṣuṇīs; the legal codes for the organization and operation of the saṃgha established in ancient India were transported as an entire corpus to the various countries where Buddhism was established.

For Buddhist women in China, the nuns' order has been a very important institution, in no small part because it has afforded women an opportunity to live a respectable, active life outside the traditional family structure (Schuster 1985b). About 516 C.E., a scholar monk, Baochang, recorded the biographies of sixty-five nuns whom he considered to be outstanding for their faith, their asceticism, or their accomplishments in meditation or in learning and teaching. His work is the Bi-qiu-ni zhuan, Lives of the Nuns (Cissell 1972; Li 1981). Like the ancient Indian Therīgāthā, the Bi-qiu-ni zhuan describes an elite group of real women who were regarded as exemplary, worthy of emulating. These Chinese nuns are praised for their own worth and accomplishments, not for the quality of their relationships with fathers, husbands, or sons, and they probably did serve as examples of personal responsibility and independence for those Chinese women who read about them.

In China, scholarship and literary expression have been highly valued since very ancient times. There have been female scholars, and there have also been reactions against the notion of education for women. However, a majority of the nuns of the Bi-qiu-ni zhuan are extolled for their erudition and their sophisticated literary skills (Cissell 1972, 87–91; Tsai 1981, 12–13; Schuster 1985b, 93–96). Although some of the nuns are reported to have been well educated in traditional secular subjects before joining the order (Cissell 1972, 149, 166, 169, 178, 244; Li 1981, 33, 45, 53, 108), it was mastery of Buddhist scriptures which was especially lauded by Bao-chang; a great many nuns' biographies celebrate their command of volumes of lengthy and important sūtras as well as of treatises and disciplinary books. The sūtras these nuns most frequently studied and mastered were the Lotus, Prajñāpāramitā, Vimalakīrtinirdeśa, Śrīmālādevī and Mahāparinirvāna (Cissell 1972, 87–89; Tsai 1981, 12; Schuster 1985b, 96); all of these texts expound a single way to full enlightenment for all beings and put forward important arguments in support of the spiritual integrity of female bodhisattvas.

Many Chinese nuns became great teachers who lectured to other nuns and to large congregations of laypeople on the sūtras, thereby becoming highly respected and extremely influential. Like monks, they often had many friends at court and lectured to and acted as spiritual guides to emperors and other members of princely families (Cissell 1972, 89–92; Schuster 1985b, 93ff.)[14] Some nuns publicly debated famous monks and defeated them. But although many nuns were extraordinary teachers, scholars, and religious leaders who held influential positions as abbesses of important convents and even as directors of the nuns' saṃgha in the capital region,[15] there is no evidence so far that individual nuns or nuns' communities made any significant contributions to the development of the Chinese Buddhist schools which were emerging by the sixth century C.E., or that they participated in the discussions on doctrine and the institution of new practices from which the Chinese schools grew. There were nuns who wrote commentaries and treatises on doctrine (Cissell 1972, 227, 258; Li 1981, 95, 118), but so far as we now know, most such works have been lost, and few extant treatises can be confidently attributed to Chinese women scholars.

So far as the records are concerned, therefore, the situation is about the same for the Chinese nuns as for their counterparts in ancient India: we know there were learned, influential, and well-respected nuns who taught and also wrote, but almost no clear evidence survives of what their actual contributions might have been. So far as history is concerned, the nuns remained on the periphery of religious events.

Buddhism reached China around the beginning of the common era. Translations of sūtras from Indian languages into Chinese commenced at once, and the assimilation of Buddhist ideas by the many Chinese converts to the foreign religion proceeded gradually over the next few hundred years. By the sixth century, genuinely Chinese schools of Buddhism were appearing which were grounded in a clear comprehension of Buddhist principles but which reshaped Buddhist concepts into acceptable Chinese forms. The Tiantai school (Japanese Tendai) was one of these, established by the monk Zhi-yi at the end of the sixth century. He adopted the Lotus Sūtra as the basic text of his school for he felt it contained the essence of all Buddhist doctrine, but Tiantai monks also studied the Prajñāpāramitā and Mahāparinirvāṇa Sūtras intensively. Tiantai stresses the totality and mutual identification of everything that is, and that all beings have the same potential to attain Buddhahood (Chen 1964, 303–13). Buddhahood is moreover attainable in this very life, and the episode in the Lotus Sūtra of the Dragon Princess attaining immediate Buddhahood after changing her sex was taken as an example of this truth (Paul 1979, 282). Tiantai commentaries on the Lotus Sūtra repeatedly assert that women can become Buddhas; some claim that there is no ncessity for an individual to change sex to become a Buddha[16] so long as she has attained the tolerance of the notion that phenomena do not, in an ultimate sense, really come into being or really cease to exist—that is, so long as she has the profound realization that all phenomena are empty of unique essence and therefore impossible to grasp by themselves (Paul 1979, 282; Schuster 1981, 30, 35, 45, 51). Thus the Tiantai school clearly perceived and unhesitatingly accepted the full implications of the basic Mahāyāna teachings as expounded in the Prajñāpāramitāsūtras; if it is not possible to distinguish beings from each other absolutely since all are equally empty of unique essence, and if all beings have the same inherent potential for full enlightenment, then beings of both sexes, all ages, and all social positions must be the same from the ultimate, true, religious point of view.

Chan (Japanese Zen) is another of the distinctively Chinese schools of Buddhism which emerged in China in the sixth century, but reached its true apogee in the Tang and Song dynasties (seventh through thirteenth centuries). Transmitted to Korea, Japan, and Vietnam, Chan remains today one of the most vital Buddhist sects in east Asia; in recent times it has also been brought to the western world. Chan insists upon disciplined, intensive meditation practice under the close guidance of a teacher, which will lead to sudden, dramatic enlightenment experiences in this life and in this body. Compared with other Buddhist schools, Chan attaches relatively little importance to the study of scriptures; nonetheless it is solidly grounded doctrinally in the Prajñāpāramitā. Chan teachers have consistently argued that the one mind of enlightenment possessed by all sentient beings is without distinguishing characteristics such as maleness or femaleness (Levering 1982, 19-20). In the Chan view, then, there are no karmic impediments which can keep an individual from attaining a moment of true, liberating insight here and now. The incident of the Dragon Princess's sudden attainment of Buddhahood in the Lotus Sūtra is often cited, and in the Chan interpretation the change of sex is not the central message of the scripture; rather, what is to be recognized is that the difference between Buddhahood and delusion is merely a single moment of right thought, and the apparent sex of the enlightened one is irrelevant (Levering 1982, 22-24). Dōgen, the great thirteenth century founder of Sōtō Zen in Japan, simply says that the Dragon Princess is a case of a female becoming a Buddha. For Dōgen and other masters, the Dragon Princess's story is not about a woman who became a male Buddha, but about a woman who became a Buddha *and is still thought of as a woman* (Levering 1982, 26-27). The Lotus Sūtra itself is ambivalent about the necessity for and signficance of the sexual transformation of the Dragon Princess. Both the Chinese and Japanese schools of Chan eliminate the ambivalence and freely avow that a woman can be a Buddha.

Chan literature preserves the records of the transmission of the dharma in various master-disciple lineages. A few women are represented in these lineages, but not many: even though Dōgen and others argued that enlightened women should without hesitation be taken as teachers by men and women, there are not many recorded cases where this was done. As mentioned earlier in this chapter, the ancient Indian Vinaya prohibits nuns from teaching dharma to monks. For reasons that were probably mostly social, the bias against women as teachers was very hard for monks to overcome. To Dōgen, a man who could not accept a woman as teacher did not understand the dharma and was certainly not living it (Levering 1982, 30). But he had to argue for this view because it was so generally opposed in his day. In the Chan records of transmission of the dharma, called the Jing-de chuan-deng lu, there is one nun who is given a record of her own, and in it occurs the often-cited case of a monk who acknowledges her as his teacher. The Abbess Mo-shan Liao-ran gained Zhi-xian as her disciple by demonstrating to him in a sharply pointed dialogue that her understanding was superior to his, and true. He knelt and bowed to her—an act forbidden in the ancient Vinaya—thus admitting she was his teacher, and under her guidance he attained enlightenment (Levering 1982, 27–30). Zhi-xian had not failed to challenge her, at their first encounter, with an incongruity between her femaleness and her enlightenment, but she countered by asserting in effect that her enlightenment has no visible characteristics, so what would be the point of assuming the characteristics of a male body? It was this rejoinder which proved to him that she was his true teacher.

Chan and Zen have had women teachers, and there are some living today, including some Western women who have become Zen masters. This is a matter of spiritual equality, of course, and has no bearing, even for Dōgen, on the matter of the relative rank of women and men outside the religious path in secular society. Buddhists in times past simply did not speak to that issue; it was never considered relevant to religious practice.

Vajrayāna in India and Tibet

Vajrayāna, or Tantric Buddhism, is, like Mahāyāna, a major movement in Buddhism, not just a sect. Also like the Mahāyāna, the Vajrayāna has itself branched into several lineages or schools, but all Vajrayāna lineages are very firmly rooted in Prajñāpāramitā thought. Vajrayāna, which means the "Diamond Vehicle," imparts many esoteric teachings; the Diamond Vehicle stresses meditative practice, as does Chan, but essential to the practice of Vajrayāna are the many instructions transmitted directly from master to disciple, instructions which cannot be learned merely by studying volumes of scriptures and metaphysical treatises. Again, like Chan and other Chinese Mahāyāna schools, Vajrayāna teaches that Buddhahood can be attained in this body and in this life; therefore extraordinary efforts in practice are fully worthwhile.

Vajrayāna Buddhism originated in northern India sometime after 400 C.E. and was widely practiced there for several centuries. Like all other forms of Buddhism, it disappeared from India after about 1200 C.E., but it had already spread to the Himalayan regions and into Tibet by the seventh century C.E., and has survived there until the present time. During the past few decades, Vajrayāna has also been brought to the West and is flourishing in this new territory.

Vajrayāna counts large numbers of famous female practitioners and teachers in its ranks, and rises above other Buddhist schools in that respect. One of the major reasons for the notable acceptance of women within the Vajrayāna is no doubt the clear recognition that women and men not only have the same human nature but share the same psychological traits. The traits normally labeled "male" and "female" are in fact part of everyone's psychological makeup, and in an enlightened person these traits are ideally balanced: thus in every enlightened individual, maleness and femaleness must both be present (Ray 1980, 228–29). Predictably, feminine symbolism is given unusual prominence in this system.

Biographies of "accomplished ones," *siddhas*, have been composed from fairly early on in the history of the Vajrayāna and are still being written about recent masters. Among the siddhas were several women, although their numbers could never compare with the numbers of male adepts. As in other forms of Buddhism throughout the world, more men than women entered the Vajrayāna path of strenuous practice. Most of the women who did follow the path remained lay practitioners. But since the Vajrayāna is far less overwhelmingly a clerical vocation than are most other forms of Buddhism, remaining in lay life was not a severe impediment to spiritual practice. Many siddhas were laypeople; nearly all female siddhas were.

Women who followed the Tantric path were certainly not free from social stress. In India and Tibet, women were expected to marry and bear children, and the biographies of female siddhas vividly recount the opposition they met from fathers and husbands and the painful relations with men which threatened to interfere with their spiritual practice. When they did break with the traditional social roles which were forced upon them, they often had to endure painful social rejection, solitude, and desolation, for following the Tantric path could and often did mean deliberately forsaking all socially acceptable ways of life and becoming an object of general disapprobation (Ray 1980, 230–33). It also meant that a woman siddha could really abandon all traditional female roles within society, even more radically than nuns did, for each siddha followed a unique path.

Vajrayāna teachings as embodied in the Tantras and in the biographies of the siddhas show less self-consciously than any other Buddhist tradition that female and male are equally respected as practitioners, teachers, and as balanced component parts of the psychology of every sentient being.

WHO KEEPS THE RECORDS?

There is ample reason to believe that there have always been a great many active Buddhist laywomen and/or nuns in every culture which Buddhism has penetrated. Yet very little concrete information about these women has come down to us; that fact leaves the strong impression that somehow women remained on the periphery of most of the important developments within the religion. As I. B. Horner suggests (1930, 165), the women were no doubt always there, in the background at least, and should have had some influence on molding the religion. But the evidence even for their presence is meager compared to what we hear about men in the religion. If Buddhist women had written the history of their own sisters or had recorded their own experiences, we might have quite a different impression about Buddhism. Why did the women leave the writing to men?

Of course there are some documents reliably attributed to women: the Therīgāthā above all, and the few sermons preached by women which are preserved in the Pali Nikāyas and Chinese Āgamas. Some scholars have suggested that even the Therīgāthā were really composed by men, an arrogant proposition which Davids (1909, xxiii) indignantly rejects as ill founded; we cannot be certain that the women said to have sung those songs were the ones who actually did so, but there seems no good reason to assume the authors were not women. Moreover, the Divyāvadāna, itself composed early in the common era, says that women wrote out Buddhist texts at night with reed and ink (de Jong 1974). This probably only means that they copied texts, and there is plenty of evidence for that from China, Japan, and elsewhere, but in any case Buddhist women were known to have engaged in literary activities. Paul (1980a, 2) cites a Chinese commentary on the Śrīmālādevīsūtra which, from internal evidence, the Japanese scholar Fujieda has concluded was written by a woman. The Bi-qiu-ni zhuan records the lives of many scholarly nuns and cites at least two who composed commentaries on sūtras, or other works, but their compositions have apparently not survived (Cissell 1972, 227, 258; Li 1981, 95, 118). There certainly were women writers in the Vajrayāna tradition, as well as women who were written about; the biography of Padmasaṃbhava, the great missionary to Tibet, was written by his outstanding female disciple, Ye-shes mTsho-rgyal, and her own biography was written by a fellow disciple, a man (Nam-mkha'i snying-po, 1983).

Men did sometimes write about Buddhist women, but not often. Bao-chang wrote the biographies of exemplary Chinese nuns early in the sixth century. Since he was commissioned by the court to compose

other historical works (Cissell 1972, 1), it is possible that he was requested to write these biographies as well. At any rate, there is no
evidence that any nun was asked to do so or that any did so of her own
volition. Significantly, too, for the meagerness of records of the history
of women in Buddhism, the monks' biographies compiled in the sixth
century were added to in later centuries, so that we have a fairly extensive record of the lives and activities of a large number of Chinese
monks over a period of several centuries. But after Bao-chang wrote
about the first generation of nuns, no successor continued his work.
There is a Chan record of one great woman teacher, the Abbess of Mo-
shan, which probably has come down to us because she had a male disciple who was willing to acknowledge that she had been his teacher and
spiritual guide. The record also says that she had female disciples
(Levering 1982, 28), but apparently none of them wrote. The Chan
records contain more anecdotes about other colorful, enlightened
women, so obviously the Abbess of Mo-shan was not unique in the
tradition. As Ray (1980) remarks of the Vajrayāna stories of the siddhas
(237), these tales were written by men and are thus told from the male
practitioner's viewpoint. These men respected their female teachers
greatly and did not hesitate to credit the women for their great contributions to their disciples' accomplishments. But Tantric women
practitioners must have had important stories to tell too, and they could
have given us insights from a woman's point of view.

Why did Buddhist women leave so few records of their lives as
Buddhists? It may be that women were not significantly involved in
major doctrinal debates, sectarian developments, or lineages of dharma
transmission. Because saṃgha rules and traditions forced them to remain on the outside, women may really have been left on the fringes of
major movements. Strict adherence to the Vinaya rules, in any Buddhist community, would ensure that nuns remained out of leadership
positions, and in none but a few Buddhist traditions have laywomen
had the opportunity to lead. Thus the time-honored institutions of
Buddhism have militated against permitting women to participate fully
in creative developments within the saṃgha. This repression is the real
fruit of the monks' efforts to keep authority in their own hands.

But it is recorded that some women were scholars and did preach
and write. There are many treatises and commentaries in the Chinese
Buddhist canon and in the Tibetan Tanjur which are quite arbitrarily
attributed to one or another famous monk's name. Is it not possible
that, hidden under that mass of anonymity and fanciful attributions,
some women have left the record of their own minds? Must we really go
on assuming that Buddhism has always been an oppressively pat-

riarchal religious institution and that therefore women were not allowed to make any contributions, and did not? I do not think that is quite the picture of the religion which emerges after closer scrutiny. There certainly were powerful efforts to keep women out of positions of real authority, and there was some bias against the idea that women could be the full spiritual equals of men. But there was also a strong and basic urge to recognize the essential equality of the sexes in matters of spiritual attainment. At this point, I, for one, prefer to assume that women did play more important roles more frequently in Buddhism than we have heretofore been willing to admit, and I believe the search for more signs of their activity is warranted.

CONCLUSIONS

The real opposition which has faced women within the Buddhist saṃgha is opposition to their taking positions of authority. More possibilities came to be offered women within some late-emerging Mahāyāna and Vajrayāna schools, for in Chan and in the Vajrayāna women could become religious teachers and spiritual guides, and when they did they were in no way second to men. Nonetheless, in all Buddhist sects throughout the Buddhist world, men have always dominated and still dominate. There have been prominent Buddhist women, and there are some living today, but they are a small minority of the Buddhist leadership.

Buddhism originally offered no doctrinal resistance to the acceptance of women and men as equally capable of spiritual attainment, and this continued to be the position of mainstream Buddhist thought through the centuries. But sometime around the beginning of the common era a real theological controversy emerged among Buddhists, revolving around a doctrinal effort to prove that women are karmically inferior to men and therefore incapable of the highest human attainment and the ultimate state of being, Buddhahood. Although the majority of Mahāyāna and Vajrayāna Buddhists decisively rejected that argument because they recognized it to be antithetical to basic Buddhist doctrine, the quarrel was not fully resolved, and the antifeminists never surrendered. Most of the main schools of Buddhism which are thriving today, however, are fully egalitarian in doctrine. Many of the problems which women in Buddhist countries actually face today have more to do with deeply rooted social values which were not originated by Buddhist theorists, but with which Buddhists have usually complied.

Buddhism has had, in comparison with some other religions, little to say about what social roles should be, since such questions have not been seen as directly pertinent to religious commitment and effort. Thus, until very recent times, Buddhists have usually remained silent about social issues.

What effect, then, might Buddhism have had on the formation of attitutes toward women in predominantly Buddhist countries, and what has it contributed to the self-image of Buddhist women themselves, and perhaps of non-Buddhist women living in societies affected by Buddhist ideas and conduct? Hard evidence is scant and suppositions can run rampant, but it surely must be true that images in Buddhist literature of women as fully enlightened beings, as quick-witted teachers, compassionate friends, self-sacrificing saints, and courageous heroines have had a positive effect on the sensibilities of women and men who have heard or read the old scriptures, poems, and popular stories. Symbolisms, too, which identify perfect wisdom as feminine, and the enormous popularity of female bodhisattvas as well as goddesses in the Buddhist pantheons of Tibet and east Asia, have probably bolstered women's self-respect. These things have certainly helped make both men and women immediately aware of the dignity and power of the feminine.

To speak of concrete events, Buddhist theory has been used to support the claims to legitimate secular authority made by women rulers in China and elsewhere, most spectacularly by the seventh century Chinese woman emperor, Wu Ze-tian, who held all real power in her hands for about forty years (Forte 1976; Paul 1980b). On the basis of Buddhist scriptural authority, Wu Ze-tian and her advisers proclaimed that she had the right to rule because she was a bodhisattva in female form and a legitimate universal monarch (rājā-cakravartin). In China, Buddhist ideas contributed often enough to the creation of revolutionary ideologies, and there is some evidence that Buddhist ideas and institutions sometimes helped women establish independent positions for themselves. In nineteenth century Guangdong, for example, scores of women silk workers refused to marry and lived together as lay-women in communal groups very like Buddhist nuns' communities (Topley 1975). These women were able to choose such a way of life because they were economically independent due to their work, and that was not owed to Buddhism; but the patterns of their lives in the community were. The nuns' saṃgha has always provided an important alternative life-style for women in China and wherever else the order was strong; these modern Chinese women simply adapted the institution further to fit their own preferences.

The study of women in Buddhism is a new field. Modern scholars have only begun to seriously examine the manifold questions relating to women's place in the Buddhist religion, and Buddhist women in Asia and the West have only begun to look hard at such questions. The next several years are certain to see important advances in our understanding of this field, and new perspectives are bound to be opened as twentieth century Buddhist women become more aware of themselves within their religious tradition, and more public about their insights.

ABBREVIATIONS

A   *Aṅguttara-nikāya*, ed. R. Morris and E. Hardy, revised by A.K. Warder. 6 vols. Pali Text Society, 1885-1910. Reprint. London: Luzac and Co., 1955-61.

D   *Dīgha-nikāya*, ed. T.W. Rhys Davids and J.E. Carpenter. 3 vols. Pali Text Society, 1890–1911. Reprint. London: Luzac and Co., 1960–67.

Dial.   *Dialogues of the Buddha*, trans. T.W. Rhys Davids and C.A.F. Rhys Davids. 3 vols. Pali Text Society, 1899–1921. Reprint. London: Luzac and Co., 1965–69.

GS   *Book of the Gradual Sayings*, trans. F.L. Woodward and E.M. Hare. 5 vols. Pali Text Society, 1932–36. Reprint. London: Luzac and Co., 1960–65.

KS   *Book of the Kindred Sayings*, trans. C.A.F. Rhys Davids and F.L. Woodward. 5 vols. Pali Text Society, 1922–50. Reprint. London: Luzac and Co., 1952–65.

M   *Majjhima-nikāya*, ed. V. Trenckner and R. Chalmers. 4 vols. Pali Text Society, 1888–1925. Reprint. London. Luzac and Co. 1960–64.

MLS   *Middle Length Sayings*, trans. I.B. Horner. 3 vols. Pali Text Society, 1954–59. Reprint. London: Luzac and Co., 1967.

S   *Samyutta-nikāya*, ed. L. Feer. 6 vols. Pali Text Society, 1884–1904. Reprint. London: Luzac and Co. 1960.

Sn   *Suttanipāta*, ed. D. Andersen and H. Smith. Pali Text Society, 1913. Reprint. London: Luzac and Co., 1965.

T   *Taishō Shinshū Daizōkyō*, ed. J. Takakusu and K. Watanabe. Tokyo: Taishō shinshū daizōkyō kanko kai, 1924–29.

Thig.   *Therīgāthā*, ed. H. Oldenberg and R. Pischel. London: Pali Text Society, 1883.

Theresa Kelleher

CONFUCIANISM

T HIS chapter will examine the position of women in Confucianism, focusing primarily on the classical period and to a lesser extent on its later phase, Neo-Confucianism. As I shall show, women played a central role in Confucianism by virtue of their place in both the cosmic order and in the family. Nevertheless, since Confucianism was a patriarchal religious tradition, its estimation of women's nature was by and large a low one. Richard Guisso has summed up the negative attitudes toward women which appear in the canonical texts of early Confucianism, the Five Classics, as follows: "The female was inferior by nature, she was dark as the moon and changeable as water, jealous, narrow-minded, and insinuating. She was indiscreet, unintelligent, and dominated by emotion. Her beauty was a snare for the unwary male, the ruination of states" (Guisso 1981, 59).

I have chosen not to dwell so much on these negative attitudes as on the actual religious path set forth for women in the tradition. I will give particular attention to the types of attitudes and behavior considered desirable for a good Confucian woman and the models put forth for women to emulate. To do so, I will draw on various instructions for women found in the classical ritual texts and in pieces written by women for women, as well as biographies of exemplary women.

There are, of course, limitations in the use of these sources. They were all in support of the dominant male teachers and were addressed to an elite group in society. Social historians have pointed out the cruel use to which some of these teachings were put at different periods of Chinese history to make the lot of women difficut. Although there were surely discrepancies between the ideals articulated in the texts and the realities of women's lives in Chinese history, we have evidence that many women did take these teachings seriously, fervently believed in them, and were even willing to die to honor them. For this reason, though other readings of the texts are possible (and even necessary) to fully understand the position of women in Confucianism, I will keep to a fairly straight-forward description of the texts and their teachings, supplying occasional critical commentary.

Since the basic religious orientation of Confucianism may not be well understood by many and since such an understanding is necessary if one is to appreciate the part women played in the tradition, I will begin with a brief overview of basic Confucian teachings. I will do so in terms of the cosmic order of Heaven and earth, the human order, which parallels the cosmic order with its roots in the family and its fullest expression in the state, and lastly, the proper response of humans to these two orders.

The cosmic order in its fullest sense is seen as comprised of the triad of Heaven, earth, and the human. Humans are intimately linked to Heaven and earth, but not in the same way as they are related to the divine in the West. The call of the human community is not to worship Heaven and earth, but to learn from them, imitate their behavior, and thus form a human order modeled upon the cosmic order. Three aspects of the cosmic order especially impressed the Confucians as lessons worth learning in the human order.[1]

First, Heaven and earth were seen as fundamentally live-giving; they continually bring new life into being, nurture and sustain it, and bring it to its completion. The fundamental optimism of Confucianism that life is good—indeed, that life is the most precious gift of all—comes from this sense of the universe as being fundamentally oriented toward the production and promotion of life.

The second aspect of the cosmic order valued by the Confucians was that everything in life is relational. Nothing comes into being in isolation, and nothing survives in isolation. Both the creative and the nurturing process depend on the coming together of two different elements in a relationship. Now the relationship between Heaven and earth is the most primal and most creative one in the universe. But these bodies do not function as equals; rather, they observe a hierarchy, with Heaven as the superior, creative element, positioned high above, and earth as the inferior, receptive element, positioned down below. What mattered was the overall effectiveness of the relationship rather than which was superior or inferior.

The third aspect of the cosmic order which impressed the Confucians was the orderly fashion in which it worked, with harmony rather than conflict prevailing among its parts. Each part seemed patterned to work for the good of the whole and yet at the same time to realize its own nature. It appeared to the Confucians that the parts observed a type of deference, or "polite form," with each other. For example, the sun dominates the day but yields its place to the moon at night with an absence of strife. Each of the four seasons gets its turn to dominate part of the year, but then gives way, or defers, to the season that follows.

In sum, the cosmic order was seen as life-giving, relational, and harmonious in the interaction of its parts. All these concepts formed the cornerstone of the Confucian ordering of human society.

The capacity of humans to be life-giving, for human life to be passed down from generation to generation in an unbroken chain was an awesome thing for Confucians. The most direct and profound experience of this for any human was the gift of life at birth from one's parents. Birth brought one into this continuum of life, which was much larger than any one individual life. One felt oneself caught up in a flow of life which connected one to countless generations before and many more to come. A worshipful attitude was thus directed toward the progenitors of life: in the most concrete sense, one's own parents, but also their parents and their parents' parents. This reverence and gratitude for life formed the basis of ancestor worship.

The family, as the nexus of this life-giving activity and the custodian of the chain of life, thus came to be enshrined as a sacred community and was reverenced in a way that few religious traditions of the world have reverenced it. All other social groupings, including the state, had their basis in the family, and indeed, were often seen in terms of the family metaphor. Since Confucianism had no priesthood or special houses of worship, the roles of husband and wife took on a sacerdotal character. Marriage was a vocation to which all were called. Just as one received life at birth, one was to pass on that life to the next generation. Not to do so was a serious offense. As the philosopher Mencius said, "There are three things which are unfilial, and to have no posterity is the greatest of them" (Mencius 4A:26, Legge 1966, 725). As we shall see, this sense of the primacy of marriage and the sacredness of the family had an immense impact on the lives of women in Confucianism.

The second lesson that Confucians learned from the cosmic order was the relational aspect of things. All humans exist in relationships; there are no solitary individuals. These relationships are not just any relationships, but five very specific ones, known as the "Five Cardinal Relationships." The family generates three of them, and society generates the other two. Man and woman come together as husband and wife. They produce children, thus establishing the parent-child relationship was well as the older-younger sibling relationship. These bonds form the basis of the poitical relationship of ruler and subject and the social one of friend and friend.

For the Confucians, these relationships were not just biological or social; more importantly, they were moral. Since humans are not like plants and animals, they need more than food and shelter to sustain themselves—they need the empathetic response and support of other humans. Confucians had a profound awareness of the capacity of humans to nurture (be life-giving) or tear down (be life-destroying) in their interactions with others. Confucius thus made as the focus of his teachings in the Analects the virtue of *jen*, variously translated as "benevolence," "humaneness," "humanity," "love," or even just "virtue." The Chinese character for jen is composed of two elements: a human being on the left and the word for 'two' on the right. The implication is that humans are structured to be in relationship, that our fundamental being is wrapped up in the existence of others. We are called upon to be as responsible and as empathetic as possible, both for the sake of the other and for our own good. One of the descriptions of jen given by Confucius explains it thus:

> Now the man of perfect virtue, wishing to be established himself, seeks also to establish others; wishing to be enlarged himself, he seeks also to enlarge others. To be able to judge of others by what is nigh in ourselves: this may be called the art of virtue. (Analects 6:28, Legge 1966, 77)

Thus the Confucians were puzzled and disturbed when Buddhism made its way to China with its monastic system, which called for males to leave home and lead a celibate existence away from any family or social context.

The actual practice of jen in the Five Cardinal Relationships varied because of the hierarchical nature of these relationships. The same sense of hierarchy that exists in the cosmic order was seen as existing in the human order. Except for the friend-friend relation, all the others were conceived of as hierarchical in nature, with one party in the superior position and the other in the inferior position. This hierarchy was seen as necessary if the relationships were to work. Those who occupied the superior positions were parents, rulers, husbands, and older siblings; those in the inferior positions were children, subjects, wives, and younger siblings. Children were exhorted to be filial to their parents, subjects loyal to their rulers, wives submissive to their husbands, and younger siblings respectful to their older siblings. While most moral teachings in Confucianism were directed to those in the inferior positions, persons in the superior positions were obliged to use their superior status for the well-being of the other.

The third aspect of the cosmic order which impressed Confucians was the order and harmony which prevailed among the various elements, the correct positioning of each part in relation to the whole. Desirous of establishing the same order and harmony in the human community, from the family up to the state, Confucians attempted to choreograph the gestures, speech, and behavior of human beings with ritual. Here ritual included not just the more overtly religious ceremonials associated with coming-of-age ceremonies, weddings, funerals, and ancestral sacrifices (the four major rituals in Confucianism), but also what Westerners would put in the category of comportment and good manners. The classical ritual texts (notably, the Book of Rites, the Book of Etiquette and Ceremonial, the Rites of Chou) are filled with directives on the correct and proper behavior for every conceivable human interaction. The range extends from details for children to follow in serving their parents on a day-to-day basis in the household to the correct protocol for officials at court. While Confucius was all too aware of the dangers of formalism to which such a heavy emphasis on ritual could lead, nevertheless, he feared leaving the carrying out of virtue to chance. How was a child to be filial? Did he have to figure that duty out anew each day? Though one's understanding of filial piety should deepen over one's lifetime, one must begin with patterns to follow, both to ensure the smooth running of the household and also to initiate a person into a sense of what filial piety consists. Similar directions could be applied to the other relationships, including that of husband and wife.

From this brief presentation of the basic teachings of Confucianism, we see that the cosmic order is the primary source of divine revelation and the model for the human order, that the family is perceived as the nexus of the sacred community, and that all humans, both male and female, operate in a highly contextual, hierarchical, and choreographed setting. Relationships and the behavior considered appropriate to them are spelled out in quite specific terms. The religious pursuit for a Confucian is not to leave the world, but to realize the fullness of his or her humanity by a total immersion in human life, beginning with the family and extending outward to society through public service. By so doing, one achieves a mystic identification with the cosmic order, and one is "able to assist in the transforming and nourishing powers of Heaven and earth" (Doctrine of the Mean, ch. 22, Legge, 1966, 399).

This, then, is the context in terms of which I will base my discussion of the role of women in Confucianism. I will show how that role was said to mirror the cosmic order, how women were identified in terms of their roles in the network of human relationships rather than as individuals, and how their behavior was informed by the elaborate ritual code.

In the cosmic order of things, the feminine as yin constitutes one of the two primary modes of being. This feminine force is identified with the earth, with all things lowly and inferior. It is characterized as yielding, receptive, and devoted, and it furthers itself through its sense of perseverence (Book of Changes, k'un hexagram, Wilhelm, 1967, 386–88). Though inferior to the masculine yang principle, the yin principle is nevertheless crucial and indispensable to the proper workings of the universe. From this cosmic pattern it was deduced that the position of women in the human order should be lowly and inferior like the earth, and that the proper behavior for a woman was to be yielding and weak, passive and still like the earth. It was left for men to be active and strong, to be initiators like Heaven. Though men were considered superior, they could not do without women as their complementary opposites.

In the human order, women were seen only in the context of the family, while men were seen in the wider social-political order. And within the family, a woman was subject to the "three obediences": as a daughter she was subject to her father; as a wife, to her husband; and when older, to her son. If the Confucian calling for men was "the way of the sages" (sheng-tao), for women it was "the wifely way" (fu-tao). The Chinese word for 'wife' shows a woman with a broom, signifying the domestic sphere as her proper place. Marriage was indeed the focal point of a woman's life, and she was identified in terms of her role as wife, along with her two related roles as daughter-in-law and mother. In theory, females as step-daughters did not have much status within their natal families because, destined as they were to join the ranks of another family at marriage, they would never be official members of their natural families (no tablet would ever stand for them on the family's ancestral altar).

All childhood education for females was solely to prepare them for their future roles as wives and mothers. In contrast to boys, who went out of the house at age 10 for their education in history and the classics, girls remained at home, sequestered in the female quarters and under the guidance of a governess. They learned good manners and domestic skills like sewing and weaving.

A girl at the age of ten ceased to go out [from the women's apartments]. Her governess taught her [the arts of] pleasing speech and manners, to be docile and obedient, to handle the hemper fibres, to learn [all] woman's work, how to furnish garments, to watch the sacrifices, to supply the liquors and sauces, to fill the various stands and dishes with pickles and brine, and to assist in setting forth the appurtenances for the ceremonies. (Book of Rites, ch. 12, Legge 1967, 1:479)

At age 15, according to this chronology, a girl would receive the hair pin in a coming-of-age ceremony. At 20 she was to marry. Three months before her marriage, a young woman was to be instructed in the four aspects of womanly character: virtue, speech, comportment, and work (Book of Rites, ch. 44).

Both for the woman and the families, marriage and the wedding ceremony were extremely important events. As mentioned earlier, marriage marked the formation of a new link in the family chain of life, the sacred passing on of one generation to the next. The emphasis was on this sense of linkage or continuity rather than on any sense that marriage was the start of something new; that is why the Book of Rites says that no one congratulates anyone at the time of marriage (Legge 1967, 1:442). In addition, the Book of Rites comments on marriage as follows:

The ceremony of marriage was intended to be a bond of love between two [families of different] surnames, with a view, in its retrospective character, to secure the services in the ancestral temple, and in its prospective character, to secure the continuance of the family line. Therefore, the superior men (the ancient rulers), set a great value upon it. (Book of Rites, ch. 44, Legge 1967, 2: 428).

Because the event had repercussions not just in the existing human order but also in the cosmic order and with the ancestors, the ceremony had to be done with careful attention to detail so that it would have its proper effect. Below are several of the most important details.

When the groom is about to set forth to fetch his bride, he receives the following command from his father: "Go meet your helpmeet, and so enable me to fulfill my duties in the ancestral temple. Be diligent in taking the lead as husband, but with respectful consideration, for she is the successor of your mother. Thus will the duties of the women in our family show no signs of decay" (I-li, or Book of Etiquette and Ceremonial, 4B, Steele 1966, 38). The groom then sets forth to the home of his bride. It is important that he take the initiative in this matter to remind all the parties that as husband, he is to be the active agent like Heaven, while the wife is to be the passive agent like earth.

When the groom arives at her house, the bride receives the following command from her father: "Be careful and reverent. Day in and day out disobey no command of your new parents." Her mother also repeats this exhortation, modifying the last line to "Disobey no rule of the household" (I-li 4B, Steele, 1966, 39). Once she leaves with the groom, the bride is no longer a member of her natural family.

When the bride and groom arrive back at the groom's family, there is great feasting with food and wine. "They ate together of the same animal, and joined in supping from the cups made of the same melon; thus showing that they now formed one body, were of equal rank, and pledged to mutual affection" (Book of Rites, ch. 44, Legge, 1967, 2:429–30). The following day the bride is formally presented to her parents-in-law, to whom she now owes perfect obedience as well as care in their old age and mourning for them when dead. On the third day, the parents-in-law fete the new bride in a ceremony which indicates that she is now the primary childbearing woman in the household, replacing the mother of the groom (ibid. 2:431). After the third month, the new bride is formally presented to the ancestors as a new member of the family, and from thereon she has a place on some ancestral line, something she never had in her natal family.[2]

Several points are worth noting about this ceremony. First, the idea of marriage is different for men and women, as can be seen both in the marriage ceremony itself and in the Chinese terms for marriage. The verb for a woman to marry is *kuei*, "to return home," implying that her rightful place is wherever her husband's family is, not her own natural family. In contrast, the word for a man to marry is *ch'u*, "to go out and fetch" someone. The second point is that the entering of marriage is more for the good of the overall family, past, present, and future, than for the personal happiness of the couple. In terms of the past, the wife and the husband must ensure the continuation of the periodic sacrifices to the ancestors; in terms of the present, the wife must dedicate herself to serve her parents-in-law; and in terms of the future, she must provide male heirs who will someday be able to carry on the family sacrifices. Third, while the new bride is deserving of respect for the crucial role she is about to play in the overall family structure, her immediate role in the hierarchy is not a very high one, so she is cautioned by her parents to be especially careful and obedient.

After the wedding ceremony, the couple was to observe a certain amount of sexual segregation in the household. They were not to mix freely, but rather to keep to separate quarters, except when sleeping.

The observances of propriety commenced with a careful attention to the relations between husband and wife. They built the mansion and its apartments, distinguishing between the exterior and interior parts. The men occupied the exterior; the women the interior. . . . Males and females did not use the same stand or rack for their clothes. The wife did not presume to hang up anything on the pegs or stand of her husband; nor to put anything in his boxes or satchels; nor to share his bathing house. (Book of Rites, ch. 12, Legge 1967, 1:470)

However, this separation of the sexes was never observed to the degree and level of strictness as the Islamic *purdah*.

Though they were to observe this type of separation, both husband and wife had to share in attending upon his parents and carrying out their orders. For example, upon rising in the morning and dressing, the couple were to proceed immediately to their parent's quarters.

On getting to where they are, with bated breath and gentle voice, they should ask if their clothes are too warm or too cold, whether they are ill or pained, or uncomfortable in any part; help and support their parents in quitting or entering the apartment. They will ask whether they want anything and then respectfully bring it. All this they will do with an appearance of pleasure to make their parents feel at ease. (ibid. 450-1)

The ritual texts also stipulate that neither the son nor his wife should own any private goods, and any gifts to them should be offered to their parents and not kept for themselves.

Marriage was regarded as such a sacred event, registered in the cosmic order and with the ancestral line, that it could not be dissolved. However, if a wife was guilty of certain behavior, she might be divorced by her husband and sent back to her family. The seven traditional grounds for divorce (literally, *ch'i-ch'u*, "seven reasons for sending out of the house") were disobedience to his parents, failure to bear a male child, promiscuity, jealousy, having an incurable disease, talking too much, and stealing. Three extenuating circumstances, however, prevented a husband from divorcing his wife. They were that her parents were dead and she had no home to which to return, she had already carried out the mourning rites for one of his parents, and he began the marriage a poor man but upon achieving riches wished to get rid of her (K'ung-tzu chia-yü 6:6a).[3]

The wife never had any grounds for initiating a divorce against her husband. Even after the death of her husband, she was supposed to remain faithful to him and never remarry.

Faithfulness is requisite in all service of others, and faithfulness is specially the virtue of a wife. Once mated with her husband, all her life she will not change her feeling of duty to him, and hence, when the husband dies, she will not marry again. (Book of Rites, ch. 11, Legge 1967, 1:439)

A good deal of the reason for this was that a woman's bond in marriage was not just with her husband, but also with his family. Thus, even with his death, she had duties to his living relations and his ancestors. Though women were encouraged not to remarry, the social sanctions against those who did, in classical and medieval Chinese history, were not nearly as heavy as they were to become in later Chinese history under the influence of Neo-Confucianism.

Such was the wifely way as outlined in the ritual texts of classical Confucianism. During the Han dynasty (206 B.C.E.-220 C.E.) when Confucianism was first made a state orthodoxy, there was a more conscious attempt to bring women into the mainstream of the tradition and to give them more specialized instructional writings and biographies of women to emulate. Specifically, we have in the Han dynasty two pieces, Instructions for Women (Nü-chieh) by Pan Chao, and Biographies of Exemplary Women (Lieh-nü chuan) by Liu Hsiang.

Pan Chao (?-116 C.E.), author of Instructions for Women, was a highly educated woman who was publicly recognized for her scholarship and intellect. She was called to court to tutor the women of the imperial family, and also was instrumental in completing the Han dynastic history her brother left unfinished upon his death. According to her Preface to the Instructions, she wrote the text out of concern that the unmarried women of her family (her daughters and nieces) were unprepared for their future vocation as wives. She hoped to remedy the situation with helpful advice that, as we shall see, fully embraces the wifely way that we have been describing.[4]

She begins by alluding to an ancient practice upon the birth of a girl which was meant to indicate the type of life she was meant to lead.

On the third day after the birth of a girl, the ancients observed three customs: first to place the baby below the bed; second to give her a potsherd with which to play; and third, to announce her birth to her ancestors by an offering. (Nü-chieh 1:2b-3a, Swann 1932, 83)

The first action indicated that as female she should be lowly and submissive, humbling herself before others, the second that she should be hardworking and diligent in the domestic sphere, and the third that she should enter fully into the wife's responsibilities to the ancestors of her husband's family.

Having thus explained these three fundamental aspects of a woman's vocation as wife, Pan Chao next focuses on the nature of the marriage bond and the wife's duty to her husband. She fully accepts the cosmological correspondences of the husband-wife relationship with that of Heaven and earth, and the implications for differentiation in sex roles. That is, the husband must be strong, firm, and dominant like Heaven, and the wife must be weak, pliant, and subservient like earth. The husband's duty is to superintend or manage the wife, the wife's duty is to serve her husband. Things will go awry if either one fails in his or her duty to the other. Thus men who fail to exert authority over their wives are just as much at fault as wives who are not willing to serve their husbands (Nü-chieh 1:4b-5a, Swann 1932, 84).

The couples owe each other mutual respect and the way to maintain respect is to observe the restrictions placed upon their intimacy by the system of sexual segregation. She warns couples of the dangers of too much familiarity, that it so often leads to excessive lust or anger.

> If husband and wife have the habit of staying together, never leaving one another, and following each other around within the limited space of their own rooms, then they will lust after and take liberties with one another. From such action improper language will arise between the two. This kind of discussion may lead to licentiousness. And out of licentiousness will be born a heart of disrespect to the husband. (Nü-chieh 1:6a-b, Swann 1932, 85)

Pan Chao goes on to describe how this loss of respect often then leads to contempt for one's husband and incessant nagging on the part of the wife, which then evokes anger on the part of the husband who then beats the wife. "The correct relationship between husband and wife is based upon harmony.... Should actual blows be dealt, how could the matrimonial relationship be preserved?" (Nü-chieh 1:6b, Swann 1932, 86).

Though there is to be this typically Confucian reserve and formality in the marriage relationship, there should also be, on the part of the wife, an element of affectionate devotion. Pan Chao quotes an ancient saying: "To obtain the love of one man is the crown of a woman's life; to lose the love of one man is to miss the aim in woman's life" (Nü-chieh 1:8b, Swann 1932, 87). Though this is so, Pan Chao cautions women not to try to win their husbands' hearts through flattery and cheap methods, but through single-minded devotion and correct behavior. Such behavior is broken down into four categories, or aspects of a woman's character. They are womanly virtue, womanly speech, womanly deportment, and womanly work.

Womanly virtue involves being pure and chaste, quiet and reserved, and acting with a sense of honor and integrity in all things. Womanly speech entails talking only when appropriate, not maligning or abusing others in one's talk, and not wearying others with too much talk. Womanly deportment, interestingly enough, focuses entirely on personal cleanliness, that is, washing one's hair and one's body regularly, as well as keeping one's clothes and ornaments fresh and clean. Lastly, as for womanly work,

> With whole-hearted devotion to sew and weave; to love not gossip and silly laughter; in cleanliness and order, to prepare the wine and food for serving guests, may be called the characteristics of womanly work. (Nü-chieh 1:8b-9a, Swann 1932, 86)

Having dealt with a wife's responsibility to her husband, Pan Chao uses the last few sections of the text to deal with the wife's responsibilities to her in-laws. In dealing with all of them, she recommends a heavy dose of modesty and acquiescence, as well as a skillfulness in pleasing them all. Specifically, in terms of one's mother-in-law, one is advised to act as a shadow or an echo to her, that is, she should go along with her in all matters and assert no will of her own. Even if what the mother-in-law commands is wrong, the daughter-in-law should still obey it. The jealousy and haughtiness of sisters-in-law (wives of one's husband's brothers) may be even more of a challenge to the new bride, so she is cautioned to humble herself before them at all times.

The rewards Pan Chao holds out to women who fully follow her advice in this text are typically Confucian: "Parents-in-law boast of her good deeds; her husband is satisfied with her. Praise of her radiates, making her illustrious in district and in neighborhood; and her brightness reaches to her own father and mother" (Nü-chieh 1:11b, Swann 1932, 88). These rewards are consonant with those usually offered to Confucian males: a good name and the happiness of one's parents.

On one level, we can read this text as a guidebook for surviving as a bride in the highly hierarchical, group-oriented Chinese family system. Being a new bride in such a system was not easy, and as Margery Wolf's research has shown, in more recent times the rate of suicide was quite high for young brides. Indeed, at one point in her text, Pan Chao decries the lack of adequate overall education for women, given the difficulties of their roles in the Chinese family system. On a deeper level, the text represents the type of spirituality required of women in the Confucian world.

The religious path presented by Pan Chao, though not as overt as in later texts by women, revolves around the full acceptance of women's inferiority and submission to the relationships involved in marriage: notably, with the husband, his parents, and other in-laws. A woman accepts her inferior status, according to Confucian logic, not because men have told her to but because the authority of the cosmic order demands it. She has a stake in the maintenance of that order just as much as a man. She also has a stake in the maintenance of the family order and thus submits to the discipline of family relationships. Her spiritual path has the same orientation as that of men, that is, that one fulfills oneself by immersing oneself in human life, not going off on one's own. As sacred community, the family is to be a woman's total area of dedication. She takes her place in the larger whole, not upsetting but rather enhancing its order. She does so by not putting herself forward but by working in subtle and humble ways. Though a woman is called upon to be "weak," she is not to be spineless and helpless. Rather what she is called upon to do requires a great amount of inner strength and courage. In fact, one might even say that Confucian women are called upon to go beyond the selflessness, humility, obedience, and dedication expected of men. As outsiders in men's families, they have to doubly prove themselves to gain acceptance. They have to work for the good of the family as a whole even though it is not their natural family; thus in many ways, their dedication is more selfless than a man's dedication to his family.

Pan Chao's Instructions for Women, though only a short piece of 7 sections, nevertheless exerted a tremendous influence on the lives of Chinese women. It became the prototype of all later instructional texts for women, and Pan Chao became the model female instructress, so much so that later women often wrote their texts in her voice rather than their own. Two of the most striking examples of this are a Ms. Ch'eng (ca. 700 C.E.)[5] who wrote the Classic of Filial Piety for Women (Nü hsiao-ching) and Sung Jo-chao (ca. 800 C.E.) who wrote the Analects for Women (Nü lun-yü). These two women capitalized both on the reputation of Pan Chao by adopting her voice in their texts and also on the popularity of the Confucian texts the Classic of Filial Piety and the Analects. The conscious modelling of women's instructional texts on mainstream Confucian classics represents a growing moral seriousness on the part of women and a sense of the need for texts as valuable for their guidance as those already canonized by the tradition for men.

Though the limitations of space preclude me from giving a detailed content analysis of these two texts, several important features of them need to be mentioned. The first one, the Classic of Filial Piety for Women opens with Pan Chao sitting at leisure, conversing with court women about the wifely way, in contrast to the original which has Confucius sitting at leisure, discussing filial piety with his disciples. Pan Chao's message to the court women elevates women's role in the Confucian household to that of moral custodian. Service to one's husband goes beyond obedience and deference to him, and now includes the responsibility for his moral character. A wife must monitor and nurture that character as needs be.

> She leads him on with respect and love and he never forgets his sense of filial piety to his parents. She presents him with a model of virtuous conduct and he improves his behavior. She guides him with a sense of modesty and deference, and he isn't contentious. She leads him on with ritual and music, and he is pleasant and easy to get along with. (Nü hsiao-ching 2:17b)

Elsewhere in the text, the court women ask her if a woman can be considered a model wife if she obeys everything her husband commands of her. Pan Chao responds in shocked, incredulous tones: "What kind of talk is that? What kind of talk is that?" She goes on to make the point that husbands are not always perfect in what they say and do, and need their wives to keep them on track, just as a good ruler needs a vigilant minister to keep him doing good all the time (Nü hsiao-ching 2:11a-b).

The text does not limit the woman's responsibilities of moral leadership to just her husband, but extends them to the entire household.

> A virtuous wife never dares demean the younger concubines, how much more is her solicitation for her sisters-in-law. Therefore they are all happy and get along with each other, and are able to serve their parents-in-law. In managing the household, she never dares mistreat the chickens and dogs, how much more is her care for the servants. Therefore those of all ranks are content with their lot and are able to serve their master well. ... In these ways, the nine degrees of relatives are kept in peace and harmony, calamities do not arise, nor disorders occur. (Nü hsiao-ching 2:17b-18a)

This passage corresponds in the original classic with a discussion of how the sage kings of antiquity used filial piety to rule the world. The implication here is that a woman's role in the family parallels that of the emperor in the political realm; both are ultimately responsible for the moral character of the group, the family and the state, respectively.

As lofty as the role for women presented in the Classic of Filial Piety is the down-to-earth nature of the same role found in the Analects for Women written about a hundred years later. Sung Jo-chao, its author, was so impressed with the life of Pan Chao that she dedicated her own life to the moral instruction of women.[6] Her Analects for Women is rich in concrete details about how to cultivate one's personal character, how to run a household, and how to handle domestic relationships. The following advice comes in the opening chapter.

> Keep your body clean and your reputation spotless. When walking, don't turn your head; when talking, don't open your mouth wide; when standing, don't shake your skirts. When you're feeling happy, don't express it in hearty laughter; when angry, don't vent it in a loud voice. (Nü lun-yü 2:2b)

The text goes on to spell out the details of such household duties as the providing of food and clothing for the household, as well as the proper hospitality for receiving guests. Instructions for the spinning and weaving of cloth, the making of silk, and the sewing and mending of clothes are given, as well as for preparing and serving meals in the proper manner. Elaborate details are also provided for carrying out one's duties to one's parents, one's parents-in-law, one's husband, and one's children. As for an example, in the section on parents-in-law, a woman is advised to rise early, open the household up, but not make any noise to disturb the mother-in-law's sleep. "Sweep and mop the floors, wash and rinse the clothes. When the mother-in-law awakens, present her with soap, tooth paste, and warm water. Withdraw while she bathes until you hear her beckon you back to remove the bathing articles" (2:9b-10a).

At the end of each section, negative models are given from which the reader is advised not to learn. These are lazy women who don't keep up with their sewing and their family members go around in ragged clothing, or self-indulgent women who get up late, stagger to the kitchen without having dressed or washed, and who don't get any of the meals served on time; or women who get drunk and gossip wildly when visiting female friends. Just as bad as these women are those who show up at their parents' funeral with dry eyes, bent only on getting the largest inheritance they can ("Such women rank with the swine and the wolves!" 2:9a), or those who don't respond to the needs of their parents-in-law ("Heaven will show no mercy to such women even if they were to repent" 2:10b), or those who fail to raise virtuous children ("It is as if they had raised pigs or rats" 2:13b).

The value of both of these later instructional texts for women was that they fleshed out the basic guidance provided by the real Pan Chao in her Instructions for Women, making it at once both more lofty and more down-to-earth. Women's moral role was elevated and the practical details of fulfilling that role were spelled out.[7]

As Pan Chao's Instructions became the prototype of later instructional texts for women, so did the Biographies of Exemplary Women kept by the scholar-official Liu Hsiang (77-6 B.C.E.) with respect to collections of female biographies. This collection, which drew upon a variety of sources from the legendary past to his own day, presents biographies of over a hundred women, grouped according to seven types. The first six types are of good, moral women (exemplary mothers, worthy and astute women, benevolent and wise women, women of propriety, women of sexual integrity, and intellectual women), and the seventh group is of bad, wicked women.

This text is fairly remarkable. Even though it groups women into types, and even though most of the women are celebrated for some contribution they make to men, still, it is no mean thing that such a large number of lively women who show themselves skillful in the arts of moral persuasion, have a keen moral sense, and are ready to act on their beliefs are honored in the sociopolitical realm.

To appreciate the distinctiveness of this text, I wish to provide the reader with a sampling of the biographies, beginning with two of the model mothers from the first chapter. These two models give us a sense of how Confucians regarded the duties of a mother. The first is T'ai-jen, the mother of one of the classical sage-kings, who was honored for her ability in "prenatal instruction." Believing that the moral character of the child was formed during pregnancy, an expectant mother was urged to pay special attention to her attitudes and behavior during that period.

A woman with child did not lie on her side as she slept; neither would she sit sidewise nor stand on one foot. . . . She did not let her eyes gaze on lewd sights nor let her ears listen to depraved sounds. At night she ordered the blind musicians to chant poetry. (Lieh-nü chuan 1:4a, O'Hara 1945, 23)[8]

Because T'ai-jen excelled in doing these things, her son "King Wen grew up and became an illustrious sage."

The next model mother is the most celebrated mother in Chinese history, the widowed mother of the great philosopher Mencius.[9] Aware of the influence the environment had on the moral formation of children, she moved their residence three times before coming on one suitable for her son's upbringing. In their first two places of residence, one near a graveyard and one near a market place, Mencius had spent his time playing undertaker and businessman, two professions a good Confucian mother would hardly want for her son. Finally, she moved near a school, where Mencius engaged in play more along the Confucian lines of teacher and ritualist (1:10a-b, O'Hara 1945, 39).

Several other incidents are given to show her vigilance in the care of her son, but the one which most endears her to women is one which takes place after Mencius was married. One day he entered his wife's room and found her not fully dressed as propriety would dictate, and he left immediately in disgust. Aware that in his stubbornness he would never return to her on his own, the wife appealed to Mencius's mother. Mencius's mother, with her down-to-earth, balanced moral sense, took her son aside and pointed out to him that while his wife might have transgressed the dictates of propriety, so had he by not giving her fair warning that he was approaching. "Mencius apologized and kept his wife. The superior person commented that Mencius's mother understood propriety and excelled in the way of the mother-in-law" (1:11a, O'Hara 1945, 41 adapted).

Elsewhere, in chapters 2, 3, and 6, we are presented with women, mostly wives, who excel in dispensing valuable moral advice to men, often in attempts to reform their conduct in the domestic or political sphere. These women are skillful in the art of persuasion, show that they are fully conversant with Confucian moral teachings, and even display a type of savvy in terms of the hard political realities of their day (which, for most of these biographies, is the chaotic and violent Warring States period, roughly 500-220 B.C.E.). Among these women, we find wives of rulers who criticize their husbands for failing in their role as father to the people, or for being inept in selecting good, capable advisors, or for shortsightedness in planning military campaigns. A daughter proves herself more astute about marriage politics than her father.

Many of these women are astute enough to realize that they must be indirect in their approach if their advice is to be taken seriously by the men in their lives. One wife, disturbed that her husband finds her so attractive that he neglects his duties at court to be with her, tried to reform him by making a public display of her guilt. In the palace tribunal, she tears off her hair ornaments and earrings, and has her governess deliver a statement of her guilt to her husband. "The stupidity and licentious heart of your wife have manifested themselves. It has come to such a pass that she causes the King to fail in propriety and to come late to court so that it is seen that the King enjoys the beauty of women and has forgotten virtue" (2:1a, O'Hara 1945, 49). In so taking responsibility on herself, she awakens the king to his own responsibility in the matter. He refuses to accept her accusation and immediately reforms his ways, thereby becoming a more effective ruler.

In contrast to those wives who excel at advising and reforming their husbands, chapters 4 and 5 are filled with women dealing with their own sense of personal honor. These chapters have a great dramatic sense, with women often taking their own lives to protect their honor. While both chapter headings have a word meaning 'chastity' (chen in chapter 4 and chieh in chapter 5), the interpretation of 'chastity' has a broader sense than the narrow one of sexual continence, embracing a more general sense of integrity or honor.

Some of these women illustrate a strict adherence to proper ritual behavior as in the case of the widow who, when her room catches fire one night, will not leave the room because, according to ritual procedures, a woman does not go out at night unless accompanied by a matron and governess. Declaring herself willing to risk death rather than go against right principle, she perishes in the fire. She is praised as one who has perfectly realized the "wifely way" (4:1b-2a, O'Hara 1945, 105–6). Another example is that of the wife of the Duke of Ch'u. While he is away from home, a terrible flood threatens his home so he sends a messenger with others to relocate his wife. But because the messenger has forgotten the proper credentials, the wife refuses to go with him. She does so even though she is aware that her refusal almost certainly means death by drowning. She does indeed die in the flood, but is celebrated by her husband and others for preserving her chastity (4:6a-b, O'Hara 1945, 117).

Other biographies deal more explicitly with the matter of faithfulness to husbands, dead or alive. There is the woman of Wei who learns only when she has reached the gates of the town that her prospective husband has just died. Though she is advised to return home to her parents, she asserts her prerogative as his wife to enter his household, carry out the mourning rites for him, and to remain on as a member of the household. Her dead husband's younger brother proposes marriage to her, but she staunchly refuses, even when her own brothers pressure her to do so. "My heart is not a stone, it cannot be rolled. My heart is not a mat, it cannot be folded away" (4:2a-b, O'Hara 1945, 106-7).

There is also the case of the wife who refuses to obey her mother's order to return home when she learns that her husband has contracted leprosy. "If my husband is unfortunate, then his misfortune is mine. Why should I leave him? The way of the bride is that after one marriage cup of wine with the groom, she does not change in a lifetime. If unfortunately she meets with one having an incurable disease, she does not change her resolve" (4:2b-3a, O'Hara 1945, 107-8).

The suicides and killings continue in chapter 5, but here women are caught in divided loyalties to the various men in their lives. In one example, a wife's brother comes and murders her husband, takes over his kingdom, and then tries to take his sister back to his own kingdom. For her, the dilemma is that if she ignores what happened to her husband and excuses her brother, she will be going against righteousness; and yet, if on account of the loss of her husband she became angry with her brother, she will go against sibling love. What should she do so that she can be true to both men? With tears to Heaven, the woman goes out and kills herself (5:5b-6a, O'Hara 1945, 138-9). A second example is that of the "chaste woman of the capital." Her husband's enemy sees a way of getting revenge by exploiting the virtuous nature of the wife. He captures her father and threatens to kill him he she doesn't help him get to her husband. Her dilemma is that if she doesn't obey her father, she will be unfilial and he will be killed; if she obeys him, she will be unrighteous and her husband will be killed. Either way she will lose. She pretends to cooperate, advising the enemy where her husband will be sleeping on a certain night. She has her husband sleep elsewhere that night and arranges that it is she who is murdered, not her husband. Thus able to be faithful to both men, the woman earns the reputation of being humane and filial (5:11a-b, O'Hara 1945, 151-2).

From this sample of biographies from the first six chapters of this text, we have seen a variety of strong, moral women. In the domestic scene, they have shown themselves to be wise and able teachers of their sons and husbands; in the political sphere, they have proven themselves to be skillful and astute advisers. Often they have appeared more faithful in carrying out their Confucian duty than have the men, some even going so far as to give their lives on behalf on some Confucian principle. These are women with moral consciences who have the courage of their convictions. Thus does Liu Hsiang honor women as custodians of family and state morality.

But if he gives most of his attention to exemplary women (trying to exercise the power of positive thinking?), he does not completely leave out evil, selfish, wicked women. The last chapter of the text is given over to examples of "dangerous" women, women whose beauty distracts men from their official duties and occasions the downfall of kingdoms. Among the examples given are the concubines of the bad last rules of the Hsia and Shang dynasties (second millenium B.C.E.), Mo-hsi, the concubine of King Chieh, and Tan-chi, the concubine of King Chou. Not only do these two women ensnare the men in a life of sensual pleasure, but they also encourage sadistic treatment of servants and ministers. When the minister Pi-kan remonstrates with King Chou about his orgies, Tan-chi goads King Chou to have Pi-kan cut open to see if it is true that a sage has seven orifices (7:1a-2a, O'Hara 1945, 186–9).

These women in the last chapter are the antithesis of the others, caring nothing for the betterment of the men in their lives, wrapped up instead in their own insatiable desires for sensual pleasure. They threaten the moral fabric of society, and rather than being the custodians of family and state morality, are its destroyers.

The texts that this paper has discussed so far can all be seen as attempts to bring women into the mainstream of male-dominated Confucianism. Though the modern reader might well have doubts as to whether they truly gave women much dignity in their own right, still, when compared with the later position of women in Neo-Confucianism, they reflect a broad and generous approach to women. We turn now to take a brief look at women and Neo-Confucianism.

With the fall of the Han dynasty in 220 C.E., Confucianism was eclipsed by Buddhism and Taoism in the area of religion. It was not to play a significant role in that area until its reemergence in the form of Neo-Confucianism in the Sung dynasty (960-1279 C.E.). When it did reemerge in this form, a great shift had occurred which was to have a profound effect on the lives of women.

The early Neo-Confucians zealously worked to revitalize Confucianism to reclaim the territory it had earlier lost to the Buddhists. Their challenge was to reestablish the family and the state as the locus of religious duty. They attacked the Buddhists for selfishly trying to escape from the world rather than direct their energies to building up the human order. Nevertheless, they were quite impressed with the depths of Buddhist spirituality. How could they blend the best of the two? The Neo-Confucianism that resulted was a more overtly religious tradition than earlier Confucianism and was concerned more with metaphysical matters, human interiority, and religious practices such as meditation. There was a new sense of the profound depths of the human self, but with it a greater awareness of the dangers and obstructions which hinder the full development of the self. They saw these dangers in terms of human desires and passions. As a result, in Neo-Confucianism there is a greater preoccupation with self-discipline and with controlling one's desires.

This great wariness about human desires and passions was directed to the area of human relationships, the cornerstone of Confucian religiosity. Ch'eng I (1033-1107), one of the leading Sung Neo-Confucians, reflects this wariness in the following statement which appears in the most famous anthology of Neo-Confucian writings, Reflections on Things at Hand (Chin-ssu lu):

> In family relationships, parents and children usually overcome correct principles with affection and supplant righteousness with kindness. Only strong and resolute people can avoid sacrificing correct principles for the sake of personal affection. (Chin-ssu lu 6:1b, Chan 1967, 173)

Here we see a new element. In classical Confucianism, one fulfilled oneself by immersing oneself in the network of human relationships. Now there is more ambivalence about these relationships, a sense that they may be a source of obstruction rather than a contribution to one's pursuit of sagehood.

Women could not but be influenced by this change, especially because one of the most intimate ties of a Confucian male was with his wife. Women came to be seen as activators of desires both sensual and affective. There was a felt need to ensure that they controlled their desires and not upset men's progress toward sagehood. Thus the moral code for women, while in many ways a continuation of the earlier, classical one, focused to an almost obsessive degree on chastity. And within this, the chastity of widows was singled out for special emphasis.

To be sure, chastity had been an important virtue for women in the classical period, as we have seen in the Biographies of Exemplary Women, and widows were exhorted to remain faithful to their husbands by not remarrying. But nothing in the classical period can match the degree of preoccupation with chastity that Neo-Confucianism exhibited. The most chilling statement in this regard was made by Ch'eng I concerning the remarriage of widows. He is asked whether a widow can remarry in the extenuating circumstance that she is poor, all alone, and about to starve to death. Ch'eng I responds: "This theory has come about only because people of later generations are afraid of starving to death. But to starve to death is a very small matter. To lose one's integrity, however, is a very serious matter" (Chin-ssu lu 6:3a, Chan 1967, 177).

The models of women presented in an influential primer for young men, the Elementary Learning (Hsiao-hsüeh), compiled by the most famous Sung dynasty Neo-Confucian Chu Hsi (1130-1200), staunchly promote this moral code. In one case, we have a woman who progressively mutilates her body with each new exertion of pressure by her parents to remarry. First she cuts off her hair, then her ears, and finally her nose, all the while defiantly asserting her determination to remain faithful to her dead husband. Another example is of two unmarried sisters who are abducted by bandits. They both resist rape, the first by hurling herself off a high cliff and the second by dashing herself on the rocks (there is plenty of blood and gore in these tales)(Hsiao-hsüeh 6:11a-12a). Since the bond of marriage is not just with the husband but with his parents as well, we are also presented with model widows who further prove their faithfulness by giving unstinting care to their mother-in-laws, even in the worst of conditions. One woman's husband dies in war while she is still young, leaving her childless. Rather than succumb to her parent's pressure to remarry, she cares for her mother-in-law even though it entails a life of poverty for her. What little she has at the time of her mother-in-law's death she sells to give the mother-in-law a proper funeral (6:10a-b). Another woman is praised for trying to ward off ten strong bandits when they attack her mother-in-law. She is able to succeed in saving the mother even though she herself is almost beaten to death (6:11b-12a).

What is noticeably absent among these models are mature, astute women of the kind who dispense good advice, who are skillful in the arts of persuasion, and who involve themselves in the political realm. There are no wise, discerning mothers. There are only nun-like martyrs in their young adulthood. This more dramatic and ascetical tone, I must add, also pervades the models set up for men to emulate.

Neo-Confucianism was not adopted as the state orthodoxy until about a hundred years after the demise of the Sung dynasty, that is, until the late Yüan and early Ming dynasties (last half of the fourteenth century). As when Confucianism became the state orthodoxy in the Han dynasty, efforts were made to bring women more into the mainstream. But in contrast to the Han emperors, the early Ming emperors were more heavyhanded in promoting Neo-Confucianism.

One aspect of the new orthodoxy was that it brought the chastity cult for women more into the public arena.[10] For example, the first Ming emperor T'ai-tsu announced that chaste widows who lost their husbands before they had reached the age of 30 and who remained chaste until the age of 50 would have a memorial arch built in their honor, and their household would be exempt from corvee labor. The biographical sections of the dynastic histories and local gazetteers are filled with documented cases of women who are celebrated for having preserved their chastity. Ming and Ch'ing China witnessed a great increase in the number of women who mutilated themselves or committed suicide rather than lose their chastity before marriage or enter into a second marriage after the death of a husband. One scholar's estimate, based on dynastic history records, is that the number of deaths by suicide jumped from 383 cases in the Yüan dynasty to 8,688 in the Ming dynasty and then fell to 2,841 in the Ch'ing dynasty. The cases of mutilation jumped even more dramatically, from 359 cases in the Yüan dynasty to 27,141 cases in the Ming dynasty and 9,482 in the Ch'ing dynasty (Tung 1970, 112).

The other aspect of the new orthodoxy worth noting is once again the popularity of texts written by women for women. The most notable one is the Instructions for the Inner Quarters (Nei-hsün) by the second empress of the Ming dynasty, Empress Hsü. Imitating the work her husband, the Yung-lo Emperor, was doing in the area of promoting Neo-Confucian texts for men, she dedicated herself to the instruction of women in the imperial family. Though much of the content of her text echoes that found in the texts we have already discussed, several features are worthy of comment.

The first is her adoption of Neo-Confucian terminology in the area of self-cultivation to discuss the duties and responsibilities of a woman. Great attention is put on one's inner life, a keeping watch over one's thoughts and desires at all times. Though this is not dealt with in nearly the detail or sophistication of texts addressed to men, still, it does go beyond the earlier texts for women where attention to personal character mostly concerned itself with propriety and comportment (be chaste and pure, don't shake your skirts when you stand, be humble and modest).

The second feature of note is that she takes seriously the Neo-Confucian notion that all human beings are called to sagehood. So she encourages women to pursue the path of female sageliness, describing it as a far more precious jewel than either pearls or jade (Nei-hsün 3:22b). As part of this female sageliness, she envisions women as playing a vital role in both family and state morality, thereby restoring to women their role of moral adviser which they had in classical Confucianism but which had been taken away by Sung Neo-Confucians.

Sometime in early or mid-Ming, this text was published together with the three earlier texts (Instructions for Women, Classic of Filial Piety for Women, and Analects for Women) as the Four Books for Women (Nü ssu-shu). Later, in the early seventeenth century, a scholar official Wang Hsiang substituted the instructional text his mother had written for women, A Handy Record of Rules for Women (Nü-fan chieh-lu), for the Classical of Filial Piety for Women, and published that set as the Four Books for Women. His action came at a time when many Chinese men involved themselves in education for women. One of the most popular texts for women was a new rendering of the Biographies of Exemplary Women from the Han dynasty brought up to date for contemporary women by a man named Lü K'un (Handlin 1975).

Although we have these examples of women who embraced Neo-Confucianism, either by writing in the spirit of its teachings or by sacrificing themselves to be faithful to its teachings, we still have to consider the fact that most women in China were Buddhists. With the rise of Neo-Confucianism, Buddhism suffered a decline, except with women who became its mainstay. Attention needs to be given to the question of what Chinese women found in Buddhism that sustained them in a way Confucianism (or Neo-Confucianism) did not. Because of the secular nature of Confucianism, there was no problem with women participating in both. Though many male Neo-Confucians had no tolerance for Buddhism themselves, they placed no restrictions on their wives or mothers who practiced it.

The legacy of Confucianism in the modern period is a complicated one. By the late nineteenth and early twentieth century, China was in a state of decline, overwhelmed by problems of poverty, overpopulation, corruption, and loss of morale in the government, and imperialism by Western powers. Radicals and reformers turned on Confucianism as one of the prime sources of their problems. Since the position of women was also seen as at an all-time low, as evidenced in the widespread practices of footbinding, female infanticide, and the buying and selling of women, women also turned against the tradition. Probably no other socioreligious tradition has been attacked in such a large-scale, systematic way. Mao Tse-tung was astute enough to see the potential in women as a revolutionary group and achieved much of his success from the support of women. The People's Republic of China has made sweeping reforms to improve the status of women in society, and has included large numbers of them in the work force and in political office. However, as several recent books have shown,[11] much remains to be done to give women full equality. The recent one-child policy has brought to the surface the traditional bias in favor of male heirs.

But the larger question for us is the future of Confucianism. Does it indeed have a future? Can it exist in a scientific and technological world that does not reflect its cosmic orientation? Can it exist apart from the traditional Chinese political and family system? Despite all the repudiation of Confucianism in modern China, do many of its teachings persist, albeit in Communist form?

If there is no future for Confucianism, then there is no use asking what future role women might play in it. Indeed, there are few Chinese women today who want to identify themselves with Confucianism, linked as it is with the oppression of women. But will there come a time when the atmosphere is not so highly charged and when Chinese women will want to evaluate the positive legacy of their tradition as well? From the outsider's point of view, there is such a positive legacy. Though Confucianism contributed to the victimization of women, it also gave them a sense of self-discipline, esteem for education, and respect for public service that has enabled them to enter into today's political and social realm in the number and with the effectiveness that they have.

The Confucian tradition, with its appreciation for the gift of life, with its profound humanistic spirit, its sense of religious practice as building the human community, and its sense of the relational quality of things, has much to contribute to our global religious heritage. The challenge of giving women a more equitable place within that tradition remains. It seems obvious that unless that challenge is met, the appeal of many aspects of Confucianism will be greatly diminished.

Barbara E. Reed

TAOISM

> The Valley Spirit never dies.
> It is named the Mysterious Female.
> And the Doorway of the Mysterious Female
> Is the base from which Heaven and Earth sprang.
> It is there within us all the while;
> Draw upon it as you will, it never runs dry.
> (Tao te ching VI, Waley 1958, 149)

ANY religious or philosophical tradition that symbolizes cosmic and personal creativity as the "Mysterious Female" has great potential for attracting women's participation. Taoism not only uses female images for creative powers, but also advocates the harmony and equality of all opposites, including male and female. Women's historical fate in Taoism is especially interesting because it developed within the extremely patriarchal culture of Confucian China.

Taoism is the native religious tradition of China. It has shaped Chinese culture along with the native philosophical tradition of Confucianism and the imported Buddhist religion. According to tradition, Taoism was founded by the legendary Lao tzu in the sixth century B.C.E. But its roots are traceable to ancient shamanistic practices, deities, and myths which were incorporated into a rich tradition of philosophy, ritual, and magic. The Taoist tradition has several interacting strands: the mystical and philosophical texts, such as the Tao te ching (compiled ca. third century B.C.E.) and the Chuang tzu (fourth century B.C.E.), the Taoist religious sects dating from the second century C.E., and various techniques of exorcising malevolent spirits and attaining immortality.

WOMEN IN TAOIST PHILOSOPHICAL LITERATURE

The two great classics of Taoist philosophy, the Tao te ching and Chuang tzu, extol the way of nature as the path to happiness. The mysterious way of nature is called Tao. One can know Tao by yielding to and following nature. One should act spontaneously, naturally, without purpose. These two Taoist texts describe similar paths to simplicity and happiness, but they address themselves to different audiences and use radically different styles. The Tao te ching uses feminine imagery and traditional views of female roles to counter destructive male behavior. Chuang tzu illustrates the Tao by describing anecdotes in the lives of individuals who manifest the Tao.

The Tao te ching is a short, cryptic text addressed to the ruler. One who has the responsibility of rule could, it suggests, create a simple and happy society by allowing the Tao to govern. The mysterious Tao can transform all things spontaneously if the ruler does not intervene with obstructive behavior. The Sage Ruler says: "So long as I love quietude, the people will of themselves go straight. So long as I act only by inactivity the people will of themselves become prosperous" (Tao te ching LVII, Waley 1958, 211). To communicate the Tao, the path of quietude and inactivity, the Tao te ching relies heavily on female imagery. Ultimately, the Tao is ineffable: "The Way that can be told of is not an Unvarying Way" (I, Waley 1958, 141). But the Tao manifests itself in creativity and in spontaneous, nonaggressive human behavior. The Tao te ching symbolizes this behavior in concrete images from nature: water, the uncarved block, the child, the female, the mother, the valley, the dark, the bellows, the door, the empty vessel, the mare, and the hen. Most of these symbols are explicitly female, and all of them point to the potentiality associated with female reproduction or the unqualified nature of motherly love. Ellen Chen has shown that in many ways the Tao represents the Great Mother, the creative power of the female (1969, 1973, 1974).

Creation in the Tao te ching is the production of all things from the womb of the Mother. The Tao is named the "Mother," the "dark," and the "mysterious." She is the "doorway" through which things enter the visible world (VI, Waley 1958, 149). All things were created by her and continue to rely on her for their sustenance. The creativity of the Tao depends on the womb of creation, on its emptiness, its potentiality. The Tao is nonbeing in the Taoist understanding of nonbeing as the potential for new being—not in the usual Western sense of the negation of being. The Tao as empty has unlimited potentiality.

    The Way is like an empty vessel
    That yet may be drawn from
    Without ever needing to be filled.

It is bottomless; the very progenitor of all things in the world.
(Tao te ching IV, Waley 1958, 146)

Tao as nonbeing is the beginning of all things and should also be
that to which all things return. Unless one realizes that nonbeing is the
sacred quality of female creative power, the return to the darkness of
nonbeing appears to be a morbid search for annihilation (Chen 1974,
52-53). The return to original nonbeing is truly the return to authentic
existence. Perhaps the goal of returning to the Tao is rooted in an earlier
worship of the mother goddess (Chen 1974, 53). Because the cycle of
return is grounded in the creative power of the Tao, it has none of the
terror or meaninglessness associated with Hindu conceptions of life in
continuing cycles. As Eliade (1959) has suggested, the terror of cyclical
views of time occurs only when the sacred nature of the cosmos has
been forgotten (107-9). The Tao te ching does not envision a primordial
beginning with specific gods and goddesses. The creative powers of the
beginning are instead symbolized by the abstract Mother, the Tao. She
provides the comfort and meaning for the return to the beginning.

Nonbeing and being are both described with female imagery. Tao as
the nameless (nonbeing) is beyond categories, but in attempting to describe it the text uses images of the dark and mysterious female. Tao as
the named (being) is the source of all things. In Ellen Chen's view, the
creativity of the nameless Tao as Mother is based on her emptiness, and
the creativity of the named Tao (being) is based on its potentiality. The
Mother is nonbeing, and her child of unlimited potential is being (Chen
1973, 411).

The spirit and creativity of the Mother is also found within all
her creatures.

The Valley Spirit never dies.
It is named the Mysterious Female.
And the Doorway of the Mysterious Female
Is the base from which Heaven and Earth sprang.
It is there within us all the while;
Draw upon it as you will, it never runs dry.
(Tao te ching VI, Waley 1958, 149)

The Taoist follows the Tao by acting as a child and clinging to the
Mother's breast (XX, Waley 1958, 169). The way to act in the world is to
follow the role traditionally assigned to women in society—to be weak,
flexible, and lowly. Creative power comes from these positions, not
from positions of strength, hardness, or superiority. "He who knows the
male, yet cleaves to what is female/Becomes like a ravine, receiving all

things under heaven" (XXVIII, Waley 1958, 178). The lowly position is identified with women but is advocated for all—particularly for the ruler, to whom the entire text is addressed. If the ruler acts passively, all things spontaneously follow the creative principle within them.

The Tao te ching takes a negative view toward the achievements of traditionally male-dominant Chinese civilization—its books, laws, and travel (Chen 1974, 53). And it views the traditional love of the mother as the model for the relationship of the Tao to all creation. The Tao, like the love of a mother, makes no distinctions; it embraces both the "good" and the "bad" (LXII, Waley 1958, 218). One who follows Tao also refrains from judgments and accepts all things that come from the mother (XLIX, Waley 1958, 202). Traditional sex roles and biological differences are recognized but denied determinative status. All people (male or female) should take the role of the infant clinging to the Mother or of the female animal beneath the male in order to live in harmony in the world and to return to the Tao.

The Tao te ching uses both female biological characteristics and traditional socially defined characteristics to symbolize the Taoist path. The biological imagery of the womb and breast dominates images of the Tao; the social role of passivity dominates the images of the person who follows the Tao.

Chuang tzu does not use female imagery to communicate the Tao. Whereas the Tao te ching uses universal female images abstracted from nature to counter the normal way of perceiving and acting, Chuang tzu teaches in concrete anecdotes. The text illustrates Tao by describing people who have lived in harmony with it. Although women are mentioned, most of the characters are men. But all those who follow Tao act in the yielding and spontaneous way suggested by the Tao te ching. Chuang tzu expands the meaning of returning to the Tao by expressing a joyful acceptance of the mysterious transformation called "death." One should yield to all things brought about by the Tao, even death.

There are two items in Chuang tzu that are particularly interesting for this investigation of women in Taoism. First, Chuang tzu mentions a myth of a utopian matrilinear society in which people "knew their mothers, but not their fathers" (XXIX, Watson 1968, 327). Second, Chuang tzu sees no sex restrictions for the immortal beings who are an important part of later popular legends and religious Taoism. Hsi Wang Mu, the Queen Mother of the West, appears as one who found Tao and became immortal (VI, Watson 1968, 82). And there is also an old woman with the complexion of a child who knew Tao and tried to teach it to a sage (VI, Watson 1968, 82–83).

The Tao te ching and Chuang tzu both reject the aggressive, highly structured societies of their times in favor of lives of simplicity close to nature. With no value placed on social hierarchy, there is no place for the denigration of women. In fact, in the Tao te ching women serve as models.

YIN AND YANG

The complementary principles of yin and yang are important in most of Chinese thought and religion. They are not unique to Taoism, but in Taoism they are fundamental. Yin is the dark side, the cold, the damp, the female. Yang is the sunny side, the hot, the dry, the male.

In Taoist thinking, yin and yang are the complementary principles of the cosmos. The ideal is balance, not the victory of one over the other. In the Tao te ching the balance is grounded in the yin, which has the lower position. In Chuang tzu the alternation of the two, such as life and death, is accepted as the transformation of the Tao. Neither is superior—the yin state of death is as acceptable as the yang state of life. One cannot exist without the other; they are both part of the wondrous Tao.

The yin-yang duality of balance is strikingly different from Western conceptions of conflict dualism. In Western dualism, the victory of good over evil is based on a conflict that separates everything and everyone into two opposing sides that cannot exist in peace. Violence, whether physical or mental, may be necessary for the victory of one side over the other. There is no room for compromise with the other side— "You are either for us or against us," as the saying goes. This conflict dualism gives great hope to those on the side of "good" because there is the assurance that good is stronger than evil. Good, usually represented as God, will win in the end. The closer the end, the more hope for the forces of good.

Taoist harmony is a radically different goal than the victory of good over evil. It is based on a complementary dualism rather than a conflict dualism. There are two sides, but they depend on each other for their existence. The goal is the balancing of the two sides, the mutual interaction of the two forces. This complementary dualism has been the core of much east Asian religion and philosophy. It is the yin-yang model that originated in ancient China. One attains harmony in society and nature through the balancing of the positive forces of yang and the negative forces of yin. The cooperative actions of male and female, summer and winter, the sun and rain are examples of this complementary dualism, in which neither side is better than nor independent of the other. Yin and yang are viewed as female and male principles or forces, but women and men contain both principles and need the harmony of the two for physical and mental health.

The idea of the balance and relativity of yin and yang is difficult to maintain. In later Confucian thought and in some religious Taoism, yang is evaluated as the superior. In the Taoist quest for immortality, the relativity of individual life and death is superseded by the development of techniques for holding off death by the accumulation of yang. Breathing exercises, special diets, laboratory alchemy, and sexual practices were all developed in the context of yin-yang theory to prolong life and to attain individual immortality.

Even though the desire for the yang principle of life dominates, however, the importance of the yin principle never dies. Taoist techniques for attaining immortality are based on the cooperation of yin and yang and maternal creativity. The union of yin and yang in sexual intercourse is one technique to produce an immortal body and serves as the paradigm for others. In laboratory alchemy, the crucible functions as the womb, the elements of cinnabar and lead as female and male sexual fluids, and the alchemic firing process as the sexual technique (van Gulik 1974, 80). The equal importance of yin and yang is central to most Taoist paths to immortality. Both yin and yang could be absorbed through the skin to further the Taoist's progress toward immortality. The Classic of the Five Sacred Talismans (Ling-pao wu fu ching) of the third or fourth century suggests that the adept "breathe" in yang from the light of the sun and yin from the light of the moon at midnight (Seidel 1983, 1039).

HISTORY OF RELIGIOUS TAOISM

The Taoist religion can be most narrowly defined as the religious organization that traces itself to the second century revelations to Chang Tao-ling. A deified form of Lao tzu, the legendary author of the Tao te ching, appeared to him. Chang Tao-ling became known as the first Celestial Master (t'ien-shih) after he ascended into the heavens. He received a new teaching that taught how to cure illness and how to create a new religious and political structure in China. This structure soon became based on patriarchal leadership, with his male descendants carrying out the religious administration as Celestial Masters.

The leadership was not totally male, however. The basic position of ritual and moral leadership was the libationer (ch'i-chiu) who served small dioceses. Both women and men served as libationers. The twenty-four dioceses were to be presided over by twenty-four male and female officials. Kristofer Schipper (1978) has suggested two possible reasons for this equal participation of men and women: the Taoist cosmology, which is based on the balance of yin and yang; and the possibility that women were historically important in the development of the Taoist organization (375).

High-level participation of women in Taoist leadership does seem remarkable. The Taoist canon contains evidence of Taoist ordination for women. Michael Saso (1978) also has a copy of a Taoist text that lists eight grades of perfection for women Taoists (284, n.15). Maspero (1981) describes the ranks of ordination in the Way of the Celestial Masters as parallel for men and women: Sons and Daughters of the Tao (tao-nan, tao-nü), Man and Woman Wearing the Cap (nan-kuan, nü-kuan), and Father and Mother of the Tao (tao-fu, tao-mu). Only the highest rank of Divine Lord (shen-chün) has no parallel female rank (378).

Perhaps more important evidence of women's participation in Taoism is the mention of individual women in historical texts. Wei Hua-ts'un (251–334) is considered the spiritual founder of the Shang-ch'ing Mao Shan sect. She was the child and wife of classically educated scholars and was herself educated in reading Taoist texts. She was ordained as a libationer in the Meng-wei tradition of Taoism before she posthumously founded a new sect. From the perspective of this sect, her life is not as important as her spiritual activities after death. After she had been dead for thirty years she appeared to Yang Hsi in a vision and passed on to him the scriptures revealed to her by the Immortals (Saso 1978, 37).

The Taoist religion as a whole grew up in the context of shamanism. Women in China have always been important in contacting the world of the spirits, so there is nothing surprising in the role of women in a new organization based on communication with the Immortals. Many of the male Taoist leaders were influenced by shamanist women in their families. Chang Lu, the grandson of the legendary First Celestial Master, was successful in expanding the new religion and was well known for the "sorcery cult" that he received from his mother (Stein 1979, 60), who was an important priestess at the court of the Wei dynasty (Schipper 1978, 375). Chou Tzu-liang, who had a series of revelations in the sixth century, had two influential religious women in his family. His grandmother was a great shamaness, and the maternal aunt who raised him converted his father to the Taoist religion (Stein 1979, 54–55).

Individual Taoist women are also mentioned in Chinese texts as great laboratory alchemists. Alchemy of the laboratory was both a means of creating an elixir of immortality and a microcosm of the transformations of the universe. The fourth century text by Ko Hung describes the wife of a Han dynasty courtier who was an accomplished alchemist. Ko Hung's own wife, Pao Ku, was also known as an alchemist from an influential Taoist family (Needham 1983, 76). A woman alchemist known as Teacher Keng was an attraction at the ninth century T'ang imperial court. She entertained the emperor with her chemical procedures and magical tricks. According to the writer who records her life history, she may have been an Immortal herself (Needham 1983, 169–71). A twelfth century work by the poet Hsü Yen-chou gives a first hand account of the Taoist alchemy of Li Shao-yün, a widow determined to perfect the elixir of immortality. She wandered from one Taoist temple to another developing her process for transforming cinnabar into a potion that would turn her into an Immortal. The poet describes her extreme thinness, the precision of the weights and measures in her procedures, and her eventual death (Needham 1983, 191–92).

Saso's research on Taoism in contemporary Taiwan shows that active roles for women in official capacities have not completely disappeared. The Taoist Master Chuang keeps a picture of his dead mother, the ordained priestess Ch'en A-kuei, on his altar. She excelled in her Taoist training but could not perform public rituals because her family was of high social status (Saso 1978, 76–79). In a less official role, a married daughter of Master Chuang also carries on the family tradition by writing out the long ritual documents for her father's use in public ceremonies (Saso 1978, 112).

Women's widespread participation in the Taoist religion must be seen in the light of the status of religious Taoism in Chinese culture as a whole. Such high level participation of women in a long continuous tradition of Chinese civilization would be truly amazing if this tradition were the primary or elite tradition. Such is not the case with Taoism. The Taoists coexisted with the Buddhists and the elite Confucians, and they were always closest to the lower levels of popular religion. Even with intermittent imperial support, Taoists were at the bottom of the social hierarchy, along with women. Chinese histories confirm this status. As Saso has noted, "Since the men who wrote Chinese history were for the most part (at least publicly) Confucian, the

Taoist was always relegated (with women) to the last place in the biographies of famous people in the dynastic histories" (Saso 1978, 4).

TAOISM, POPULAR CULTS, AND SHAMANISM

The three Chinese traditions of Confucianism, Buddhism and Taoism are difficult to separate into distinct strands because, unlike Western religions, they were seldom seen as mutually exclusive. It is even more difficult to separate organized Taoism from the diffuse, unorganized popular religion of the Chinese. Confucian historians have been quick to associate anything not strictly Confucian or purely Buddhist with the Taoist tradition. Religious practices considered immoral were often labeled "Taoist" by officials. Such is the fate of any religion that loses a struggle for dominance (Stein 1979, 53). Popular religion and Taoism strongly influenced each other, but the Taoists drew a clear line between themselves and what they considered excessive, immoral cults. Taoist adepts converted people in the local cults to the more highly organized Taoist religion—sometimes to encourage political rebellion and sometimes to lead them to more civilized rituals without the wild shamanist trances or animal sacrifice (Miyakawa 1979, 101). Taoism prohibited participation in the "excessive" cults but encouraged the masses to continue many popular communal and domestic rituals important to women and men—worship of ancestors, of the soil god, and of the god of the stove (Stein 1979, 77).

Taoist priests have not only encouraged much Chinese religion, but also have served as its ritual specialists. Taoist priests initiated into the esoteric literature and liturgy of Taoist sects have the unique role in Chinese religion of performing the elaborate rituals of cosmic renewal (chiao). The chiao is a ritual performed in the classical Chinese language to renew the community's relationship with the deities—especially at times of temple repair. Women who have participated in this esoteric ritual tradition have already been mentioned, but public ritual performance by women is now rare. Many more women serve religious functions outside this literary ritual tradition. In both traditional and modern Chinese societies, a large number of the shamans who serve on the margins of organized religion have been female. Shamanesses (wu) and female mediums predated Taoist sects, influenced them, and were rejected by them, but continued to operate on the periphery of the movement.

Shamanism, which was central to ancient Chinese religion, centered around women. The Chinese word for shaman—wu—originally referred exclusively to a woman. In the Chou dynasty (1122?-256 B.C.E.), she danced and sang in the fields to invoke the deities and thereby brought the needed rain and fertility for the crops (Chow 1978, 65–68). During this ancient period, she was a figure of great power who probably personified the great goddesses of rain and fertility. The official cults later rejected her, and she was left to perform her spiritual craft on the margins of Chinese society (Schafer 1951, 156–57).

Female shamanism influenced organized Taoism both through the families of Taoist leaders and through its belief in communication with the supernatural as a basis for Taoist revelations from Immortals. Shamanesses cannot perform the high liturgies of the initiated priesthood, but they can perform many of their ordinary functions of exorcism, healing, and communication with many deities and ghosts. They use many of the same deities and are associated with the same Taoist temples. Shamanesses, shamans, and Taoist priests function more at different levels in the same religion than in completely different religions. Initiated priests and priestesses are the educated functionaries of popular religion; modern shamanesses are the typically uneducated women who come to serve the same community, often after suffering psychological or social crises.

Research on contemporary Cantonese shamanesses yields valuable information on their careers and relationship to Taoism (Potter 1974, 207-31). The three shamanesses of Ping Shan in the New Territories of Hong Kong all began their work as intermediaries to the spirit world only after extreme crises. The most respected of them resigned herself to life as a medium only after her seven young children had died, her husband had died, and the spirits of her dead children continually possessed her and made her momentarily "die." She finally accepted the social and financial role of village medium with the help of an older spirit medium. The second Ping Shan woman became a shamaness after her four young children died and she was possessed by two of them, who fought over her fate. Her husband refused to let her become a shamaness until the possessing spirits caused her to "die" several times one evening. She entered the profession with the assistance of a Taoist priest. The priest helped her establish her own altar to the deities demanded by her childrens' spirits. He addressed the deities as follows: "Here is a woman who, with the aid of her children's spirits, wishes to become a spirit medium. Please help her" (Potter 1974, 227). The Taoist priest spoke to the same deities as the woman and encouraged her in her religious profession. The third woman became a shamaness after the death of her 9-year-old son and her subsequent illness of three years. She was apparently the only Ping Shan shamanist with a history of shamanism in her family. Her grandmother's sister was the spirit medium who taught her the profession. This older woman was a respected medium who lived to be 120 years old (Potter 1974, 228).

These Cantonese women serve the religious, psychological, and social needs of their community. They communicate with the spirits of the dead from village families. They protect the health of children vulnerable to soul kidnapping or evil fates. They take care of the spirits of the unmarried girls of the village who are denied support and a place on their family altars (because women do not belong to their parents' family but are destined for the family of their husbands). And they even predict the future (Potter 1974, 207). Taoist priests may also serve in some of these roles, but they are not as available. A family of Ping Shan who had been plagued by a brother's spirit paid a famous Taoist priest from a nearby town to exorcise the spirit. The priest failed. Later during a séance with the shamaness the spirit told his brother that if he would hang a piece of silver paper with his name inscribed on it by the ancestral altar, then the spirit would bring the family good fortune. In this instance a shamaness and a Taoist priest attempted to accomplish the same task, and the shamaness alone succeeded (Potter 1974, 208–9).

In dealing with the guilt and fears associated with dead relatives, old women are in a better position to "exorcise" these demons. They know the village gossip and have become sensitive to others' emotions in the way required by people who live dependent on others. They must understand the feelings of the living and the dead. Most evil ghosts are female, and the reasons seem obvious (Potter 1974, 229). The frustrations, anger, and jealousy of Cantonese women mistreated by mother-in-laws, abused by husbands who take second wives, or ignored by families in preference to their brothers have few public outlets. Surely these emotions are felt by the community, especially by the women, and surface through their "spirits" or psyches.

In Taiwan today, women often serve as mediums for Redhead Taoist priests, who are so named because of the color of their caps. These priests are considered heterodox by the Blackhead priests, who can trace their lineage back to the founders of their sect and have received complete registers of deities to call on for formal rituals. The Redhead priests are less involved in the literary traditions and closer to popular religious practices. The popular San-nai (Three Sisters) Sect of Redhead priests trace their history back to three legendary women who practiced exorcism and spirit possession (Saso 1978, 60). In the Lu Shan sect, a female medium surnamed Wu is possessed every morning at 10

A.M. by the goddess Ch'en Nai-ma and serves as the intermediary to the spirit world for local Redhead priests. The priests interpret the illegible spirit writing she produces while in a trance. In this way Redhead priests remain closely tied to the spontaneous shamanism rejected by both elite Taoism and Confucianism in China.

VIEWS OF THE BODY

Religions often associate women more closely than men with the physical body. Whenever body is contrasted with spirit, this association means lower status for women. Fear and guilt about the body is then transferred to the female sex. Taoism does not have a body-spirit dualism. The complementary duality of yin and yang is within nature. The physical world is highly valued, and the physical human body in its most purified form is the Taoist's goal.

The natural universe is the transformation of yin and yang. It is the body of the Tao. The individual human body is a microcosm of the universe, and it undergoes the same transformations, is controlled by the same forces, and is of highest value. The goal of immortality in religious Taoism is not the immortality of a disembodied spirit; it is the prolongation of life in a purified physical body. Just as gold is the incorruptible and highest form of metal, the bodies of the highest Celestial Immortals are of the purest, most incorruptible substance.

The division of male and female in the body of the universe is most clearly the division of Heaven and Earth. Heaven and Earth are the father and mother of the macrocosm and are equally important. In the earliest Taoist scripture, the T'ai-p'ing ching, the Master says, "Father and mother are equally human beings, and Heaven and Earth are both 'celestial'" (Kaltenmark 1979, 37). The respect for Mother Earth is as important as that for Heaven, which traditionally had been associated with moral law and natural order. In this scripture, followers are prohibited from digging wells because it would be equivalent to wounding one's own mother. People must be content with the natural springs which serve as the nipples of Mother Earth (Kaltenmark 1979, 37). This Taoist vision of the world is clearly wholistic. Each being is part of the larger body of the universe, and to harm any part of the universe is to harm oneself, one's siblings, or one's own parents.

Taoism views even women's bodies and sexuality positively. Women's menstrual blood is powerful, not impure as in many religions. Menstrual blood is the essence (ching) of the woman, which she can use to increase her life span if she can nurture it; semen serves the same function for men. The bodily fluids of men and women are equally valuable as the sources of natural life and immortal life. Both menstrual blood and semen provide the raw material for creating an embryo for an immortal body (Needham 1983, 240). Human sexuality is valued as the obvious means of creation and is given religious and philosophical meaning. Sexual intercourse is the primary form of the interaction of yin and yang and thus represents the mysterious Tao.

The female body as symbol for creativity in the Tao te ching is not lost in the religious movement of Taoism. The Tao as the dark womb of creation is often given more mythological form. In a fifth century Taoist text (San-t'ien nei-chieh ching), creation proceeds from nonbeing, which produces the Three Breaths, which in turn produce the Jade Mother of Divine Mystery. The Jade Mother then gives birth to the legendary Lao tzu, who creates the world (Schipper 1978, 362–63). In this type of myth, the creativity of the Tao manifests itself as a specific woman—the mother of Lao tzu. Early birth legends of Lao tzu do not mention a father but only his mother, from whom he took the surname Li. Elsewhere Lao tzu himself is Mother Li and gives birth to himself (Schipper 1978, 363).

If the female body represents the creative power of the Tao, then it could be the model for all Taoists. In some instances, men apparently tried to imitate the physical characteristics of women. This imitation goes beyond the use of women's traditionally passive social role as a model. The Hsiang-erh commentary on the Tao te ching says that men should cultivate a female character, and modern lore tells of Taoist practices leading to the atrophy of male genitals or to old Taoist men urinating in a female position (Schipper 1978, 365). In Chuang tzu, when the Taoist character Lieh tzu reaches the highest level of understanding he takes the place of his wife in the kitchen (VII, Watson 1968, 97), but even more extreme is the case in the Lü-chu chih in which the man Lü T'ung-pin actually claims he is pregnant (Schipper 1978, 364). Pregnancy is a basic Taoist model for attaining immortality. A Taoist, male or female, creates and nurtures an immortal embryo within the corruptible physical body. According to this model, males must become females, at least metaphorically, to achieve their goal of deathlessness.

Sometimes sexual transformation did go the other way in Taoism. A text from about the eighteenth century proposes Hsi Wang Mu's ethical and physiological path to immortality specifically to women Taoists, but the end of the path is the rejuvenated form of a young boy rather than a young girl (Needham 1983, 237).

FEMALE ADEPTS

Women such as Hsi Wang Mu attained the secret of Tao and thus immortality in legendary times. Chinese literature is full of women who have learned the secrets of Tao in historical times, either accidentally or through the study of alchemy or meditation. One source for these stories is Pao p'u-tzu, written by Ko Hung in the fourth century (Ware 1966). He was a scholar who defended the claims of esoteric Taoism, especially the belief that normal human beings can attain the status of Immortals through Taoist arts. He argues that just because some people have not seen Immortals is no proof that they do not exist; they do exist, because people have reported their existence. Some of the stories he offers as proof describe female adepts who have learned the secrets of immortality.

Ko Hung reports a second-hand story of a 4-year-old girl who learned the secret of prolonging life. Her father, Chan Kuang-ting, had to flee from disaster, but his young daughter was unable to make the difficult trip. He abandoned her in a tomb with a few months' supply of food and drink and then fled. After three years the father returned and went to the tomb to collect his daughter's bones for burial. At the tomb he found his daughter alive and well. She explained that at first she was hungry but that then she imitated a large tortoise in the corner of the tomb that stretched its neck and swallowed its own breath (Ware 1966, 57–58). This story is used to prove that tortoises, known for their longevity in China, possess specific techniques leading to long life. It also demonstrates that gender is not relevant to the ability to master the Taoist arts leading to extreme longevity.

Another story tells of an amazing 200-year-old woman captured by hunters during the Han dynasty (202 B.C.E. –220 C.E.). She was naked and covered with thick black hair. When questioned, she told her unusual story.

I was originally a Ch'in concubine. Learning that with the arrival of bandits from the East the King of Ch'in would surrender and the palace would be burned, I became frightened and ran away to the mountains where I famished for lack of food. I was on the point of dying when an old man taught me how to eat the leaves and fruits of pines. At first it was bitter and unpleasant, but I gradually grew used to it until it produced lack of hunger and thirst. In the winter I suffered no cold, and in the summer I felt no heat (Ware 1966, 194).

Unfortunately this woman, who proved to be nearing immortality, was taken back to the court and fed a normal diet, whereupon she lost her hair and died. Ko Hung tells us that if left alone she would have become an Immortal.

The last story of a woman using Taoist arts in Pao p'u-tzu is that of a girl from a family who possessed the esoteric knowledge of Taoist alchemy. A Han courtier, Ch'eng Wei, married her but failed to convince her to give him the secrets. She believed her own efforts in the laboratory were successful because she was fated to master the Tao, but she did not believe that he was so fated. He harassed her to give him the secrets until she went crazy, fled, and later died (Ware 1966, 264–65).

A tale from the I-yüan gives further evidence of female adepts (Miyakawa 1979, 85–86). The tale tells of a shrine to a certain Lady Mei-ku in the third century B.C.E. Mei-ku was an accomplished Taoist master who could walk on water. She once broke the law of the Tao, and her husband killed her in rage and threw her body in a lake. A shaman placed her corpse in a lakeside shrine, and thereafter she would appear twice a month standing on the water. Fishing and hunting were then prohibited in this area because the shaman said that Lady Mei-ku hated to see animals suffer and die as she had (Miyakawa 1979, 85).

These four stories have one thing in common: all the women have experienced crises within a family relationship. The crisis that motivates or ends the practice of Taoist arts is caused by a male member of her family—father, husband, or patron/lover. These stories linking the practice of Taoist arts with family crises and the need for survival are similar to the stories of modern shamanesses who seek communication with the spirits only after family crises and financial necessity.

Not all women experienced crises in their search for the secrets of the Tao. The Taoist canon contains several texts that describe meditation techniques for any woman to follow. Women are important in these meditation texts as both practitioners and as representations of visualized deities.

The meditation techniques of religious Taoism demonstrate that the spiritual powers are not identified with one sex. The spirits that rule the internal world of the body and the external world of the universe are both male and female. Neither immortality nor spiritual powers are gender specific. The female spirits include various jade maidens, fairies, goddesses, and powerful spirit-generals who aid women and men in their meditation. These female spiritual beings are as diverse as the male spirits. Many are beautiful and even erotic maidens. Some are terrifying and ugly female spirits. An example of the diversity is found in Michael Saso's description of a ritual to counter black magic used by a contemporary Taoist priest (Saso 1978, 156–60). Of the six spirit-generals called on to fight the battle against evil, two are women. General Hsiao-lieh is a beautiful woman: "She is eight feet tall, and her face is white and clear complexioned, with pretty features and delicate eyes" (Saso 1978, 159). General Kang-Hsien is hideous: "She is ten feet tall, with the face of an ugly woman, yellow hair, and large protruding white teeth" (Saso 1978, 158). However, although differing in beauty, both women are courageous and strong. Here beauty is not associated with weakness.

Some meditation texts have separate spirits for women and men. The goals and techniques of the meditation are the same; only the register of spirits to be visualized differs. In the T'ai-p'ing ching women and men may both meditate on the Primordial one, or women may visualize the internal spirits that control the body as female and the men may visualize them as male (Kaltenmark 1979, 41–42). Another example of separate but equal participation in meditation requires marriage for the highest level of participation. When first initiated into the sect, young children receive a register of 1 or more spirit generals for meditation. At the second childhood initiation, they receive a register of 10 generals. At adolescence, sex distinctions begin, and women receive a register of 75 Superior Powers while the men receive 75 Superior Immortals. The highest station is not for the individual but for the married couple whose combined register amounts to 150 spirit generals (Schipper 1978, 377). This practice follows the model of the complementarity of male and female, yang and yin, in which both are equal and necessary.

Sexual techniques were also used to prolong life and sometimes even to form an incorruptible embryo for a new existence. The state of Taoist texts and current research make it difficult to fully understand women's participation in the sexual techniques or their understanding of them. Much literature focuses on male techniques of preventing ejaculation and using the yang semen and the yin essence absorbed from the female during intercourse. All people have an essence within them, and when it is exhausted, they die. The essence for the man is his semen; the essence for the woman is her menstrual blood (Maspero 1981, 518). Sexual intercourse is important for the nourishing of the essence, but only if it is done right. The Immortal P'eng-tsu recommends to men that they choose young women who do not know the techniques themselves because women who known the technique will seek to prolong their own lives and not give up their essence (Maspero 1981, 530). The physical techniques for women are not as clear as the sugges-

ted male techniques for preventing ejaculation. But women were obviously using these techniques for their own benefit, as they used other
Taoist meditative disciplines. Lest these Taoists seem to be involved in
continual sexual orgies, we must add that the texts contain many restrictions limiting when these practices could be performed. The restricted days, based on regular monthly and yearly prohibitions, number over two hundred a year. In addition, there are restrictions based on
weather and personal circumstances that reduce the possible days to
only a few per year (Maspero 1981, 532–33).

Taoist women found communal living most conducive to following these methods leading to immortality. Life in convents appealed
even to high-ranking women during the T'ang dynasty (618-907 C.E.).
Daughters of T'ang emperors T'ai Tsung and Jui Tsung chose to
become Taoist priestesses. A new convent was built for Jui Tsung's
daughters, who took the Taoist titles "Jade Realized Princess" and
"Golden Transcendent Princess" (Schafer 1978a, 7). Many T'ang Taoist
priestesses were known for their beauty and dressed in the same rich
costumes worn by the immortal goddesses whom they sought to imitate. T'ang poetry depicts them in their crowns and splendid cloaks as
they seek their true love—immortality:

> To go off in search of transcendence—
> Halcyon filigrees and golden comb are discarded:
> She enters among the steep tors;
> Fog rolls up—as her yellow net-gauze cloak;
> Clouds sculptured—as her white jade crown.
> (Hsüeh Chao-yün, Schafer 1978a, 45-46)

Sexual intercourse was one form of inner alchemy practiced in
Taoist convents that created, not surprisingly, suspicion and hostility in
outsiders. This form was later superceded by an inner alchemy for combining the yin and yang within a woman's own body without intercourse. A text written around 1798 by Liu I-ming explains that a
woman's menstrual blood alone was enough to create an immortal body
(Needham 1983, 240). By this time, Confucian and Buddhist influences
had permeated Taoist communal life. A list of rules for Taoist nuns
from the late eighteenth century requires them to abstain from wine
and meat, remain celibate, and preserve their hymens if possible
(Needham 1983, 237).

Even with the increased restrictions, some Chinese continued to
see Taoist nuns as models of transcendence. Liu T'ieh-yün (1857-1909)

in the last chapters of his novel *The Travels of Lao Ts'an* (translated as "A nun of Taishan" by Lin Yutang, 1950), depicted a young Taoist nun as the embodiment of the freedom, self-determination, and compassion that he sought in a new China.

FEMALE DEITIES

Taoist texts, Chinese mythology, and popular literature are filled with female divinities. Most have been related to Taoism at either the popular level or in the rituals. Ancient China was filled with powerful dragon women, river goddesses, and rain goddesses who lived on the cloudy peaks of mountains. Edward Schafer (1980) has shown how the state cult of medieval China turned these goddesses into abstract and asexual deities (58-61) and how T'ang prose and poetry depicted them as man-destroying evil creatures often disguised as beautiful women (187-89).

One example of a transformed creature is Nü-kua, a dragon goddess who, according to ancient Chinese mythology, created humanity and repaired the world. Huai-nan-tzu, the eclectic Taoist work of the second century B.C.E., contains the legend of her saving the world.

> In very ancient times, the four pillars [at the compass points] were broken down, the nine provinces [of the habitable world] were split apart, Heaven did not wholly cover [Earth] and Earth did not completely support [Heaven]. Fires flamed without being extinguished, waters inundated without being stopped, fierce beasts ate people, and birds of prey seized the old and weak in their claws. Thereupon Nü-kua fused together stones of the five colors with which she patched together azure Heaven. She cut off the feet of a turtle with which she set up the four pillars. She slaughtered the Black Dragon in order to save the province of Chi [the present Hopei and Shansi provinces in North China]. She collected the ashes of reeds with which to check the wild waters (Bodde 1961, 386-87).

Nü-kua not only saved the world; in another myth, she also created humanity out of yellow mud (Bodde 1961, 388-89). The fate of this powerful and benevolent dragon was unkind. She was preserved primarily as one of the three emperors of the golden age—covered with robes and deprived of her serpentine and female characteristics.

Some early goddesses survived better. Hsi Wang Mu (Queen

Mother of the West) was first mentioned in Chuang tzu, and a full mythology and cult devoted to her developed by about 100 C.E. (Loewe 1979, 88). Chinese artists depicted her with a royal headdress and seated on a half-dragon and half-tiger creature (Loewe 1979, 101–12). As symbols of yin and yang, the tiger and dragon represent the cosmic transformations over which Hsi Wang Mu reigns. Chinese worshippers believed her to be the source of immortality: she could provide the desired potion to eliminate death. Her gift of immortality was first mentioned in the third century B.C.E. text Mu t'ien tzu chuan, which describes the meeting between the divine Queen of the West and the earthly King Mu of Chou (Loewe 1979, 92–93). King Mu offered precious gifts, and she responded with the promise of immortality and marriage. Hsi Wang Mu's meetings with King Mu are part of a larger cycle of Chinese myths of seasonal meetings between rulers and goddesses or between stellar gods and goddesses (Loewe 1979, 112–26). These myths also reflect the ancient Chinese fertility rites, during which young men and women celebrated the beginning of the new season with poetry contests and sexual intercourse (Granet 1932, 147ff.). The seasonal interaction of yin and yang brings both agricultural and human fertility.

The attraction and mythology of Hsi Wang Mu continued, and she became the Fairy Queen of all the Taoist Immortals. A biography of her from the fourth or fifth century describes her life and paradise in detail. Her paradise in the K'un-lun mountains is filled with magical beauty: jade towers, silk tents, charming music, and the youthful men and women who serve as attendants for the benevolent Queen (Bauer 1976, 180). Hsi Wang Mu was also known for her concern for women's problems: she was invoked in Taoist rituals to dispel the White Tiger deity who causes miscarriages in women (Hou 1979, 218). Hsi Wang Mu's cult did not survive, but she continues to exist in Chinese literature and art as the Queen of all Immortals who cultivates the peaches of immortality. She is one of the characters in the popular novel *Journey to the West* (Yu 1977–83).

Nature goddesses have also survived—the Mother of Lightning (Maspero 1981, 98), the Old Woman Who Sweeps Heaven Clear (97), the Woman in the Moon (96), and the Mother of the Pole Star. Stellar deities are central to Taoist rituals, and the Mother of the Pole Star, Tou-mu, is one of the most important. As patroness of the contemporary Taoist Master Chuang, she appears on his altar as an eight-armed, four-headed goddess—a deity of awesome power (Saso 1978, 121).

Chinese domestic rituals often involve goddesses, usually paired with a male god to reflect yin-yang duality. The kitchen god and his wife keep records of the deeds of the household to ensure that justice is done—his wife is responsible for the records of the women of the family (Maspero 1981, 113). Another couple, the Lord and Lady of the Bed, are worshipped for fertility and marital happiness (Maspero 1981, 118). A solitary goddess, the goddess of the latrine, is sometimes worshipped by girls seeking a good husband. Although Taoism has encouraged such domestic rituals, there is nothing in them unique to Taoism.

Two goddesses enshrined in Taoist temples continue to be important in providing protection for the individual. The Empress of Heaven (T'ien-hou) protects sailors, aided by a deity who can see for one thousand *li* (Chinese mile) and one who can hear for one thousand li (Maspero 1981, 145–46). Her cult has been popular since the eleventh century. The Sacred Mother (Sheng-mu) or Lady Mother (Nai-nai niang-niang) protects women and children and is assisted by the popular goddess who brings children to women who worship her. These two Taoist goddesses avert disaster and send children just like the Buddhist *bodhisattva* Kuan-yin, who is given female form in China.

TAOISM TODAY

The Tao te ching and Chuang tzu have won their way into the world's canon of literary and philosophical classics. They will surely influence future generations of Chinese and non-Chinese readers. The future of Taoism as an organized religion is not so clear. Taoist activity in the People's Republic of China appears to be minimal. However, activity in Hong Kong, Taiwan, and other Chinese communities continues. After the arrival of the sixty-third Celestial Master in Taiwan in 1949 (who was succeeded by the sixty-fourth in 1970), Taiwan has seen increased participation and building of temples. Taoism in Taiwan has married priests from a diverse group of sects that recognize the authority of the present Celestial Master. Laywomen serve in various ways in the temples. At the Hsing T'ien Temple in Taipei, the temple courtyard is filled with blue-robed women carrying out the faith healing for which the temple has gained its reputation. They lay hands on the sick or on clothing brought by the families of those too sick to come in person. Women also serve on the margins of organized Taoism—as mediums for the Redhead priests or as independent mediums communicating with the spirits for the aid of their clients.

Organized Taoism in Hong Kong centers around the Lung-men

lineage of the Ch'üan-chen order of celibate priests and priestesses living in convents (Strickmann 1979, 164). These women and men recognize the First Celestial Master Chang Tao-ling as the founder of their religion, but they are unconcerned with the man in Taiwan who claims descent from him. Organized Taoism even continues in Honolulu, where there were three active Taoist priests when Saso surveyed the situaton (Saso 1978, 61).

Religious Taoism today survives with a cosmology based on the power of the female and interdependence of male and female. The creative principle is symbolically female because the Tao, like an empty womb, is the origin of all things. Harmony in this world depends not on male domination of female, but on male-female mutuality symbolized by the balance of yin and yang principles. The contemporary Taoist pantheon still recognizes female representations of power, benevolence, and creativity. However, in their views of women's sexuality and public leadership, the earlier positive attitudes of Taoism have long since been modified by the Chinese Buddhist and Confucian traditions.

Denise L. Carmody

JUDAISM

SINCE whole books have been written on the place of women in Judaism (for example, Swidler 1976), I should emphasize from the outset that this chapter has only the modest aim of providing an overview of the historical evolution of Jewish attitudes toward women. The materials it treats divide conveniently into those that show biblical, talmudic, and modern attitudes.

BIBLICAL ATTITUDES

The religious culture of biblical Israel spans perhaps one thousand years (ca. 1200-200 B.C.E.), but clearly many of the memories and traditions recorded in the Hebrew Bible reach back much further. When Israelite culture came to maturity, its center was a strong monotheism that was based on the conviction that the one true God had made Israel his special people. The form of this special relationship was the covenant—the quasi-contractual arrangements made between God and Moses, the people's representative (see Exodus and Deuteronomy).

This covenantal monotheism explains most of the Jewish people's strong ethnic self-consciousness throughout their long history. The covenant gave them a special identity and a special reason to survive. With such a reason, they were moved to emphasize procreation and family life. As a result, the prime raison d'être of the Jewish woman throughout history has been motherhood. To this day, Orthodox Jewish feminists can write sympathetically of the Jewish women who sacrifices personal fulfillment for the sake of her people's national survival (Poupko and Wohlgelernter 1976, 48–49).

From early biblical times, the Jews' concern for a stable family life led to a strong effort to control women's sexuality. For example, Israelite women were not allowed access to the Goddess religion that flourished in the ancient Near East. Not only did the Goddess religion challenge Jewish monotheism, but is also threatened the male dominion that patriarchal Israel assumed was necessary for social order. If women were allowed cultic prominence, and the cult itself stressed female sexuality, male control of the lines of descent and inheritance, as well as the priesthood, might well slip away. Therefore the Israelite prophets fiercely attacked the "harlotry" of Canaanite religion, attempting to destroy the statues of the Baals and Astartes, which represented a fertility religion at variance with the family structure that the covenant implied.

This family structure also led to the early marriage of Israelite girls. Normally, an Israelite girl married shortly after puberty. The bride was expected to be a virgin (the same was not true of the groom), and if her husband could prove that she had not come to him as a virgin, he could have her stoned. The discussion of this situation in Deuteronomy 22:13-21 shows that the Israelites took some care to defend brides against false charges, but it also shows that the basis for stoning a bride proven not to have been a virgin was that she had committed "an outrage in Israel by playing the prostitute in her father's house" (NEB). In other words, she had injured the rights and good name of the man under whose control she had been living, her father.

When a woman married, she passed to the control of her husband. She was then in effect her husband's property, a conception that explains the Hebrew understanding of adultery (McKenzie 1965, 14). An adulterer, male or female, could be put to death (see Leviticus 20:10-11), but in both cases the basic reason was the violation of male property rights. The adulterous man violated the property rights of the woman's husband if she were married, or of her father if she were unmarried. (A man violating an unmarried girl, however, was only obliged to marry her, after obtaining her father's consent and paying a brideprice. As a further punishment for his deed, he could not divorce her. See Deuteronomy 22:28-29). The adulterous woman violated her husband's property rights.

If a man suspected that his wife had committed adultery but could not prove it, he could have her brought to trial by ordeal (see Numbers

5:11–31). While the ordeal itself—drinking water prepared ceremonially—was not painful, the psychological burden of the priestly
prayers, the oath taking, and the common belief that a guilty woman
would be rendered sterile must have been severe. In early times husbands who accused their wives falsely seem not to have been punished.
In later times they were beaten and forced to pay a fine (which went to
the woman's father). Men were not subject to such an ordeal because
wives could not accuse their husbands of infidelity (prostitution was
indulged in, though prostitutes were maligned).

The baseline in the biblical attitude toward women, therefore, was
that a woman was the property of her father or her husband. Still, certain Israelite laws and customs softened this attitude. Women were distinguished from slaves, who, though they too had certain legal rights,
were lesser citizens that free Israelites. Women also had certain protec-
tions under Israelite law. For example, although a woman could not initiate divorce proceedings, she was not to be divorced without a substantial reason or a formal decree (Deuteronomy 24:1–4). A woman
with a wealthy father or a strong intelligence and will usually was able
to gain respect in society, for wealth, intelligence, and strong will were
qualities that biblical Israel admired. More tenderly, husbands were enjoined to love their wives, and Genesis (2:24) speaks of the marital bond
as stronger than the bond between parent and child. In the marital
bond, the spouses became "one flesh." For that reason, the marital bond
is used by prophets (such as Hosea) to symbolize the covenant between
Yahweh (the husband) and Israel (the wife).

Genesis also expresses a sense of how the sexes were first created
and then "fell" into their present condition. The two creation accounts
(1:1–2:4a and 2:4b–25) both stress that man and woman were willed
into existence by the direct action of God and that they represent the
high point of creation. The accounts also teach that man and woman
are complementary, so that only their union makes a full humanity.
Symbolically, the woman is created from the man's rib; she is one substance with him, and so is manifestly a "helper" fit for him. Obviously,
the Genesis accounts reflect patriarchal assumptions of male pre-
dominance, but granted this point of view, they picture women quite
positively. In effect, they have the primal man say, "This woman is just
what I need." Indeed, Genesis intuits a basic equality between the sexes
and their equal share in human dignity, and feminists from within the
biblical religions rightly count its symbolism more an ally than an
enemy.

This interpretation also holds true for the account in Genesis 3 of
human sin and dividedness. Whatever the misanthropy latent in this
account of the Fall, it is not specifically a misogyny. Rather, the account

depicts Adam and Eve as types of early Israelite behavior, male and female, who both miss the mark of God's command. Eve, intelligent and practical, decides that the fruit is good to eat, a joy to behold, and a possible source of wisdom. In other words, she sees it as a bargain. Adam simply eats what his wife sets before him, considering this domestic matter her affair. Both half-knowingly neglect God's command. Both therefore sin and merit punishment.

In the Genesis account, some such primordial rupture of intimacy with God, of paradisaical perfection, is the cause of the painful elements in the lives that men and women now live. Men have to work hard, earning their bread by the sweat of their brow, while women have to bear their children in pain. Later tradition, such as that recorded in Ecclesiasticus 25:24 ("Woman is the origin of sin, and it is through her that we all die," NEB), shows a sour view of woman, but the original story tends to treat the sexes equally, saying that they share responsibility for a life much less than intuition says it "ought" to be.

This positive interpretation of Eve, the protowoman, is in keeping with the portraits of other women we meet in the Hebrew Bible. They too are intelligent and decent. Bathsheba is clever, as is the woman from Tekoa whom Samuel uses to reconcile David and Absalom (I Kings 1:11–31; II Samuel 14:1–20). Deborah is a mighty prophetess, Ruth is a noble daughter-in-law, and Esther is the saviour of her people. In the wisdom literature, as we saw in Ecclesiasticus, there are misogynistic strains, but the same work that says of the contentious woman, "To restrain her is to restrain the wind or to grasp oil" (Proverbs 27:16, RSV), praises the good wife almost extravagantly four chapters later: "Who can find a capable wife? Her worth is far beyond coral" (Proverbs 21:10, NEB). As the rest of Proverbs 31 shows, the model laid before Israelite women (and all subsequent Jewish women, who heard Proverbs 31 each Sabbath) suggested that good men would prize all their wives' fruitfulness, not just their sexual productivity. The ideal wife would be industrious, a good manager, and a wise counselor.

On the other hand, it is also obvious that biblical Israel harbored some fear of women, especially strong women. Proverbs 31:12 ("She does him good, and not harm, all the days of her life," RSV) suggests that women were thought capable of injuring even a weighty paterfamilias. The foreign woman, who came into the household as a cultural stranger, was especially threatening. Like Delilah, who used her beauty and guile to bring Samson low (Judges 16:4–21), the foreign woman was exceedingly dangerous. She might even tempt the Israelite male to abjure his faith and take up her gods (I Kings 11:1–8; Judges 3:5–6). Thus King Solomon's foreign wives turned his head and Jezebel corrupted Ahab.

Beyond her industriousness or potential troublemaking, however, the Israelite women provided the Israelite man with his most prized possession, his children. The greatest good a wife brought her husband was progeny. For that reason, the greatest affliction an Israelite woman could suffer was barrenness: it made her pitiable, one judged harshly by God. (Recall that the ordeal of a secret adulteress supposedly would result in her barrenness.) If she did not soon become a mother, a young Israelite wife wondered how she had sinned before the Lord. In early times her husband often had a concubine, and if the concubine proved more fertile than she, the wife's troubles were multiplied, for this lesser wife probably would be favored.

Perhaps the most abject figure in biblical Israel was the childless widow, for she had no one close to care for her. Many of the biblical stories from the patriarchal period (stories about the hoary fathers Abraham, Isaac, and Jacob) use barrenness as an occasion to show God's greatness. Thus Sarah, Abraham's childless wife, is made to conceive in her old age so that God's promise that Abraham will have progeny as numerous as the stars in heaven may be miraculously fulfilled (see Genesis 15–21). Although patriarchal polygamy slowly gave way to monogamy, the childless woman then suffered all the more, because barrenness became a legitimate basis for divorce (Deuteronomy 24:1–4).

The general biblical view of sexual love is that within marriage it is right and good. Thus the Song of Songs praises erotic love, reaching a biblical high-water mark regarding healthy sexual attitudes. Most scholars are of the opinion that the Song of Songs originally was secular love poetry, and for our purposes its most remarkable quality is the lovers' mutuality (Terrien, 1985). The female is able to pursue the male without fear of being branded a harlot; the male is able to submit to the female without being branded unmanly. Insofar as the Song of Songs was taken to be an allegory for Israel's relations with God, it placed sexual passion near the heart of the covenant. The biblical God therefore became very different from the apathetic God of Greek philosophy. Yahweh could yearn, suffer, and lament the transgressions of his beloved, like a wronged husband (see Hosea).

Nonetheless, the biblical wife was not primarily her husband's lover. Far more pressing than his erotic satisfaction was the need to build up a house with children. An Israelite woman especially served her husband, her nation, and her God by bringing forth sons. (Another mark of biblical culture's patriarchy was its predilection for male offspring.) The mother of an Israelite male had some say in selecting his wife, and a mother played a role in the dedication of her husband's offspring to God's service. The machinations of the biblical queen mothers show how a mother's jealousy of her son's inheritance rights could become a powerful force. On occasion a queen mother would even seize power herself, as when Athaliah ruled for six years after the death of her son Ahaziah (II Kings 11:1-4).

Maternal love became a strong metaphor in biblical theology, involving a passage "from the wombs of woman to the compassion of God" (Trible 1978, 34, 38). In the Hebrew scriptures, the wombs of women belong to God. In the story of Abraham's betrayal of Sarah (Genesis 20:1-18), God "closed every womb of the house of Abimelech," the innocent corrupter of Sarah, because of Abraham's pandering. When things are made right, God opens the wombs he has closed. Similarly, in Genesis 29:31-34, God opens the womb of Leah, who was unjustly hated by her husband Jacob (because her father Laban had used her to trick Jacob). Later God remembers Rachel, Jacob's other wife, and also opens her womb (Genesis 30:22). In I Samuel 1:1-20, we meet Hannah, who, though loved by her husband, is sad because she is barren. Hannah puts up with the derision of her fertile rivals and prays to God, and in time Yahweh, who had mysteriously closed her womb, remembers her and gives her a child. The first point to note, therefore, is that God controls human fertility. Human fertility is a mysterious blessing secreted away in the depths of divine creativity.

Indeed, God himself works in the womb to form human life. Thus, in the poetry of Jeremiah, God says to the prophet: "Before I formed you in the womb I knew you for my own; before you were born I consecrated you, I appointed you a prophet to the nations" (1:4-5, NEB). Job (31:15) has the same notion: God fashions each of us in the womb of our mother. When Jeremiah laments his fate, he curses the day that he was born, wishing that God had made his mother's womb his grave (20:17). Job again has the same thought, wishing that he had not come forth from the womb but had expired (3:11). Psalm 22 speaks of God as the one who takes us from the womb, the one who has been our God from the womb of our mother (v. 10). Finally, Isaiah (46:3-4) uses the womb imagery as part of a poetic symbolism for God's providence: God carries the remnant of the house of Israel from the womb to its old age. As Trible (1978, 38) summarizes these biblical passages: "God conceives in the womb; God brings forth from the womb; God receives out of the womb; and God carries from the womb to gray hairs. From this uterine perspective, then, God molds life for individuals and for the nation Israel. Accordingly, in biblical traditions an organ unique to the female becomes a vehicle pointing to the compassion of God."

God's compassion is one of his foremost qualities. In fact, the phrase "Yahweh merciful and gracious" runs throughout the entire

Hebrew Bible like a divine signature. The root of the adjective *merciful* (*rahum*) signifies the womb. Concretely, therefore, it connotes being moved in one's womb. The prophetic literature uses this figure abundantly. Thus Hosea names one of the children of Gomer, the faithless wife, "not pitied" (from the same root), for God has decided to show compassion on the house of Israel no more (1:6). As Trible's extended analysis (40-50) of Jeremiah 31:15-22 shows, the poet plays back and forth between male and female imagery for both God and the representatives of Israel. Verse 20 reaches a high point that she translates as follows: "Therefore, my womb trembles for him; I will truly show motherly-compassion upon him" (1978, 50). The speaker is Yahweh, moved with the most intense maternal love.

Second Isaiah, author of Isaiah 49, is another prophetic voice using maternal imagery. To show God's care for Israel, he recurs to the figure of the nursing mother: "Can a woman forget the infant at her breast, or a loving mother the child of her womb? Even these forget, yet I will not forget you" (v. 15, NEB). Third Isaiah, author of chapter 63, also uses the womb in association with compassion. Where the RSV translates verse 15 as "the yearning of the heart and thy compassion," Trible (1978, 53) suggests "the trembling of thy womb and thy compassion."

Overall, this maternal imagery ensures that the God of the Hebrew Bible is both masculine and feminine. In other words, when it came to expressing its sense of the divine, even the highly patriarchal culture of biblical Israel was moved, at least in its poets, to sense a tenderness, an association with the origins of life, that brought divine motherhood to mind. However much it held back from the fertility religions, whose female divinities manifested various aspects of "Mother Earth," Israelite religion followed through on the notion (Genesis 1:26-28) that humanity, male and female, was created in God's image. The result was that its anthropomorphism made God both male and female. To picture God in fully human terms, it had to include the feminine. The God "merciful and gracious" was as much a mother as a father.

The wisdom of God dominates the sapiential books of the Hebrew bible, and usually that wisdom is portrayed as feminine. Proverbs 7:4 says, "Call Wisdom your sister" (NEB), while Proverbs 8 has Lady Wisdom standing at the crossroads to cry out the plain truth about life's real treasure. This treasure is understanding, which is better than coral, gold, or jewels. Life's real treasure is Wisdom herself: shrewdness, knowledge, and prudence. Still, Lady Wisdom implies more than practical skill, for 8:22-31 places her at the beginning of creation. Before the earth, the oceans, and the mountains, Wisdom was fashioned and born. She was there when God put the heavens in place and when he girdled the oceans. "Then I was at his side each day, his darling and delight, playing in his presence continually, playing on the earth, when he had finished it, while my delight was in mankind" (8:30–31, NEB).

As a feminine way of ordering things, close to the heart of creation, Wisdom laid the basis for a very positive view of women's intelligence. True, she is subordinate to the masculine creator, and somewhat his plaything. But her play is of the highest order, like the *lila* of Indian religion or Plato's divine puppetry. It reflects an intuition that divine creativity is effortless, an outflow of energetic, witty love. That the Hebrew Wisdom also delights in the human world is a further graciousness. It implies that the play of divine creativity loves what human beings can do and become with the freshness of a sprightly young girl.

In the sphere of religious activities, Israelite women were far from equal to men, but they did have some independence. For example, women could prophesy. Deborah and Huldah both received credit for helpful prophecy, while Novaliah was accounted a false prophetess. Therefore, when it was a question of charismata, direct gifts from God, women stepped outside the normal social constraints.

The Bible also mentions women as professional mourners (Jeremiah 9:17), midwives (Genesis 35:17), temple singers (Ezra 2:65), and nurses (Ruth 4:16). Since Israelite society tolerated prostitution, some women worked as prostitutes, but they had little social status. Sorcery was associated with women and was a dangerous profession, for Deuteronomy (18:12) calls it "an abomination to the Lord" and Exodus (22:18) says that a sorceress should not be permitted to live. If parallels with other marginalized women, such as Christian witches (see Daly 1978, 193–95) are to hold, sorceresses and cult prostitutes may well have been women of some influence. Working outside the accepted power structure, they may have posed enough of a threat to incur its special wrath.

It was probably their potentiality for such deviance, as well as the ritual impurity consequent on their menstruation, that excluded Israelite women from the priesthood. Exodus 35:22–29 shows that women were recognized as generous contributors to the tabernacle but that menstruation was thought incompatible with service at the altar for animal sacrifice. Like many other archaic peoples, the ancient Israelites regarded blood with a special reverence and dread. It was so close to the lifeforce that a wrongful contact with it was polluting. In later times this pollution was largely a legal matter, apparently stirring little emotion. In earlier times it probably carried considerable emotional clout.

An Israelite woman was considered unclean during her menstrual flow and for seven days thereafter. By contrast, seminal emission made a man unclean only until evening (see Leviticus 15:16). After childbirth, a woman was considered menstruous for seven days, and then for thirty-three days more if the child were a male. If the child were a female, both figures were doubled (Leviticus 12:1–8). After these times of purification, she was bound to seek out a priest to make atonement for her.

In general, women were held to the same moral and dietary regulations as men (Leviticus 11). Apostasy meant death for either sex, and it seems that women offered guilt sacrifices. It was optional for women to attend the three annual pilgrimages, but compulsory that they attend the seven-year assembly. So long as their husbands or fathers did not object, they might take the Nazarite vow of special consecration to God (Numbers 30:4–16). If a male were consecrated, he was worth fifty shekels. If a female were consecrated, she was worth thirty shekels. Most of the Bible's many laws, however, overlook the Israelite women, making her a "legal non-person" (Bird 1974, 56). The laws apply only to men because, apart from her status as a mother, the Israelite woman had only a dependent existence derived from that of her father or her husband.

Nevertheless, there are some biblical landmarks in the struggle for women's rights, and David Daube's (1978) two illustrations from the Hebrew Bible are worth presenting. The first is the provision in Deuteronomy 22:22 that imposes the death penalty on an adulterous couple. This is a landmark insofar as it treats the woman as equal to the man. By contrast, the law of adultery in many other cultures evolved in a way that never granted the woman fully human status. For example, ancient Greece placed the erring wife in the hands of her master, who was usually her husband or father. The wronged master then had to extract justice from the adulterous male, for the community at large made no move. The result frequently was a blood feud between the two houses involved.

With time, the community sometimes took control of these matters, making the punishment of the offending male its business. Nonetheless, usually the erring woman remained in the hands of her master, who could punish her as he saw fit. "He may wring her neck, cut off her nose, or let bygones be bygones. She is his puppy, if exaggeration be permitted. Think of a thief who gets your dog to follow him by means of a slice of pepperoni. The authorities will come down on the thief, not on the dog: it is for you to decide whether to give him a thrashing or pat him on the back" (Daube 1978, 178).

This is the state of affairs we meet in Homer's description of Menelaus's forgiveness of Helen. Though her adulterous elopement with Paris had caused the ten years of the Trojan War, she does not suffer the consequences as a full person would. In the evolution of Israelite culture, we also find this stage in Abraham's getting Sarah into the king's harem and in David's slaying of Uriah after adultery with Uriah's wife Bathsheba. Neither Sarah nor Bathsheba is brought to account. Neither is considered human enough to be a coconspirator. Thus when Deuteronomy goes out of its way to make the woman coresponsible for adultery, it promotes her to a higher status, a more nearly equal humanity, than previously had been the case.

Daube's second landmark dovetails with some of our previous discussion. It focuses on Second Isaiah's picture of God as a mother with her suckling (49:15) and Third Isaiah's feminist views of the messianic era. The former we have already met, and its significance is that by picturing God as a mother, the Bible gives femininity the highest possible status. The latter amounts to lifting the primeval curse laid on Eve (Genesis 3:16), for Third Isaiah's vision is that in the messianic Zion birth will be instantaneous, without labor pangs. Regardless of how literally the prophet meant this imagery to be taken, it shows that his vision of religious fulfillment embraced the situation of women as much as men. In other words, like Deuteronomy, he considered women fully human, with the result that their fulfillment had to be part of any "salvation" worthy of the name.

To link this treatment of biblical attitudes to those of the talmudic period, we may note that Abbahu of Caesarea, a rabbi who championed women's causes around 300 C.E., drew on Third Isaiah's text for support (Daube 1978, 183). He wanted to put women on the same level as men regarding the duty of procreation, and he taught his daughters Greek. But he did not prevail, as the feminist portions of Third Isaiah did not prevail over the male chauvinist portions. For when Third Isaiah pictured the spontaneous birthing that would occur in messianic Zion (66:7), he said, "Before the pangs of labour came to her, she was delivered of a male." It is all too like Genesis 35:17, where the dying Rachel is consoled by the news that she has another son (at a time when her husband Jacob already has eleven sons and only one daughter). Biblical women's "equality" never reached the state when a daughter was as welcome as a son.

TALMUDIC ATTITUDES

The Talmud is a vast, sixty-three-volume compendium of legal opinion, folklore, scholarship, medical and scientific theory, philosophy, theology, biography, anecdotes, and more. In effect, it is the en-

cyclopedia of Jewish culture, an efflorescence of the many-sided effort
the rabbis made to adapt convenantal life to the conditions of the Diaspora that obtained after 70 C.E., when the Temple was destroyed and the
Jews were cast out of Jerusalem. The word *Talmud* itself means "the
teachings," and it calls to mind Torah. God's guidance for covenantal
life. Many commentators date Judaism proper from 70 C.E., when the
synagogue definitely replaced the Temple, but others place it in the
sixth century B.C.E., when the Israelites returned from exile in Babylon
(see Parrinder 1971, 145–46). Either way, since it was the Pharisaic
party that provided the link from pre-Diaspora to Diaspora Judaism, we
may begin our survey of talmudic attitudes by noting how the Pharisees
tended to regard women.

Swidler (1976), drawing on the pseudepigraphal books probably
written by Pharisees and the writings of Flavius Josephus, comes to the
view that "the Pharisees thought of women as 'in all things inferior to
the man,' and 'evil,' as 'overcome by the spirit of fornication more than
men,' as ones who 'in their heart plot against men,' and that every man
should 'guard (his) senses from every woman'" (56). From the two
pseudepigraphal works that he studies, The Book of Jubilees and The
Testaments of the Twelve Patriarchs, both of which were composed between 109 and 106 B.C.E., comes corroborative evidence. Uppermost in
the minds of the authors of both books is the avoidance of fornication,
particularly with foreign women. Thus both authors combine xeno-
phobia with the notion that most women are nymphomaniacs. In the
author of Jubilees' own words: "For all their deeds are fornication and
lust, and there is no righteousness with them, for (their deeds) are evil"
(25:1). Later in the book the attack on sexual contact with foreign
women escalates, charging that all people involved in intermarriage, including a Jewish father who gives his daughter in a mixed marriage,
should be killed (30:7). The reason for this severity is that Israel is holy
to God and marriage with foreigners would defile it.

With at least some of the Pharisees, then, holiness became so pressing and legal a matter that fornication, one of the principal ways to sully
holiness, became an idée fixe. For this mentality it was but a short step
to the notion that woman is a temptress, a prime occasion of sin. The
Testament of Reuben (5:1–2) not only takes this step but goes on to see
women as intrinsically evil: "For women are evil, my children; and
since they have no power or strength over man, they use wiles by outward attractions, that they may draw him to themselves. And whom
they cannot bewitch by outward attractions, him they overcome by
craft."

This attack on women is in the spirit of the worst misogynism of
the Old Testament Apocrypha, for instance, that of Ecclesiasticus

(which is from the same century). The likely cause for this attitude was a fierce Jewish particularity. In the face of Hellenistic influences, which these writers thought threatened Jewish identity, there was a backlash that included violent opposition to movements for women's greater equality with men. When one couples this attitude with Ecclesiasticus's exaltation of studying Torah, from which women were excluded, one has the basis for the book's depreciation of women.

Swidler's general conclusion, drawn from his overall study of the attitudes toward woman in early Jewish literature, is that the positive views one can find in the Hebrew Bible, especially in its depictions of woman before the Fall, gave way to more negative views. Early Jewish views were not all negative, and bibilical views, as we have seen, were far from being all positive, but a shift occurred. It is noteworthy that this shift ran counter to the trends of contemporary Egyptian, Hellenistic, and Roman cultures, in which the lot of women was improving. Apart from the particularism cited above, it is not clear why Judaism should have opposed the going trend.

At any rate, from the return from exile in the sixth century B.C.E. through late biblical and early rabbinic times, misogyny appears to have intensified. The improvements in Jewish women's lot, such as the elimination of the death penalty for adulteresses (Swidler apparently doesn't consider Deuteronomy's legislation a landmark) and the elimination of the trial by ordeal for suspected adulteresses, were counterbalanced by such negative developments as the increasing restriction of women in the Temple and the synagogue, the rise of haremlike customs in Alexandria, and the rise of antagonistic attitudes such as those of Ecclesiasticus and some of the Pharisees.

In dealing with the Mishnah, the document forged by some of the rabbis who took over the care of the Diaspora community after 70 C.E., Jacob Neusner (1979) offers another explanation for early Jewish views of women. Since Mishnah became the foundation of the Babylonian and Palestinian Talmuds, it is a document of great historical influence. In itself it is a six-part code of rules formed at the end of the second century C.E. It was put forth as a constitution for Judaism under the sponsorship of Judah the Patriarch, head of the Jewish community in Palestine, and "Women" is one of six divisions under which it encompasses the Jewish world.

Neusner attempts a systematic description of the Mishnaic worldview, trying to show how this text "defines the position of women in the social economy of Israel's supernatural and natural reality" (85). The key point is that at which a woman becomes or ceases to be holy to a particular man—the point at which she enters or leaves the marital union. Thus the formation and dissolution of the marital bond is the capital issue. In these transactions, God and man are the active principles, and woman (along with earth, cult, and the realm of the clean) is the inert, passive principle. "Holiness" seems to mean an ordered, nonthreatening relationship: when things are in their place, they are holy. Throughout the Mishnaic system, woman's relationship to man is the criterion of significance. "Woman's relationships to other women never come under discussion, except as a realm from which a woman may not be wholly cut off at her husband's whim" (94).

When he comes to a deeper analysis, Neusner adopts Simone de Beauvoir's notion that woman is an anomaly, something abnormal. For the men who framed the Mishnah, masculinity was the normal form of humanity and femininity was deviation. As with other documents that come from a scribal and priestly source, such as the Priestly Code of Leviticus 1–15 and the Holiness Code of Leviticus 17–26, the Mishnah excludes women from the centers of holiness. "They cannot enter the sensitive domain of the cult, cannot perform the cultic service, and cannot participate even in the cultic liturgy. Likewise, in time to come, when Rabbinic Judaism comes to full expression so that study of Torah comes to be seen as a cultic act, the Rabbi as equivalent to the priest, and the community of Israel assembled for study as equivalent to the holy Temple, it would be perfectly 'natural' to continue the exclusion of women" (Neusner 1979, 96). In other words, for the priestly mind that continues on in the rabbis, women are irregular and threatening. Since the irregular and threatening must be sanctified (restored to ordinariness and so made nonthreatening), women become a special focus of sanctification. Basically, they are sanctified by being made subject to men, who express ordinary, normal humanity.

More precisely, it is the women who step out of their usual roles, which usually entail subordination to men, who demand sanctification. "About woman as wife Mishnah has little to say; about woman as mother, I cannot think of ten relevant lines in Mishnah's division of Women" (Neusner 1979, 98). The crucial times are when a daughter leaves her father or a wife leaves her husband: betrothal and consummation of marriage, divorce or the husband's death. These changes of state, with the property changes that they entail, dominate the Mishnaic treatment. However, beneath this prevailing interest lies women's sexuality, the essence of her abnormality: "The goal and purpose of Mishnah's division of Women are to bring under control and into stasis all of the wild and unruly potentialities of sexuality, with their dreadful threat of uncontrolled shifts in personal status and material possession alike" (Neusner 1979, 99).

The value of Neusner's systematic description is that it makes the early Jewish world of thought sufficiently tidy to provide us the possibility of discovering the relationships among that world's component parts. The value of a thematic description such as Swidler's, which Neusner goes out of his way to deprecate (89), is that it lets more of the untidiness of actual history flow into its analysis. Moreover, Swidler does not back off from evaluating the choices made by the subjects he studies. Because Neusner thinks that scholarship has no place cataloguing choices as "positive" and "negative" (89), he probes neither the deepest significances of the Mishnaic subjugation of women nor the relevance of this subjugation to current Jewish women's agitation for religious equality.

As we shall see in the next section, many Jewish feminists find the traditional subjugation of women highly relevant to their second-class citizenship today. The question of deepest significance is almost by definition speculative and dependent on one's theological anthropology, but what occurs to me at the present juncture is the cabining of religious instinct that the priestly and rabbinic legal theory entailed. The price for the sort of order the Talmudists wanted, and the price for the community protection this order secured, was a distancing from the moments where novelty and change force a daunting confrontation with God, the unmasterable ultimate reality. A prime index of this distancing is the Mishnaic understanding of the holy as the ordinary: in primitive (rough and creative) religious situations, the holy is the *mysterium tremendum et fascinans*. It is fearsome and alluring. If Neusner is correct, the men who controlled the Mishnaic world could not admit the awesome or alluring even in so mild a form as the sexuality of a free woman.

One has only to be slightly sensitized by Marxist studies of "ideology" to seek out who gained power from the Mishnaic scheme and who lost. That women paid most of the price for the religious control the Mishnah sought is obvious. But perhaps the gains and losses went deeper than the Mishnah sensed they would. Perhaps they led to a culture that tended to deprive half its populace of the chance to obtain deep religious consolation. That likelihood is one reason for the anger of current Jewish feminists.

Before turning to current trends, however, let us fill out our picture of talmudic attitudes. Granted the subordinate status she inherited from the Mishnah, the talmudic woman did not fare horribly. If she were a good wife and mother, she could expect the rabbis' praise. However, the context of Jewish life had changed from the biblical period. Throughout the talmudic period, Jewish life centered on the study of torah. The impact on Jewish women was direct: "Wherewith do women acquire merit? By sending their children to learn torah in the synagogue and their husbands to study in the schools of the rabbis" (Ber. 17a).

Marriage continues to be the normal state for both women and men. Indeed, it was widely held that "an unmarried man is not a man," for he lives "without joy, without blessing, without good" (Jeb. 62a). A woman without a husband was considered a *golem*, a shapeless lump (Sanh. 22B). One was even permitted to sell a scroll of the torah to secure a marriage (Meg. 27a), and the matchmaker was such an important figure in the Jewish community that the Holy One was said to have created the universe in six days and been busy ever since arranging marriages.

The ordinary talmudic term for marriage was *Kiddushin* ("Sanctification"), which fits the Mishnaic scheme we have seen. The husband consecrated his wife, making her something dedicated to the sanctuary (Kid. 2b). The wife also deserved honor because blessings flowed to a house on her account (B.M. 59a). Indeed, "a man should spend less than his means on food and drink for himself, up to his means on his clothes, and above his means for honoring his wife and children" (Chul. 84b). Not surprisingly, therefore, wives had explicit rights to conjugal satisfaction (Kid. 19b), financial support, medical care, a specific sum of money in the case of divorce or the husband's death, and burial. Were a wife kidnapped, a husband was obliged to ransom her, no matter what the cost. Though all inheritance went to his sons, his will was also supposed to provide for his daughters.

The wife's obligations to her husband were, essentially, to provide for his physical needs and to enable him to study torah. Thus Rabbi Eleazear's wife cooked him sixty different kinds of food when he was sick. Giving the male sexual satisfaction was important, since the Talmud thought that men were easily seduced ("A man should walk behind a lion rather than behind a woman"). The clever wife therefore calculated how to minimize the inconveniences of menstruation, during which sexual contact was forbidden.

Some authorities held that a man was obliged to teach his daughters torah, but the prevailing view was that he should not: "Whoever teaches his daughter torah is as though he taught her obscenity" (Sut. III, 4), and "Let the words of torah rather be destroyed by fire than imparted to women" (Sut. 19a). The result was that wives labored to free their husbands to study Torah rather than study it themselves. Men were counseled to appreciate this self-sacrifice, as in the story of Rav Rachumai, who became so absorbed in his books that he forgot to come home for the Day of Atonement. At the drop of his wife's first tear, the balcony on which he sat reading collapsed and he fell to his death (Ket. 62b).

As in biblical times, sterility was a heavy burden for the talmudic woman. Indeed, to be childless was to be as one dead (Gen. R 71:6). By contrast, the blessings of fruitfulness were celebrated in the hyperbole that "in the hereafter women will bear children daily" (Shab. 30b). The rabbis permitted contraception in cases where pregnancy was likely to harm the mother (Jeb. 12b), but they stressed that children *(banim)* are the builders *(bonim)* of both the family and the nation (Ber. 64a). Children were special gifts from God, as Rabbi Meir's famous wife Beruriah reminded him at the death of their two sons: "The Lord gave and the Lord hath taken away, blessed be the name of the Lord." Sons, however, were better gifts than daughters: "Happy is he whose children are sons and woe to him whose children are daughters" (B.B. 16b). The main concern a mother had for her son was that he become learned. Thus Rabbi Dosa ben Harkinas's mother carried his cradle to the academy so that he might hear torah from infancy.

Divorce was a major concern of the Talmudists. Their basic instinct was to limit this prerogative to men but to be solicitous for women's interests. Only the adulterous woman had to be divorced, and talmudic lawyers tended to delay in other cases to maximize the chance for a reconciliation. The detailed procedures for preparing the *get*, or bill of divorce, and the necessity of paying the *ketubbah*, or marriage settlement, also protected against haste. However, women who gave scandal could be divorced without a *ketubbah*, and scandal could include appearing in public with an uncovered head, being loud-mouthed, or spinning in the street (Ket. 7:6). To ease the situation of the suffering wife, the rabbis held that "the court may bring strong pressure to bear upon the husband until he says, 'I am willing to divorce my wife'" (Arach. 5:6). Among the causes for which the court was likely to favor a woman's divorce petition were the husband's impotence, his refusing sexual relations, and his staying away from home longer than business demanded. Other causes included the husband's being afflicted with leprosy, goiter, or boils. If the husband were a tanner, a coppersmith, or a collector of dog dung, even the wife who knew before marriage that her husband's occupation would cause him to smell bad could plead, "I thought I could endure it, but now I find that I cannot" (Ket. 7:10). Desertion, however, was not a cause for divorce. Unless a woman could muster two male witnesses to testify to her husband's death, she could not remarry. (A relaxed interpretation sometimes mitigated this law to one witness, and that even a woman).

Women were not held to the positive commandments that entailed actions at specific times (for example prayer), because these could conflict with their household duties. They could not be counted in a *minyan*, the quorum of ten necessary for a prayer service, and they could not preside at a prayer service. Although there was no law against women being called to read torah, they were not called because of "the dignity of the community" (Meg. 23a). Even small religious roles were discouraged, for the Talmud included the harsh saying, "Cursed be the man who lets his wife recite the blessing for him Friday night" (Ber. 20b).

Nonetheless, women were obliged to recite the prayers that welcomed the Sabbath and bid it farewell, to attend a *seder* meal on Passover, and to hear the reading of the book of Esther on Purim. They were also obliged to visit the ritual bath seven days after menstruation, to separate the dough to make the Sabbath loaves, and to light the Sabbath candles. Because they were responsible for preparing the food, many women became quite expert in the kosher laws. Overall, however, the female domain of home and family was considered material. The spiritual, religious domain of study and worship belonged to men.

In terms of the self-image it offered women, the Talmud ran a full gamut. Instances of hyperbolic praise include the story that when the people asked Rabbi Abba Hilkia to pray for rain, the first cloud to appear came from the direction where his wife was praying (Ta'Anit 23a, b). When Mar Ukba and his wife were in physical danger, she confided in him that they would come to no harm because of her many kindnesses to the poor (Ket. 67b). Women therefore could be saintly, despite the talmudic instinct that saintliness demanded learning. They could also be clever. A man about to divorce his wife for barrenness told her she could take back to her father's house any object she desired. When he awoke, he found himself in her father's house. Beruriah, wife of Rabbi Meir, chastized him for praying that all sinners should perish, since Psalm 104 asks for the disappearance of all sin, not all sinners.

This same Beruriah stands out as a learned woman, "the exception that proves the rule" (Swidler 1976, 97–104) that women did not study. She was remembered as having mastered three hundred laws a day, and as being so zealous for scholarship that she kicked a student who was studying silently, since she knew that oral recitation improved learning. However, when Beruriah scoffed at the rabbinical saying "Women are lightminded" (Kid.80b), she provoked her husband to test her. According to later, probably vilifying tradition, she yielded to the student whom her husband encouraged to seduce her, and then committed suicide from shame. In the same way, other prominent women came in for misogynistic denigration. Thus Deborah was called "haughty" and "a hornet," and Huldah was called a "weasel."

At their most negative, the rabbis drummed out the theme that woman is a temptress. The female voice, hair, and legs were especially bothersome. The sages tended to see women as sexually insatiable and to accredit a mythology of female spirits of seduction. Thus one reads, "It is forbidden for a man to sleep alone in the house, and whoever sleeps alone in a house will be seized by Lilith" (Shab. 15b), the disobedient protowoman. Furthermore, women gave off a negative force. Excessive conversation with a woman could cause a man to lose his good memory, and if a menstruous woman passed between two scholars at the beginning of her period, she would kill one of them. Two women sitting facing one another at a crossroads surely were engaged in witchcraft (Pes. 111a), for the "majority of women are inclined to witchcraft" (Sanh. 67a). This negativity led to such character assassination as "Four qualities are ascribed to women: they are gluttonous, eavesdroppers, lazy and jealous" (Gen. R 58.2). In the same vein, "Ten measures of speech descended to the world; women took nine and men one" (Kid. 47b).

To say the least, then, the talmudic attitude toward women was ambivalent. The misogynism of the priestly tradition, which correlated femaleness with religious uncleanness, continued to exert a strong influence on the rabbis. The mother still symbolized God's covenantal love, but also one met with such harsh descriptions of woman as "a pitcher full of filth with its mouth full of blood" (Shab. 152a). Still, some Talmudic women fought back. For instance, when Rabbi Judah patronizingly asked an old woman if she knew his teacher Samuel, she replied, "O yes. He was squat, potbellied, and largetoothed." For this Judah excommunicated her (Ned. 50b).

MODERN ATTITUDES

Talmudic attitudes towards women formed most of Jewish culture until the nineteenth century, when modern ideas of enlightenment and emancipation started to affect traditional European Jewry. Women were usually cherished in private and treated with respect in public, but Maimonides summarized the continuing legal view when he lumped women with the ignorant. The Jewish medieval mystical movement called the "Kabbalah" stressed a female aspect in divinity (the *Shekhinah*, which Kabbalists would honor by reciting Proverbs 31:10-31, the praise of a good wife. However, the Kabbalists also equated the feminine with the passive, left side of reality, which was the side most susceptible to demonic influence. Neither Kabbalism nor Hasidism (the eighteenth century pietistic movement that arose in eastern Europe) gave women access to Torah, though both movements' stress on the emotions offset talmudic dryness to some extent. In the small village, life's three treasures continued to be Torah, marriage, and good deeds, the last two defining the women's orbit.

As Beruriah stood out among the women of the Talmud, so Oudil stood out for the Hasidim. She was one of two children of the Baal Shem Tov, the founder of Hasidism. But where her brother was shy and withdrawn, unwilling and unable to succeed the Baal Shem Tov as the head of a rapidly expanding movement, Oudil was an extrovert. "No woman is as romanticized, as admired in Hasidism, as she was. She brought to the movement an added dimension of youth and charm" (Wiesel 1978, 34). Thus Hasidism came to honor her as though she were a rabbi herself. Indeed, she was always at her father's side, full of life, ideas, and enthusiasm. The Hasidim, who loved life and fervor, said that the Shekinah rested on her face. She married a rabbi and was able not only to care for him, two sons, and her father, but also to run their grocery store. Once when she was with her father at a celebration, she noticed that a disciple was leaving the dance circle because his shoes had come apart. Her father said to her, "Promise him a pair of new shoes, if he promises you another son." That was how Oudil became the mother of the great rabbi Baruch.

At the Breslau conference called by Reform Judaism in 1846, a movement emerged to make women equal in all areas of religion, but it was little heeded, even within Reform Judaism. Individual women such as Henrietta Szold, the founder of what became the Hadassah Medical Organization, distinguished themselves, but the bulk of women continued to be limited to the domestic sphere. Rabbi Isaac Mayer Wise, who established Hebrew Union College in Cincinnati as a Reform theological seminary, was one of the first American Jews to champion women's rights. In 1846 he admitted women into the choir of his congregation in Albany, and during his presidency of Hebrew Union College he encouraged women to attend. None of his female students sought ordination, however, and only in 1921 did the issue of women as rabbis come to the fore. The leadership of Hebrew Union College debated the issue, being pressured by Reform Judaism's stated commitment to women's religious equality, and a number of the faculty adopted the following resolution: "In view of the fact that Reform Judaism has in many other instances departed from traditional practice, it cannot logically and consistently refuse ordination of women" (Umansky 1979, 340). A number of women completed the theological course, but it was only in 1972 that a woman, Sally Priesand, was admitted to the rabbinate. As Umansky's article shows, however, a number of American Jewish women did remarkable work in the late nineteenth and early twentieth centuries.

In Conservative and Orthodox Judaism the position of women has evolved more slowly. Samuel Heilman's *Synagogue Life* 1976, a socio-logical study of an Orthodox synagogue in the Northeastern United States, shows the distinction of the sexes that continued as late as 1973: "Whenever the members get together to affirm in some way their collective membership in the Jewish world, they segregate the sexes" (69). . . . Thus during the meal after services, men and women would stand at different tables, the women occupying the space closest to the kitchen and the men going to the interior of the room. "When a woman breaks this barrier, she does so with an obvious display of purpose. Thus, a woman holds a garbage bag as she comes into the interior, and thereby signals she is coming into the area to clean up; or she holds some food on plates, to indicate she is going to serve. The man who is passing through the women's area stands in such a way that his forward motion is exaggerated: he is passing through, not staying" (70).

Strict Orthodox women still have few positive religious respon-sibilities, and it is still through their men that they fulfill their public ritual requirements. The men wear sanctified prayer garb, lead prayers, chant the Torah scrolls, and make the benedictions at meals. "In the segregated atmosphere of the kiddush [meal] room, for example, it is not unusual to find several women standing around a man who holds a drink in his hand over which he makes the kiddush benediction, which all, including women, must hear before eating but which only men may recite. For a moment, the women, often led by the man's wife, approach the man, listen to his kiddush [blessing], and then move away again" (Heilman 1976, 71). Women still cannot be part of the minyan, and they are still free from many legal requirements, but in the home, without which the shul (synagogue) "remains an empty fortress" (72), the Jewish woman reigns supreme. In forming faith, therefore, she remains the paramount influence.

Strong feminist demands have only come to Conservative and Orthodox Judaism quite recently.The large influx of Jewish im-migrants to the United States before World War II for the most part brought with them the traditional ways of the *shtetl* (small village), and those who fled Hitler tended either to lose their faith entirely or to reaf-firm very traditional values. Only through the protest movements of the 1960s and early 1970s did Jews develop a strong consciousness of the sexual injustices to which their religion was prone. True, many educated Jews had had serious question about Orthodox faith since the Enlightenment, but the religious inferiority of the Jewish woman, measured in terms of institutional, official status and power, was slow to come into popular focus. Since the early 1970s, however, many Jewish feminists, women and men alike, have been vocal critics of the traditional sexism.

As we have seen, the Talmud, which continues to be Judaism's main authority, severely restricts women's roles and offers them an ambivalent self-image. Therefore, many efforts to upgrade women's status have focused on reinterpreting the talmudic legislation (Berkovits 1978). If women are to observe all the commandments, become rabbis, initiate divorce proceedings, be witnesses in the courts, and the like, *halakhah* (Jewish law) has to be revised. It is not surprising the Reform Judaism, which has generally loosened the hold of halakah, should have taken the lead in Jewish women's liberation. However, many Conservative and Orthodox Jews feel that Reform Judaism dilutes the religious tradition that has bound Jews together for millennia. For this reason, feminists among the Conservative and Orthodox are willing to work at the more tortuous task of reforming halakhah from within (Greenberg 1976).

Specifically, the reformers argue persuasively that today's Jewish women do not need to be exempt from time-bound obligations, for two reasons: their housework is less onerous than in the past, and today's Jewish men should share the burdens that remain. Behind this argument is the reformers' conviction that the exemptions have, at least in modern times, tended to signal to women that their prayer is not important. By making the shul solely for men (Heilman 1976, 73), traditional Judaism has told many women that their spiritual lives are inferior to men's. Thus the reformers want to open the shul to women, making women eligible for the minyan, for *aliyah* (going up to read the Torah), and the like. In particular, those women who have no husband to pray for them, such as single women, widows, and divorcees, need a chance to *act* as part of the religious community.

Of course, tied integrally to much fuller ritual participation is greater opportunity for biblical and talmudic studies. Since learning is extremely important in Judaism, women can never become equal to men without full access to Torah. And, until Jewish women do become equal to men in functional or institutional terms so that they serve as rabbis and judges, one is not likely to see the legal reforms necessary to remove the misogynism of the past. For example, only if women's scholarly voice sounds loud and clear are the mythic taboos associated with the menstrual bath likely to be lifted from the Jewish psyche. Originally menstruation was but one source of impurity, only slightly more polluting than the loss of semen. Historically, however, menstruation became a cardinal focus of the rabbis' fears and sexism. By the time of the dictum "The uterus is a place of rot" (Nid. 57b), women were clearly the victims of a terrible legal and self-image. The lingering effects of such a saying are likely to fall away only if a solid percentage of the religious leaders and judges themselves menstruate.

Women still need relief in several areas of Jewish civil law, too, for this law is often commingled with halakhah. With the deaf-mute and the idiot, many Jewish women are still "protected" in civil law—prohibited from appearing in court, for instance. Moreover, many Jewish women still do not have equal inheritance, marriage, and divorce rights. For example, the deserted wife still cannot obtain a divorce and permission to remarry unless she can prove her husband's death. In Israel, this civil statute has resulted in a double affliction for the widows of the three recent wars. Not only have they lost husbands to combat, but because no bodies were recovered, many of them have also lost the legal right to remarry. If men were bound by such legislation, the cynical say, things would have changed long ago. The continuing affliction of Israeli women testifies that male chauvinism and patriarchy still disfigure the Holy Land.

On the psychic front, current feminists have also been devising new religious rituals so that the image of the Jewish woman, in her own eyes as well as in those of the community, might change from that of an underling to that of a mature, equal participant (Koltun 1976, 21–102). For example, in the traditional wedding ceremony, the bride is totally silent, projecting an image of effacement or nonpersonhood. The new feminist rituals aim at showing that women and men are copersons, in the spirit of Genesis's affirmation that God created humanity male and female. In the same spirit, feminists are devising new rituals for the female life cycle so that key moments in a girl's life will be solemnized, as they have always been for boys. This change means celebrating a daughter's birth with a special blessing, paralleling the gift giving for a boy's "redemption" with one for a girl's, working out bat-mitzvah rituals in which girls read Torah on coming to maturity, and so forth. It is a matter of social justice to give young women these experiences, feminists say, and many Jews now seem prepared to agree.

The conflict between ancient traditions and new claims for social justice are especially clear in today's Israel. The Declaration of Independence ensures complete equality of social and political rights, without regard to religion, race, or sex. The Women's Equal Rights Law of 1951 gives married women equality in owning property and being guardians of children. It also makes unilateral divorce, against the wife's will, a criminal offense. The Equal Pay for Equal Work Law of 1964 applies to both private and government employment. However, many of these civil rights, especially those concerning marriage, have been diluted or vitiated by the religious courts, which will not give up the old talmudic ways. As a result, a determined husband can still keep his wife from obtaining a divorce. The Orthodox are willing to play tough politics with these issues, withholding their support from any civil regime that bucks the old ways (and their religious authority). Thus, if a woman marries without Orthodox sanction, a large percentage of the population will consider her children illegitimate. Therefore the children, in turn, will not be able to marry legitimate offspring.

In the field of labor, Israeli women are still protected "as women." The effect is that they are forbidden to engage in night work and heavy labor, and also that they have earlier retirement than men. Since postnatal care of children and child raising still devolve almost completely to women, the labor legislation has done little to break sexual stereotyping (Lahav 1977). Even in the kibbutz, the vaunted laboratory of equality, women do not share equal power with men. In a recent study, fewer that 10 percent of the kibbutz women worked in the valued areas of production, which were tied into the leadership roles and important committee work. The result is that the kibbutzim are largely run by men alone, while women staff the nurseries, laundries, and kitchens. In 1972, only 14 of the 220 university students from kibbutzim were women. The return to segregated roles has made kibbutz women start to worry again about their sex appeal, for observers report a marked increase in their interest in cosmetics (Blumberg 1976). It remains to be seen whether industrialization, feminism, or the need for population control will change this trend in the future.

Optimistically, we may conclude by affirming that Jewish tradition offers women considerable resources for their development toward full equality with men. We have surveyed some of the biblical and talmudic resources, to which we could add the feminine imagery for the divine Spirit and the Torah (Swidler 1979, 49-54). Were they to empower a determined political reform, these resources might enable Jewish women to accomplish the most difficult of tasks: to change a profound mythological and ritualistic system without destroying it. It is no secret that many radical feminists do want to destroy traditional religion. Naomi Goldenberg (1979), for instance, thinks that feminism should mean the end of the biblical God (1–25). Judith Plaskow (1977) sketches a transformation of theology less radical and, to me, more compelling. It involves bringing feminine sensibilities and insights to bear on transcendence, the "going-beyond" that makes the human person ineluctably religious, so that "divinity" and "humanity" become as much female as male. Taken with all its social, psychological, and political implications, this sort of theology might advance Judaism to a new stage. The advance would build on the positive elements of both the bibilical and the talmudic traditions, but it would not hesitate to slay those traditions' misogynism. In the best of scenarios, it would replace the traditional morning prayer, "I thank Thee, God, for not having made me a woman," with an enlightened successor: "I thank Thee, God, for having made me the Jew that I am."

Rosemary Radford Ruether

CHRISTIANITY

IN this essay I propose to survey the major periods of Western Christian development from the perspective of the theology and practice of male-female relations in the Church. This is a very complex history which encompasses twenty centuries and diverse cultures and religious movements. I will not attempt to do justice to the Eastern Catholic and Eastern Orthodox traditions, which have not, to any extent, begun to enter this dialogue or to generate historical research on this subject. Confining the essay to Western Christianity, Roman Catholic and Protestant, is sufficiently complex. This essay will necessarily involve great simplification. I will organize the main lines of development around the theme of the conflict between two motifs in the theological understanding of male-female relations: subordination and equivalence.

The conflict between these two themes was already explored in one of the earliest books of feminist critiques of Christian theology, Kari Børreson's *Subordination and Equivalence: the Nature and Role of Women in Augustine and Thomas Aquinas,* published originally in French in 1968.[1] Børreson chooses the term *equivalence* in preference to the word *equality* because 'equality' suggests sameness, while 'equivalence' leaves open the possibility of physiological and psychological differences but rejects the notion that these differences are to be hierarchically interpreted. Rather, both men and women, although different in various respects, are nevertheless human *persons of equal value.*

This conflict between two views, one affirming the equivalence of man and women as human persons and the other defining women as subordinate to men, socially and even ontologically, can be traced through the whole of Christian history. The clash between the two views is rooted in the Christian Bible, or New Testament. What I propose to do in this essay is to define the two basic perspectives of subordination and equivalence and then to trace the conflict between these two views of male-female relations in successive periods of Western Christian Church history: (1) the New Testament period, (2) the patristic and medieval periods, (3) the Reformation and early Protestantism and (4) the modern period, beginning in the nineteenth century.

The theology of subordination is based on the notion of 'male headship of the order of creation.' This notion basically identifies patriarchal social order with the natural or divinely created order. Male headship is thus regarded as rooted in the intrinsic nature of things and willed by God. Any effort to upset this order by giving women autonomy or equal rights would constitute a rebellion against God and would result in moral and social chaos in human society. This notion that male headship is the order of creation usually carries with it the hidden or explicit assumption that God is male or at least properly represented by symbols of paternal authority. Female symbols, therefore, can in no way be regarded as equivalent images for God. Paternal authority, as a power of sovereignty and rule over others, expresses the nature of God. This assumption is doubtless the primary underlying reason for the hostility toward the new inclusive language lectionary recently released by the National Council of Churches.[2]

Social order, according to this view, demands the sovereign authority of men as husbands and fathers over women as wives and children. The proper relationship between the sexes is one of rule and obedience, however softened it may be by love or kindliness. Women must not initiate ideas or exercise their will independently but essentially must act as obedient followers and complements to the male, carrying out his commands and mediating them to the children (and slaves or servants). Even when the male exercises his power violently, arbitrarily, or sinfully, woman is not justified in rebellion or autonomous life, but serves the social order and obeys God by silent and prayerful suffering, attempting to better the male by her compliance and good example.

The theology of subordination buttresses this view of male headship as the order of creation by various insinuations that woman is, in fact, morally, ontologically, and intellectually the inferior of the male. Her subordination is not merely one of social office, but of actual inferiority. She is less capable of independent life in all respects than the male. Moreover, her inferiority leads to sin when she acts independently. Thus a key item in the theology of subordination is the scapegoating of woman for the origin of sin. Woman, acting on her own, caused the fall of humanity. This idea reenforces woman's subordination by making it not simply a voluntary but now an enforced relationship which must be suffered by woman as a punishment for sin and as a curb against further sin.

Woman's moral status in the theology of subordination, then, is highly ambivalent. On the one hand, woman is called to a kind of heroic ethic of humility and suffering, chastity and self-abnegation which is not required to the same extent of men but which closely approximates the Christian ideal of Christ. On the other hand, woman is regarded as the moral inferior of the male: willful, lacking self-control of her passions and appetites, a temptress to the male, and therefore needing to be kept under control, both for her own good and to prevent her from subverting the higher capacities of male rationality and virtue. This notion is expressed in the bifurcated image of woman in Christianity as Mary, the virgin mother obedient to God, and Eve, the disobedient woman who caused sin to come into the world. At the most extreme, the witch images the negative view of woman as the handmaiden of the Devil, in contrast to Mary, the handmaiden of the Lord.

This construct of themes associated with the theology of subordination has never been the sole view of women in Christianity, although for much of Christian history it has been the dominant and official view. A theology of equivalence has also been present, although generally championed only by minority movements. Only recently has it come to be seen as the dominant view, and only by liberal churches. The theology of equivalence takes the creation story of Genesis 1:27, where both male and female are created in the image of God, as normative for its view of male-female relations. Both men and women possess the image of God equally as human persons.[3] Both are given sovereignty over the lower creation. Neither is given dominance over the other. They stand as copartners before God and stewards of creation.

This understanding of shared humanity in the image of God is seen as having been restored in Christ. Galatians 3:28, where baptism into Christ is seen as making all humanity one, male and female, Jew and Greek, slave and free, is the charter of the Christian theology of equivalence restored in redemption. In the light of Christ, male dominance and all forms of ethnocentrism are seen as sinful. The curse upon Eve, that she should bear children in sorrow and be under the domination of her husband, is read not as divinely intended punishment, but as a historical statement of the fallen state of humanity, which distorts the authentic cohumanity of male and female. This equivalence, restored in Christ, is further extended by the Pentecost text of Acts 2:17 (Joel 2:28), where the spirit of prophecy sent by the risen Christ to be with the Church is given to both the "maid servants and the men servants." These three texts form the keystones in the theology of equivalence. One can find them cited century after century in movements that seek to affirm women's equal humanity with the male, as well as her calling to the ministry.

THE NEW TESTAMENT

Although the New Testament has been traditionally read as the foundation for the theology of subordination by patriarchal Christianity, the basis for this theology appears primarily in the post-Pauline texts of the New Testament; in the earlier strata of Christian development, theology of equivalence is present. The vehement statements justifying women's subordination must be read today as expressions of a post-Pauline patriarchalizing Christianity which is in conflict with the heirs of this earlier egalitarian Christianity. This theology of equivalence is implicit rather than explicit in the Gospel stories. It is significant that since no texts justifying women's subordination appear in the Gospels, patriarchal religion has typically relied on deductions drawn from the Law and the order of creation, as suggested in the second creation story of Genesis 2-3, rather than on dominical teaching.

However, there is evidence that early Christianity originally did not read itself this way but rather regarded the redemption announced by Jesus as overturning systems of social discrimination and bringing all persons, male and female, Jew, Samaritan, or Gentile, learned or unwashed, into a new status before God. The core of Jesus' messianic announcement was understood as "good news to the poor" precisely in the sense of overthrowing views of special privilege and favor with God enjoyed by the learned scribal or priestly Jewish male. In contrast to this traditional view of divine favor upon the pious elite, Jesus' mission was to those who were left out of this system of privilege: the poor, the ritually unclean, the socially outcast, and the people of the nations.

Often the Gospel stories radicalize this good news by portraying these outcast groups through female representatives: the woman with the flow of blood, the widow, the Samaritan woman, and the Syrophoenician woman. As women of these despised groups, they form the bottom of the existing hierarchy of religious privilege. It is precisely these outcasts who are to be "first in the Kingdom of God." They are the ones who hear the message of God's prophet "gladly" when the representatives of the official system of religious privilege—the priests, the scribes, and Pharisees—reject it. Thus the key to the Gospel vision is a message of iconoclastic transformation of the existing social and religious order of Jesus' milieu; the last will be first and the first last.

This Gospel vision is not consciously feminist in the sense that it does not isolate women as a special problem group. Rather, it recognizes that women form a subgroup within social groups who suffer from particular, additional abuses. It uses examples of such women to illustrate its radical vision of the good news which "puts down the mighty from their thrones and lifts up the lowly" (Luke 1:52). This perception is found not only in particular parables and stories where outcast women figure as the hearers of the gospel, but also in the basic story line of all four Gospels. All the Gospels are shaped by a dramatic form in which Jesus as God's messianic prophet is successively rejected by his family and home town, by the religious leaders, by the fickle crowds who once heard him, and finally, by his own male disciples, a betrayal which is climaxed by Peter's denial. The women disciples thus constitute the "faithful remnant" who remain with him at the cross and who are the first at the tomb to witness the resurrection and to bring the good news back to the trembling male disciples in the upper room.

However much modern scholars may question the exact historicity of this pattern, especially the empty tomb story, what is significant here is the consciousness of that early Christianity which shaped the Gospel material into this dramatic pattern, thus illustrating in the entire drama of Jesus' life and death the basic message that "the last shall be first." Those who have no honor and are not even accounted worthy to be witnesses in the dominant religious system are the faithful remnant and first witnesses of the resurrection.

There is also evidence that this early Christian consciousness of being called out of an old order into a new order of redemption was expressed in patterns of ministry which included women. In contrast to what was to become the dominant patterns of the synagogue, the early Christian Church included women in the catechetical community. Women, equally with men, were called to study the new Torah of Jesus, to teach and to preach. Evidence for this equality is seen in the Mary and Martha pericope of Luke 10:38–42, where Mary's right to study with the male disciples around Rabbi Jesus is justified over against the traditional role of the woman in Judaism, who frees men for study by cooking and serving. Although this text has been much misinterpreted in Christianity, it is likely that its original context was a justification of the inclusion of women in the Christian catechetical community. The presence of women in the learning and teaching community is also probably reflected in the pattern of the double parables that appear in the Gospels, where the same idea is illustrated by male and female examples, such as the woman seeking the lost coin paired with the shepherd seeking the lost sheep, and the woman who sows leaven in a measure of flour paired with the farmer sowing seed in a field.[4]

The Pentecost narrative of Acts 2:17, to which I have already alluded, reflects the early perception that the gift of prophecy was given to men and women alike. We know by the references to the four prophet daughters of Philip that early Christians recognized women as prophetesses.[5] When it is recognized that Paul himself lists prophets after apostles in the hierarchy of spiritual gifts, that many Christians well into the second century regarded a prophet as the appropriate person to preside over the Eucharist[6] and to call down the gifts of the Spirit upon the gifts, this inclusion of women in prophecy is no small matter. It was through the prophet and the martyr in particular that the living presence of Christ was present with the Christian community. Women's equivalence in both roles was always acknowledged, and indeed has never been denied by patriarchal Christianity, although both roles were gradually marginalized from ministry as an officially recognized office. Early Christianity, including Pauline Christianity, however, did not make this distinction between charisma and office, but saw ministry as rooted in charismatic gifts of the Spirit.

It is generally assumed that Paul is the author of a Christianity of female subordination. But more recent studies have shown that the historical Paul in fact continued most of the assumptions and practices of early charismatic, inclusive Christianity.[7] Indeed, most of the New Testament evidence that women functioned as local leaders, as well as traveling evangelists, is to be found in the Pauline letters. Paul addresses almost an equal number of women along with men (sixteen women and eighteen men) in his greetings to Church leaders in Romans 16. He mentions two women, Euodia and Syntyche, as having preached the gospel "with Barnabas and me" in Philippians 4:2–3. He addresses a woman named Junia by the title of "apostle,"[8] and constantly refers to the husband and wife team, Priscilla and Aquila, as "Church leaders," usually naming Priscilla first. He also speaks of the prominent woman Phoebe by the title of both "deacon" and "*prostasis*," or leader, of her community.[9]

Paul received from the early Church both a practice of thus including women in the ministries of catechesis, prophecy, local Church leadership, and traveling evangelism (the role Paul calls that of "apostle"), and also a baptismal theology of male-female equivalence in Christ as reflected in the Galations 3:28 reference. This formula was not original with Paul; he cites it from early Christian tradition. The

Galatians baptismal text expresses the early Christian vision of the new humanity in Christ. It was consciously moulded to contrast with the traditions of rabbinic piety, adapted from Hellenistic philosophy, in which the Jewish male thanks God for having been born male and not female, free and not slave, and Jew rather than gentile.[10] By declaring that in Christ these divisions had been overcome and all these groups made "one," the early Christian stated the essence of his or her new identity as one where the equivalence of all humans in the image of God had been restored.

Although Paul accepted this theology of equivalence of women with men in redemption and the practice of including women in ministry, he remained ambivalent about the theological basis for this position. Paul accepted from his rabbinic background a theology of the orders of creation which regarded the subordination of women and slaves as the created order. This hierarchical ordering of the cosmos is evident in I Corinthians 2–3, where the headship of man over woman is paralleled with the headship of Christ over man and God over Christ. Paul is uncertain about the status of this cosmic patriarchal order. In one sense, he regards it as still intact, and in another sense he sees it as having been relativized by the coming eschatological order in Christ.

In I Corinthians 7:17–40, Paul equates not being married or being freed from marriage through the death of a husband with being released from slavery. Both women and slaves are under the yoke of paternal authority as long as their masters have authority over them. In the case of the slave, this authority is broken by manumission. In the case of the woman, it is broken by the death of the husband. This parallel of the wife and the slave shows that Paul equates both female subordination in marriage and the subordination of the slave to servitude as marks of the passing form of this world. This servitude is still intact as long as this present created order continues. But it belongs to a world order which is passing away and whose end Paul expected to come very soon.

Paul accepted the fact that this new eschatological equivalence of all persons was expressed in baptism and ministry. But he was reluctant to allow women or slaves to translate this equivalence into efforts to change the social system by seeking manumission or freedom from husbands. Paul himself remained uncertain about the relationship between the creational theology of subordination and the eschatological theology of equivalence. His equivocations in I Corinthians 11:2–12 show that he was troubled and dissatisfied with his own formulations in this regard. Although he himself did not systematize such a split, the Pauline legacy laid the basis for dualism that has haunted subsequent

Christianity to the present day: namely, a bifurcation between a creational theology of subordination and an eschatological theology of equivalence.

The post-Pauline Christianity which laid claim to the Pauline inheritance did not move solely toward a more explicitly patriarchal Christianity. Rather we should see deutero-Pauline Christianity of the period 85-135 C.E. as moving in two opposite directions, both claiming to be followers of Paul. On the one hand, a charismatic, prophetic Christianity continued the belief in the equivalence of men and women in Christ, their equal endowment with prophetic gifts, and their call to preach and even to baptize. This Christianity increasingly expressed itself in ascetic (but not necessarily gnostic) form. Radical Christian conversion was seen as expressed by a call to chastity and martyrdom. For women, chastity dissolved their subordination to males, whether fathers, potential husbands, or the authority of the state. Liberated by Christ from their subordination to paternal authority, they renounced marriage, flouted the demands of family, left home to preach and baptize, and even expressed their dissolution of female status by adopting male dress. The classic legend that expresses this type of Pauline Christianity is the Acts of Paul and Thecla, written about the middle of the second century, but probably going back in oral tradition to the late first century.

A second type of Pauline Christianity is encapsulated in the pastoral Epistles. This type of Christianity had moved from the charismatic ministry of the historical Paul—of apostles, prophets, and teachers—to the institutionalized ministry of bishops, presbyters, and deacons. It still included women in the order of deacons, but probably restricted this female deaconate to ministry to women, such as helping baptize women, bringing the Eucharist to women, and catechetical instruction of women. Its concept of the Church was modeled after the patriarchal family. The primary qualification of a bishop, presbyter, or deacon was that he should be a proven father of a family, a husband of one wife. This paternal status was given priority over any spiritual gifts.

As in the rabbinic tradition after which it is modeled, the primary role of bishop and presbyter in the pastoral Epistles is teaching. Women are explicitly excluded from this teaching ministry. The basis for this exclusion is a patriarchal interpretation of Genesis 2-3, which sees women's secondary status in creation and priority in sin as decreeing a historical position of silence and servitude. In the pastoral Epistles and in other Epistles, such as I Peter of the same period, we find the household codes which reiterate the subordinate status of women, children, and slaves to the patriarchal authority of men as husbands, fathers, and masters. The reiteration of these dicta in this strata of the New Testament suggests a Christianity that sees itself to be threatened by a conflicting view which believes that the new humanity in Christ in some way dissolves this paternal authority.[11]

A recent study of these two Pauline traditions by the New Testament scholar D.R. MacDonald, *The Legend and the Apostle*,[12] has shown that the legend of Paul and Thecla was already current in oral Christianity at the time the pastoral Epistles were written. The author of the pastoral Epistles writes consciously to refute this radical version of the Pauline tradition and to assert a patriarchal Paulinism as the authentic Pauline tradition. Thus he writes in the name of Paul, shaping his epistles as Pauline letters. Moreover, this same patriarchal deutero-Paulinism was doubtless responsible, not only for the collection of the Pauline letters, but for their editing. This editing has been shown to include certain interpolations into earlier letters, such as I Corinthians 14:34–36, where the enjoining of women to keep silence is inserted into earlier passages that actually included women in speaking and prophecying in the Christian assembly.[13]

Such contemporary study of the pastoral Epistles in the light of contemporary noncanonical material such as the Acts of Paul and Thecla allows us to relativize the authority of the pastoral Epistles and to recognize that there existed a different and conflicting tradition about Paul that made equal claims to the Pauline heritage. Nevertheless, the historical importance of the pastoral Epistles cannot be underestimated. In effect, this patriarchal Paulinism represents what, by the middle of the second century, is already the victorious Christianity which is asserting itself as the "orthodox" line of apostolic teaching through episcopal succession. Although the radical Paulinism of the Acts of Paul and Thecla was never itself declared heretical and continued to be venerated into the Middle Ages, its heirs were increasingly marginalized and condemned as heretical.

Thus patriarchal Paulinism not only won historically, but it also succeeded in defining the final strata of the New Testament canon, which provided the lens through which the entire New Testament would subsequently be read—not only Paul himself, but also Jesus and the earliest apostles. One cannot challenge the authority of the pastoral Epistles as the authentic reading of Paul without to some extent challenging the authority of the canon which was defined by this victorious,. patriarchal deutero-Paulinism. Noncanonical material such as the Acts of Paul and Thecla can be allowed to critique and relativize the pastoral Apostles in our account of the true "apostolic teaching" only if this deutero-Pauline perimeter of the New Testament is thrown into question as the definitive line of apostolic teaching.[14]

THE PATRISTIC AND MEDIEVAL PERIODS

The theology of inclusion did not vanish in the patristic and medieval Church, but it became identified primarily with sectarian or heretical forms of Christianity. A truncated version of it survived in monastic movements, especially in women's monasticism. The equality of men and women in Christ was associated in these movements with an eschatological humanity and heavenly order transcendent to creation. This eschatological equivalence was expressed within history by the renunciation of marriage and sexuality and a life style of celibacy and asceticism. This concept of eschatological equivalence could be expressed in prophetic popular movements or mystical and gnostic movements. The prophetic version drew on the ancient roots of Christianity, which saw the Church as a messianic community of the "last times" in which the spirit of prophecy had been poured out on all flesh and both men and women had been given prophetic powers.

Various popular early Christian movements carried on this prophetic tradition. The Montanists of the late second century are the most notable example. Two women, Maximilla and Priscilla, were acknowledged by Montanists as prophetic revealers of the movement. The Spirit of Christ was seen as continuing to speak to the Church through the prophet or prophetess. One surviving prophecy from Priscilla images the appearance of Christ to her in the form of a shining female. Montanism thus anticipated movements of the later Middle Ages where the renewal of prophecy was seen as a new dispensation of the Spirit which completes the revelation through Jesus as the Christ. The notion that the Spirit will be represented as a female often appeared in such movements. This notion reflected the sensibility that the representation of women in Christ and in the Spirit had been excised from patriarchal Christianity and that a new dispensation was necessary to complete the revelation of God and the making of the new redeemed humanity.

This kind of prophetic, apocalyptic Christianity finds reverberations in much of the literature of popular Christianity. It was never condemned as sectarian or heretical. The martyr literature bears strong affinities with this type of Christinity, and women figure prominently among its heroes. Since the martyr is seen as a second Christ, representing for the Christian community the ultimate imitation of Christ, martyr literature does not hesitate to say that women martyrs also represent Christ. Thus, in the *Acts of the Martyrs of Lyons and Vienna*, the martyr Blandina is described as inspiring the other witnesses to steadfastness in suffering, "for in their conflict they beheld with their outward eyes in the form of their sister the One who was crucified for them."[15]

The popular Acts of the Apostles, such as the Acts of Paul and Thecla, as well as many other acts of this genre, frequently have a female or females as the central figure. These women are described as having been converted by an apostle. They renounce marriage, shake off dependency on the family, and take to the road to preach and witness. The women are frequently described as being persecuted by the authorities of both family and state, triumphantly surviving these trials, and having their ministry ultimately acknowledged by the apostle. A recent book on these popular Acts has suggested that this is essentially a literature produced by and for Christian women, its possible authors being deaconesses and widows who formed the catechetical order that taught and ministered to women.[16] This literature held up to women the vision of a new equality in Christ and a heroism available through rejection of family and state authority and the adoption of celibacy.

Although Christian gnosticism had elements in common with this popular asceticism, it differed in its use of speculative mystical and cosmogonic theories. Gnosticism was generally based on a creational dualism which saw the material world itself as coming into existence through a fall from a higher spiritual unity. Humanity was originally androgynous and spiritual. The separation into male and female was seen as coming about through the fall into material embodiment. Christ represents the restoration of the original spiritual, androgynous humanity. The gnostic seeks to follow Christ by renouncing marriage and sexuality and thereby returning to androgynous, spiritual unity.

The gnostic champions the equality of women in redeemed humanity; however, woman is saved only by transcending her specific femaleness. This transcendence is often referred to as having become "male" (maleness being equated with spirituality).[17] The notion that the female ascetic casts off her female characteristics and becomes male also is found in orthodox Christian mysticism and monasticism.[18] The difference between gnostics and official monasticism, however, is that ascetic women, as well as men, are given the leadership roles. Patriarchal Christianity in the third and fourth centuries accomodated itself to asceticism only by setting the ascetic aside as a special vocation and distinguishing this vocation to holiness, which was available to both men and women, from ecclesiastical office, which was reserved for males.

Patriarchal Christianity never totally renounced the belief in the equivalence of male and female in Christ. However, it identified this equivalence with the spiritual and eschatological plane which is to be realized only in heaven. It identified male and female embodiment with a hierarchical differentiation. Although women might be potentially equivalent in soul and in capacity for holiness, in their embodied form they represent the lower self of the bestial appetites and material, corruptible existence. This imaging of male and female as symbolic of the hierarchy of mind over body is typical of most of the Church fathers. It is particularly evident in Augustine, who believed that woman had been subordinate to man even in paradise. In his treatise on the Trinity, Augustine even states that woman in herself does not possess the image of God because she is the image of the body. She possesses the image of God only when taken together with the male, who is her head, whereas the male possesses the image of God without regard to his relation to the woman. Thus we see clearly in Augustine the theological anthropology that makes the male the image of normative humanity and woman the "other" in the sense of the lower and incomplete.

This tradition became more explicit and pseudoscientific in the scholastic theology of medieval theologians such as Thomas Aquinas. Aquinas adopted Aristotelian biology, which declared that the generation of the human species comes solely from the male semen.[19] Woman contributes only the material flesh, which is formed by the male seed. Femaleness comes about through a defect in which this formative process fails to "take" completely and a "misbegotten male," or female, results. Woman is then defined as inferior in her essential biological and psychological nature. She is weaker physically, lacking in moral self-control, and inferior in reasoning powers. Thus she is by nature fitted to a servile and dependent relationship to the male.[20] How this view of woman as not only physically but also morally and mentally inferior could be reconciled with an affirmation of woman's equal redeemability and capacity for holiness becomes problematic. Nevertheless, medieval theology continued to hold that women were capable of equal holiness and would be rewarded accordingly in heaven, where gender-based hierarchy would disappear.

However, patriarchal Christianity assumed that woman aspired to such holiness only by the strictest subordination and self-abnegation to male authority, especially male ecclesiastical authority, which was permitted to abrogate paternal familial authority over women in recognizing a woman's vocation of monastic life. The early Christian notion that conversion to Christ permitted the female ascetic to rebel against familial authority thus survives in medieval monasticism only in a very diminished form. The female saint is frequently described as having a vocation to virginity from earliest childhood and repelling her parents' efforts to arrange her marriage. Her struggle against them, however, takes the form of a suffering compliance with their every wish, except the one demand that she marry. Eventually this struggle is rewarded by the recognition of the woman's vocation by the bishop, who then allows her to leave her family and depart for the convent.[21] The convent, needless to say, is understood by such episcopal Christianity as strictly cloistered and regulated by the male hierarchy.

However, there is evidence that a more autonomous form of female monasticism continued into the twelfth century. Female monastic orders in the early Middle Ages were often founded by women of the gentry upon independently endowed bequests of land which these women possessed in their own right. The women's monastery became a self-governing female world in which the abbesses possessed many of the rights and titles of landed nobility: the right to rule over dependents (villages and towns), to coin money, raise armies, and even, in some cases, to be represented in parliament.[22] Abbesses were also accorded some of the ecclesiastical prerogatives of bishops, such as the mitre and crozier and the right to credential priests to function in their territory.[23] Such great abbeys were centers of independent learning with schools and libraries. A stream of writing came forth from the pens of these learned women: treatises on mysticism, but also plays, poetry, and treatises on humanistic learning and on medicine.[24]

Gradually, in the later Middle Ages, the independence of female monasticism was subdued by male ecclesiastical authority. With the transfer of learning from monastic schools and libraries to the universities, where women were forbidden to study, female monastic learning faded. Strict rules of cloister were applied to female orders. New religious orders were reluctant to allow female branches. The right to appoint male confessors of nuns and an ecclesiastical supervisor to run the financial affairs of the convent and to supervise its internal governance was asserted. The rules of female orders had to be submitted to the bishop or eventually to Rome to see that they had these provisions for female subordination to male ecclesiastical authority. In the Counter-Reformation, Roman Catholic ecclesiastical law triumphed in its efforts to regulate female monasticism.[25]

As a result of these restrictions, new female religious communities began to spring up in the later Middle Ages. These women often belonged to the urban merchant or working classes. They took simple vows, without restrictions of cloister, and often made a living through their own manual labor. Since these Beguine-houses were continually under ecclesiastical suspicion as hotbeds of dissent and heresy, they often ended by attaching themselves to male orders, such as the Dominicans, to win acceptance and protection.[26] The Beguine-houses can be seen as the beginning of a continual struggle between Catholic religious women and male ecclesiastics which has continued down to the present time. In this struggle, women frequently have founded new orders which have evaded some of the restrictions of the old type of convent, with an eye to giving themselves a freer possibility of learning and ministry in the society. But this original effort to create a freer community was often modified and eventually suppressed in the struggle to win ecclesiastical approbation or to avoid condemnation.

The later Middle Ages saw the rise of many popular reform movements aimed at restoring a freer and more prophetic Christianity. Some of these, like the twelfth-century Waldensians, took the form of popular preaching movements that sought to restore a life-style of simplicity or poverty. Following the ancient Christian tradition that women as well as men were given the spirit of prophecy, such groups often included women as equals in this work of preaching and evangelism. For the official male ecclesiastical hierarchy, the female preacher became the mark of the heretical movement.

Among the Spiritual Franciscans and other monastic reform movements of the later Middle Ages, the doctrine developed by the twelfth century monk Joachim of Fiore that a third age of the Spirit would supercede the present age of the Church ruled by clerics, became increasingly a language of dissent against the ecclesiastical hierarchy.[27] Popes and bishops were pictured as having departed from apostolic poverty and simplicity and as having given themselves over to corruption. The clerical Church was seen as having become the Anti-Christ. The true Church was a Church of monastic or evangelistic reformers who were persecuted by the present corrupt Church. A few female-led groups arose that even suggested that, in the new dispensation of the Spirit, the Spirit would be disclosed in female form and women would be included in the ranks of priests and bishops.[28]

Thus medieval Christianity moved toward increasing sectarian strife and dissention between a hierarchical Church which had grown ever more repressive and popular and monastic reform movements which grew ever more alienated, each condemning the other as apostate. This sectarian strife of the later Middle Ages set the stage for the full-blown schism in the medieval Latin Church, along both national and sectarian lines, in the Protestant Reformation of the sixteenth century.

EARLY PROTESTANTISM

The Reformation as a whole cannot be said to have had a liberating influence on women. Magisterial Protestantism (Lutheranism, Calvinism, and Anglicanism) inherited trends of both ecclesiastical and sociopolitical subordination of women in the early modern period (fifteenth to seventeenth centuries). This period saw women lose some of the economic and political rights they had enjoyed under a feudal system, where women had sometimes been given the prerogatives associated with landholding. In the evolution of the nationstate, these feudal rights were abolished for a more uniform concept of citizenship which excluded women.[29] The economic trends were also removing women from independent guild membership or professions that they had previously exercised by apprenticeship or popular folkknowledge (such as medicine, midwifery, and pharmacy) and were restricting women more and more to dependency as housewives within a male-controlled economy.[30]

The mainstream Reformation abolished celibacy and Christian monasticism, which had been the mainstay of an independent female vocation in the early and medieval Church. But it did not substitute a new inclusion of women in the Protestant married clergy. Instead the Reformers adopted the patriarchal reading of the Pauline tradition, which enjoined silence and submission on women as their vocation, both within the order of creation and as punishment for the sin of Eve. Luther drew from the monastic tradition a belief in the original equivalence of Eve and Adam in paradise. But he used this doctrine of original equivalence only to accentuate the subordination of women on the basis of her guilt for the Fall. Because of her primacy in sin, woman has lost her original equivalence with males and is subjugated to the rule of husbands. Woman may complain against these pains and inconveniences, but she must learn to accept them as the just punishment visited upon her by God.

> The rule remains with the husband and the wife is compelled to obey it by God's command. He rules the home and the state, wages war, defends his possessions, tills the soil, builds, plants, etc. The woman, on the other hand, is like a nail driven into the wall. She sits at home. . . . The wife should stay at home and look after the affairs of the household as one who has been deprived of the ability of administering those affairs which are outside and concern the state. . . . In this way Eve is punished.[31]

The Calvinist tradition, by contrast, continued the line of Augustine, which saw woman's subordination as part of the original order of creation. Her subordination did not simply arise from the Fall; woman would have been subordinate even in paradise, although her situation must now be doubly reenforced as punishment for sin. But Calvinism did not follow the medieval scholastic tradition in attributing this subordination to any genetic inferiority. Rather, it stressed that women and all persons of every social status are spiritually equal before God. All possess the same capacity, or rather, incapacity, for holiness. Election by God takes place irrespective of gender or social status.

However, Calvinism sharply distinguished this spiritual ranking of election and grace from the created social order. The social order was defined as a hierarchy of men over women, parents over children, and masters over servants, and was drawn from the New Testament household codes. It had nothing to do with natural or spiritual superiority or inferiority. Rather, it was a positive system decreed by God to restrain sin and to keep order. In this ordained order, every person had his or her appointed place as servant or master, husband or wife, parent or child.[32] For servants and wives, this order meant a permanent status of subordination to their rulers in the family, submission to the divinely given place, not only when their rulers were kind, but even when they were harsh and arbitrary. The husband and master was in turn enjoined to be kindly and benevolent, although his right to rule was in no way dependent on these virtues.

Late sixteenth and seventeenth century English Puritanism elaborated this view of male-female relations in treatises on marriage and family, or "domestic economy." In these treatises, the husband is enjoined to be a benevolent ruler, looking out for the spiritual and material welfare of his dependents. Wives are in turn called to be the docile helpmates to their husbands in all things. This role of helpmate is seen as both spiritual and social. The wife is envisioned as a subordinate partner in the family economic enterprise, as well as a subordinate partner with the husband in the spiritual journey of salvation and pious governance of the family. With the husband, but always under him, the wife also administers the affairs of the family and helps inculcate piety in children and servants.[33] Puritanism in this period did not yet envision women as more pious than men or as the primary religious teachers of the family. The husband was the "little minister," and the family was a "little church" governed by him, although he in turn was to be duly submissive to the higher authorities of Church and state. But woman had a spiritual role as companion of her husband, encouraging him (discreetly) in piety and mediating his teaching role to servants and children.

This Puritan vision of family harmony, based on compliance to one's appointed role in the social hierarchy, also had its dark side in its constant suspicion that women (and servants) were secretly rebellious against constituted authority. Thus William Perkins, foremost Puritan divine, complemented his earlier work *Domestical Oeconomie* (1590) with a treatise in 1596 entitled *The Damned Art of Witchcraft*. Although Perkins allows that witchcraft is to be found in both sexes, he says it is more frequently found among women because that woman is the "weaker vessel," as is shown by the fact that the Devil more easily prevailed with her in the beginning and continues to resort to woman as the easier victim of temptation. Perkins goes on to specify that one of the main reasons women easily succumb to the blandishments of the Devil is that they are naturally insubordinate and wish to reject their divinely appointed subordination to men. This spirit of insubordination makes them an easy target for the Devil.[34]

Thus Puritanism laid the basis for an identification between witchcraft and female insubordination and patriarchal authority in the family, the Church, or the state. The effects of this link can be seen particularly in the struggles of New England Puritanism in the sixteenth century (1630-1700). Although Puritanism enjoined strict subordination upon women in the social order of the Puritan family, church, and state, it contradicted this rule by championing the lay conscience, including the female lay conscience, in the case of conflict between a disestablished Puritan community against an established Anglican (or Roman Catholic) state. The woman may rebel against husband, cleric, or ruler when that authority is heretical and fails to accept the purification of the Reform.

This championing of the lay conscience in interecclesiastical strife undoubtedly strengthened the role of women in many dissenting congregations during the Puritan Civil War. Many of these congregations were gathered predominantly by women, who took the lead in organizing them and providing the means to call and pay the preacher (such Puritan preachers would have been outside the official Anglican system of stipendiary support). Some more radical Puritan groups, such as Baptists and Fifth Monarchists, even championed the right of women to preach during the religious struggles of the seventeenth century.[35] Such dissenting Puritans reclaimed the ancient Christian identification of preaching with the gift of prophecy given to men and women alike on the basis of charismatic gifts. This identification allowed anyone male or female who manifested such gifts to preach.

John Rogers, a Fifth Monarchist preacher during the Puritan Civil War, wrote a treatise in which he championed the equality of women with men in all affairs of ministry and church governance. He based this view on the spiritual freedom and equality given to all persons in Christ, using Galatians 3:28 as his key text. While in the civil order there may be distinctions of class, in the spiritual community all such distinctions of class, race, or gender are abolished. Women are given equal redemption with men. This equality means that, in the spiritual government of the Church, women should exercise equally with men all the rights and privileges of ministry, both in the teaching office and in the administration of the affairs of the Church, voting equally in church assemblies and objecting or making proposals in such assemblies.[36]

It was Quakerism, or the Society of Friends, that synthesized these charismatic and egalitarian tendencies of radical English Puritanism of the Civil War period. This synthesis was due in no small part to the influence of Margaret Fell, patron of George Fox and eventually his wife, who not only supported the early Society of Friends financially, but who developed its theology of male-female equivalence in Christ. In her treatise, *Womens' Speaking Justified, Proved and Allowed of by the Scriptures* (1667), Margaret Fell develops the classical texts of the theology of equivalence. Woman is made equal to man in the image of God and thus shares with man a humanity of equality, dignity, and worth.

According to Fell, subordination of woman to man is the result of the Fall. But even in the Hebrew scriptures, woman continues to exercise the office of prophetess. She has been liberated from the yoke of servitude and restored to the glorious liberty of the children of God by Christ, who chose to reveal the glad tidings of the Resurrection first to women. Thus women's right to preach the gospel has its charter in the primacy of their witness to the Resurrection itself. Unless men choose to believe the preaching of women, they cannot receive the good news from its very beginning. Margaret Fell goes on to show how the ministry of women was continued in the early Church, citing many of the texts already mentioned in this essay of women's role in the Pauline ministries. Those who refuse to accept women's right to preach contend against Christ himself and are the spokesmen of the powers of darkness or the Devil.

For early Quakerism, this equality of women took the form of allowing women to share in the evangelistic ministry. Many Quakers of both sexes preached throughout England and increasingly carried their message into the new worlds of America, the Caribbean, and the Middle East.[37] The message also took the form of the Woman's Meeting, whereby women as a group were organized to share in the administration and governance of the Societies of Friends, both administering their own budgets for certain charitable purposes and sharing in the spiritual oversight of persons, especially in matters of marriage and family life.[38] The Society of Friends in the seventeenth century fostered female literacy, since every women's meeting was expected to make a careful report and also to circulate exhortations to other meetings. At least seventy-five Quaker women wrote published tracts in the seventeenth century defending their faith. Many of these tracts include a particular defense of women's equality in the redemptive community. These writings are preserved in the Friends' Library in London, but are unread and unknown today even within the Society of Friends.

The clash between patriarchal and radical egalitarian Puritanism was to be played out particularly in the New England colonies in the period of 1630-1700. It took the form of three types of strife between these two expressions of Puritanism: (a) a struggle against antinomianism and free church radicals, (b) a struggle against Quakerism, and (c) the witchcraft persecutions. The Puritan colonies of New England brought with them from England many strong and independently minded women who had sharpened their skills of theological debate and had developed their sense of spiritual autonomy through their leadership as members of a dissenting sect against the authorities of the established Church and state. These strong minded women did not easily subordinate themselves to the Puritan concept of the family and the theocratic state once they arrived in America. The struggles over antinomianism and the free church views that broke out in the 1640s must be seen as the consequences of trying to adapt a dissenting sect to Puritan theories of an established reformed society.

The name of Anne Hutchinson is best known among the leaders of the antinomian movement. But it must be recognized that she was only the most prominent among many Puritans of New England who believed that spiritual life and teaching did not depend on the authority of ordained ministers but rather could be dispensed by spiritually minded Christians generally, both male and female. Anne Hutchinson gathered a group in her home for prayer and spiritual guidance, and this group increasingly took on the form of a dissenting congregation which included men as well as women.

The official pretext for her indictment for heresy was a somewhat technical dispute over the relationship of the covenant of grace and the covenant of works. Hutchinson contended that the covenant of grace freed the Christian from the covenant of works. Since the covenant of works was associated with the patriarchal social order and women's place in it while the covenant of grace was seen as transcending this social order and dispensing revelation in the Spirit directly, without male ecclesiastical mediation, Hutchinson's position was quickly seen as both a lay and a female rebellion against ecclesiastical patriarchalism. Since the dominant Puritan group regarded this patriarchal order as divinely established, such efforts to supersede it through redeeming grace were a heretical rejection of God's revealed will. That this was the chief issue is evident in the trial record of Anne Hutchinson, where she is continually questioned as to her acceptance of women's subordination and her duty to keep silent and not to teach.[39]

Among the followers of Anne Hutchinson who left the Massachussetts Bay Colony as a result of her condemnation in 1638 was one Mary Dyer, who then moved with her husband to Rhode Island. In the 1650s Mary Dyer became joined to the Society of Friends and was imprisoned for this offense on her return from England. In 1659 Mary Dyer returned to Massachussetts to continue her war of conscience against the New England Puritan establishment. She was ordered to be hung, but was reprieved at the last minute and banished again, although her two male Quaker companions died at the gallows. But Mary Dyer returned again to Massachussetts to challenge the Puritan theocracy, and this time was hung on Boston Common.[40] Thus Dyer not only illustrates the struggle of radical egalitarian Puritanism against patriarchal Puritanism in New England, but also establishes, in her own person, the link between this Quaker-Puritan struggle and the earlier antinomian disputes of 1537-40.

The link between these struggles over independence and equivalence of men and women and the witchcraft persecutions that broke out in the last decades of the seventeenth century in New England is less evident. Yet there is continuity here also. It is notable that when Mary Fisher and her female companions, two other Quaker women preachers, were arrested on shipboard in Massachussetts in 1656 on their way to Barbados, they were not only accused of being Quakers, but were also pricked and examined as witches.[41] In the official Puritan mind, a woman who dissented from male Church authority was not only a heretic, but very likely a witch as well, for only the promptings of the Devil could so strengthen the frail female that she would contend against male authority in this way.

We have seen already that in 1596 William Perkins equated witchcraft in women with insubordination to men in the family, Church, and state. This link became evident in the witchcraft trials in New England, where one of the primary charges against women as witches was accusation of insubordination. Thus Ann Hibbens was first excommunicated and later executed for witchcraft in 1656 primarily from charges stemming from her contention with town authorities over carpentry contracts. The trial attempted to prove that, in her contentiousness, she proved herself insubordinate to her husband's authority as well.[42] Recent demographic studies of witchcraft in New England have shown that those most likely to be accused and eventually executed were women between 40 and 60 years of age, widows with property, or women otherwise independent in the administration of their affairs and who exhibited a spirit of independence to authority, either by having no husbands or by appearing to rule their husbands rather than being ruled by them. These women were able to flout the authority of neighboring male landholders and church leaders.[43] In other words, the woman most likely to be accused of witchcraft was the woman who did not fit into the Puritan theory of female subordination in the "domestic economy" of the patriarchal, theocratic society.

Although dissenting Protestantism was crushed in Massachussetts by the end of the seventeenth century, it continued to raise its head elsewhere. In pietist reform movements in Germany and England in the seventeenth and eighteenth centuries, new mystical and communitarian sects arose which often adopted versions of the ancient gnostic anthropology of the androgynous Christ. An important source of this renewed mystical vision was the Protestant mystic Jacob Boehme (1575-1624). Boehme believed that the original Adam was androgynous. Only with the Fall did division into sexes appear, along with the need for carnal union, reproduction, sin, and death. With redemption, the androgynous Adam has been restored in Christ. The redeemed will renounce sexuality and marriage and return to the original state of spiritual androgyny.[44] Mystical sects such as the Rappites or Harmonists adopted celibacy and a communal life style and immigrated from Germany to America to find free space for their version of the "New Jerusalem." Women, along with men, were seen as sharing in this redeemed, androgynous humanity. Sects inspired by Boehme also placed emphasis on a mystical communion with divine Wisdom, or the female side of God.[45]

From the perspective of female leadership, the most important sect in this tradition of Protestant mysticism was the Anglo-American Shakers, or United Society of Believers in Christ's Second Appearing. The Shakers, who developed under the leadership of Mother Ann Lee in England in the 1770s and immigrated to America in 1774, gathered up all the themes of gnostic and prophetic theologies of equivalence from Scripture and Christian history and synthesized them into one clear expression. For the Shakers, the theology of equivalence started with God. God is androgynous, having both a male and female side. The creation of humanity in the image of God, both male and female, expresses this androgynous divine nature. Sin appears with the fall of humanity into carnal sexuality. Christ comes to deliver us from this sin of carnality, but redemption is incomplete as long as God has been revealed only in male form. It is necessary that a female Christ, the revelation of the mothering or Wisdom side of God, appear to complete the revelation of God and the redemption of humanity. This revelation, the Shakers believed, had happened in Mother Ann Lee. Through her, the messianic humanity was being gathered.

This redeemed humanity will return to its spiritual unity by renouncing sexuality. The androgynous nature of God and redemption must be expressed, moreover, in a religious leadership of paired orders of men and women. Shaker women and men lived in spiritual community but in separate sections of the household, each led by their own leadership of men or women. All the ranks of leadership of men over the male community were paralleled with a similar ranking of female leadership over the female community of Shakers. Shakerism was the most explicit effort of mystical Christianity to work out the theology of equivalence in terms of the doctrine of God, anthropology, Christology, and Church polity within the framework of the classical assumptions of an eschatological transcendence of patriarchy as the order of (fallen) creation

MODERN WESTERN CHRISTIANITY

As we have seen, the dilemma bequeathed to Christianity by the legacy of Pauline Christianity lay in the assumed dualism between a patriarchal order of creation associated with marriage and procreation, and a theology of equality in Christ associated with transcendence of creation through renunciation of marriage and sexuality. Both patriarchal and radical Christian groups acceded to this basic dualism, although in different ways. For patriarchal Christianity, the patriarchal order should govern the order of the Church as well as a historical community. Equivalence is reserved for heaven. For radical Christians, equivalence begins on earth, but only within the redeemed community of prophetic witness, usually associated with celibacy. It does not extend to an equality of women within the civil order.

This dualism between a patriarchal order of creation and an egalitarian order of redemption began to be overcome only in the Christian movements of the nineteenth century, which took their clue to the order of creation from the Enlightenment. The Enlightenment is significant in this regard because it broke the connection between the theology of creation and patriarchalism. In Enlightenment thought, the original order of creation is associated with the *imago dei*, in which all humans are created equally in the image of God and none is given domination over others. All humans, equally and collectively, are sovereign over creation and all enjoy the same human nature, which the Enlightenment identified with reason and free will.

The Enlightenment also broke with mystical gnosticism in no longer regarding this original equality as a transcendent, spiritual, androgyne prior to the division into male and female embodiments. Rather, this original equality is the embodied, created order of nature. The old theory of embodiment and sexual division as a fall into sin and subordination is eliminated. The sin of domination and division arises, not through embodiment, but through the entry into social arrangements of civilization which distort the original order of nature into a hierarchical order of privilege and servitude.

Having located the sin of humanity in hierarchical social ordering, it follows from Enlightenment thought that society itself can be reformed to restore the original, egalitarian order of nature. Through the triumph of human reason, a new social contract can be written which reorders social institutions in such as way as to be compatible with the egalitarian order of nature. Since all persons have the same human nature, it follows for liberal thinkers that all should have the same human rights.[46] A just social order is one which creates legal and social structures whereby this equality of nature and rights is embodied in reformed political structures.

Enlightenment thought thus allowed modern Christians, for the first time, to identify the Christian view of redemption and equality in Christ with a reform of the social order in the direction of egalitarian justice of rights and opportunities. Salvation is no longer other-worldly, available only in heaven. Nor is it associated with a sectarian, redemptive community who anticipate the eschatological order by transcending the civil and familial order. Rather, redemption can now be conceived as a reform of the civil and even the familial order in such a way as to vindicate the equivalence of all persons with equal access to political power and economic and cultural opportunities for self-expression. This shift in the relationship of the theology of creation and redemption is basic for all modern theologies of liberation, including feminist theology.

The first to formulate clearly the theology of liberal feminism was the generation of American feminists who arose in the 1830s and 1840s within the abolitionist movement, figures such as Sarah and Angelina Grimké, Lucretia Mott, Elizabeth Cady Stanton, and Susan B. Anthony.

All these nineteenth-century feminist leaders must be recognized as exponents of a theology of Christian feminism. Their vision of feminist reform of all social institutions of the state, society, the family, and the Church, was based on the liberal feminist understanding of creation and redemption that I have outlined above.

Sarah Grimké laid out what she understood as the biblical basis of women's equality in her *Letters on the Equality of the Sexes and the Condition of Women* (1836-1837). These letters were written in response to a pronounement by the Massachussetts Congregational clergy denouncing the sisters for their public speaking in churches on behalf of abolition. The clergy claimed that women's dependence on the male was the ordained nature of things. By speaking publicly, the sisters had violated nature and God's command.

Grimké replied by defending an egalitarian interpretation of original nature based on Genesis 1:26-27. In the original plan of creation, men and women were created equal, endowed with the same human nature. Both shared in the dominion over nature, but neither was given dominion over the other. It was not they, but male domination which violated nature by subverting this divinely ordained equality of the sexes:

> The lust of domination was probably the first effect of the Fall, and as there was no other intelligent being over whom to exercise it, woman was the first victim of this unhallowed passion. ... All history attests that man has subjected woman to his will, used her to promote his selfish gratification, to minister to his sensual pleasures, to be instrumental in promoting his comfort, but never has he desired to elevate her to that rank which she was designed to fill. He has done all that he could to debase and enslave her mind and now he looks triumphantly on the ruin he has wrought and says that the being that he has thus deeply injured is his inferior.[47]

For Grimké, the appearance of women's inferiority in intellect or leadership ability is the product of distorted socialization, not of nature. Once released from unjust bondage and given equal rights and opportunities, women can develop into the equality with the male that is her authentic potential.

> I ask no favors for my sex. I surrender not our claim to equality. All I ask of my brethren is that they will take their feet from off our necks and permit us to stand upright on that ground which God has designed us to occupy.[48]

In 1848 these early women's rights leaders met in Seneca Falls, New York, to draft a *Declaration of the Rights of Women* based on the American *Declaration of Independence*. The women took over and extended the liberal doctrine of Original Nature to claim equality in rights for women as well as men, protesting against the millenia of male tyranny and usurpation of women's rights. The declaration ends with a final resolution which calls for the "speedy overthrow of the male monopoly of the pulpit."[49] Thus early feminism saw the Church as one among other social institutions which must be reformed to include women in those rights to education, profession, and decision-making which should be theirs by nature.

In 1853, this demand for equal opportunities in the Church was realized in the first ordination of a woman to the Congregational ministry. She was Antoinette Brown, a graduate of Oberlin College, the first theological seminary to admit women. The sermon delivered on that occasion by Luther Lee, an evangelical preacher, typifies the blending of liberalism and radical Protestantism in this nineteenth century egalitarian Christianity. Lee took as his text Galatians 3:28, "In Christ there is neither male nor female." But he also drew heavily on the themes of the Pentecost narrative of Acts 2. For Lee, preaching is essentially the prophetic ministry. And since it can be shown from the New Testament that the ministry of prophecy was conferred by Christ upon women equally with men, it has always been wrong for the Church to deny women the ordained ministry. In ordaining Antoinette Brown, Lee declared, we are not innovating, but simply returning to the original mind of Christ.

In the nineteenth century, however, this egalitarian Christianity was confused by a contrary movement that stressed the different and complementary natures of men and women. According to this anthropology, women were not inferior. Indeed they were in many ways superior, but different, from men. Femaleness was equated with love, altruism, spirituality, and piety, in contrast to male rationality and force. In this viewpoint, feminine virtue became closely equated with Christian virtue, and both were located in the private, domestic sphere set apart from public life. This view reflected the increasing domestication of middle-class women, the secularization of society, and the disestablishment and privatization of religion.

Both Christian and secular conservatives used female altruism and piety as arguments for women's unfitness for public power. Women, like religion, should be kept at home. However, Christian women used this increasing influence of women in religion to build voluntary benevolent societies and women's home and foreign missionary societies, thus shaping female church institutions by which they could lay claim to public roles in the Church and society. Instead of accepting the conservative view that women's more spiritual nature made them unfit for public life, these reform feminists argued that female virtues were exactly what the public order needed. Women must organize to win the vote and to establish themselves in all arenas of public leadership to purify the social order from vice and corruption and to uplift it to the higher standards of female virtue.

The Women's Christian Temperance Union, under the leadership of Frances Willard in the late nineteenth century, was the classic example of this use of the idea of female moral superiority as the basis of a crusade, not just for temperance, but for a whole panoply of social reforms, culminating in the abolition of war.[50] Most Victorian feminists continued to be rooted in a belief that Christianity was the charter of female equivalence. They tended to argue for women's rights on the basis of women's equality as a human person and her moral superiority as a female.

Although a few Christian denominations began to ordain women in the nineteenth century (such as the Congregationalists, the Unitarians, the Universalists, and the Methodist Protestants), mainstream Protestantism (Methodists, Presbyterians, and Lutherans) refused to ordain women. The order of deaconesses and the roles of women in home and foreign missionary work were used to siphon off the zeal of women for Christian service. In 1956 this historic refusal was reversed when the Methodist Church (a merger of the Methodist Protestants and the Methodist Episcopals) voted to ordain women. The Presbyterian church likewise agreed to women's ordination in that same year. Over the next decade and a half, most other Protestant churches in American and throughout the world followed suit, with the Episcopal church voting for women's ordination in 1975. Only conservative fundamentalist Protestant groups and the historic traditions of Eastern Orthodoxy and Roman Catholicism still cling to the tradition of excluding women from ordained ministry.

Between 1968 and 1983, this historic shift was reflected in increasing numbers of women in theological seminaries. In Protestant seminaries which ordained women, female students rose rapidly to equal numbers with men. Even more conservative seminaries saw a notable increase of women theological students. This increase was soon followed by an increase of women in theological teaching and the development of feminist criticism of theological education and Church tradition. All branches of Christianity today feel themselves under increasing pressure from women to accept full equality in all levels of the Church's polity and to expunge from their teaching and language the theological denigration of women.

This mounting feminist movement in Christian churches has not happened without resistance, however. In the last decade reactionary movements have been everywhere evident. Protestant fundamentalists have dusted off the historic arguments of male headship as the order of creation and women's subordination as an expression both of nature and of divine punishment for the sin of Eve.[51] Roman Catholic and Orthodox theologians write new versions of the traditional arguments for the male priesthood based on the maleness of Christ.[52] Liberal Protestants today are often caught in the middle, accepting the mounting demands for inclusion of women and for inclusive theological language, and, on the other hand, tending to conform more and more to historic patterns of hierarchical ministry in their pursuit of ecumenical alliance with the Catholic and Orthodox traditions.[53] It is by no means evident that the gains of feminism in the Church will continue and will not be sold out by a male-defined ecumenism based on historical patriarchal patterns of ministry. Thus the Christian Church stands today at the crossroads between a tradition of hierarchical order that has traditionally subordinated women and excluded them from the ministry and the full and systematic renewal of the Christian message and mission based on a theology of equivalence.

Jane I. Smith

ISLAM

To attempt to talk about women in Islam is of course to venture into
an area fraught with the perils of overgeneralization, oversimplifica-
tion, and the almost unavoidable limitations of a Western bias. The first
problem is simply one of raw numbers. There are perhaps close to half a
billion Muslim women inhabiting all major areas of the world today. Is
it possible to say anything that holds true for all of them, let alone for
their sisters over the past fourteen centuries of Islam?

Then one must consider all the various elements that comprise the
picture of Islamic womanhood. Many of these elements are directly
related to the religion of Islam itself, such as past and present legal
realities, roles permitted and enforced as a result of Muslim images of
women, and the variety of Islamic and hetero-Islamic rites and practices
in which Islamic women have traditionally participated. Other elements contributing to the full picture of women in Islam—such as
education, political rights, professional employment opportunities, and
the like—have less to do with the religion per se but are still influenced
by it.

The Holy Qur'ān (sometimes transliterated as "Koran") still forms
the basis of prevailing family law in most areas of the Muslim world. It
has always been and still is considered to be the last in a series of divine
revelations from God given in the seventh century C.E. to humanity
through the vehicle of his final prophet Muhammad. The Qur'ān is
therefore the literal and unmitigated word of God, collected and ordered by the young Muslim community but untainted with the

thoughts and interpretations of any persons, including Muhammad himself. It is obvious, then, why the regulations formulated by the Qur'ān in regard to women have been adhered to with strictness and why changes in Muslim family law are coming about only very slowly in the Islamic world.

The circumstances of women in pre-Islamic Arabia are subject to a variety of interpretations. On the one hand, certain women—soothsayers, priestesses, queens, and even singular individuals—did play powerful roles in society.[1] On the other hand, whatever the earlier realities for women in terms of marriage, divorce, and inheritance of property, it is clear that the Qur'ān did introduce very significant changes that were advantageous for women. Contemporary Muslims are fond of pointing out, quite correctly, that Islam brought legal advantages for women quite unknown in corresponding areas of the Western Christian world.[2] What, then, does the Qur'ān say about women?

The earliest messages of the Qur'ān, and the twin themes that run through all the chapters, are of the realities of the oneness of God and the inevitability of the day of judgment.[3] All persons, men and women, are called upon to testify to those realities. (Tradition has it that Umm Salama, one of the wives of the Prophet, reminded him that he was saying "men" only, after which he clearly identified both believing men and believing women as fully responsible for their religious duties and fully accountable at the time of the final resurrection and judgment.)[4] Religiously speaking, then, men and women are fully equal in the eyes of God according to the Qur'ān.

Before looking at the specifics of the legal injunctions for women, it is necessary to consider two verses that have caused a great deal of consternation to Westerners. One is 2:228, which says literally that men are a step above women, and the other is 4:34, clarifying that men are the protectors of women (or are in charge of women) because God has given preference to one over the other and because men provide support for women. Perhaps because these verses have been so troublesome for non-Muslims (especially feminists), they have been subject to an enormous amount of explanation and interpretation by contemporary Muslim apologists eager to present a defense of their religion. These writers, men and women, affirm that it is precisely because men are invested with the responsibility of taking care of women, financially and otherwise, that they are given authority over the females of their families. And that, affirm many Muslim women today, is exactly the way it should be. We will return to this perspective later, particularly in light of what a desire for liberation means—and does not mean—for many Muslim women.

Turning then to the Qur'ānic legal injunctions for women, we find that they are clustered around four major issues: marriage and related topics, divorce, inheritance and ownership of property, and veiling and seclusion. These form what is called the "personal and family law" part of the total complex of legal realities in Islam. Islamic law (the *shari'a*) is based primarily on the Qur'ān, secondarily on those things that the Prophet is supposed to have said and done (chronicled in a body of literature called the *hadīth*), and to a lesser extent on analogy and legal reasoning. The four major schools of law in the Sunni tradition (which makes up 85 percent of the Muslim population) are in general agreement on most aspects of the law and differ only on relatively minor points in personal and family law. Elements comprising personal law are more specific in the Qur'ān than many other aspects of the shari'a and so have been more resistant to change in contemporary times. Of the non-Communist Islamic countries, only Turkey now has a secular law including family and personal law. In most other countries there is a kind of dual system of a secular civil and a religious family code.

According to the Qur'ān, a man may marry up to four wives, so long as he is able to provide for each equally.[5] He may marry a Muslim woman or a member of the Jewish or Christian faith, or a slave women.[6] A Muslim woman, however, may marry only one husband, and he must be a Muslim. Contemporary Muslim apologists are quick to point out that these restrictions are for the benefit of women, ensuring that they will not be left unprotected. In Islam, marriage is not a sacrament but a legal contract, and according to the Qur'ān a woman has clearly defined legal rights in negotiating this contract. She can dictate the terms and can receive the dowry herself.[7] This dowry *(mahr)* she is permitted to keep and maintain as a source of personal pride and comfort.

Polygamy (or more strictly polygyny, plurality of wives) is practiced by only a small percentage of the contemporary Muslim population, and a man with more than two wives is extremely rare. Many countries are now taking steps to modify the circumtances in which a husband may take more than one wife, although only in two countries, Turkey and Tunisia, are multiple marriages actually illegal. Other countries have made such moves as requiring the husband to have the permission of the court (as in Iraq and Syria) or to get the permission of the first wife (as in Egypt), or permitting the wife to write into her marriage contract that she will not allow a cowife (as in Morocco and Lebanon). It seems reasonable to expect that other countries will make changes and modifications. It is interesting to note that while for some finances have dictated monogamy—most husbands have simply not been able to afford more than one wife—changing economic realities may again dictate that a man contemplate the possibility of having several wives to work and supply income for the family.

Muslim women traditionally have been married at an extremely young age, sometimes even before puberty. This practice is related, of course, to the historical fact that fathers and other male relatives generally have chosen the grooms themselves, despite the guarantee of the Qur'ān that marriage is a contract into which male and female enter equally. While it is true that technically a girl cannot be forced into a marriage she does not want, pressures from family and the youth of the bride often have made this prerogative difficult to exercise. Today, the right of a male member of the family to contract an engagement for a girl against her wishes has been legally revoked in most places, although it is still a common practice, especially in rural areas.

In the past, the members of an engaged couple have not been allowed to see each other until the wedding. This practice is now changing, even in the most conservative places. Saudi Arabian *ulema* (religious leaders), for example, are realizing that the divorce rate can be lowered if both parties know more clearly what they are getting into. In most Muslim countries today the minimum age for marriage is around 18 for young men and somewhere between 15 and 17 for young women.

On the basis of some rather obscure references in the Qur'ān, birth control has generally been frowned upon by Muslim religious leaders, and abortion and sterilization are strictly forbidden. However, a number of family-planning efforts are now taking place to halt the rise in the high fertility rate (the average Muslim woman has around seven children). Among Middle Eastern countries, Egypt, prerevolutionary Iran, Tunisia, and Morocco officially have adopted population control policies, and a number of the ulema are attempting to show that birth control is permissible in Islam.[8] Western images of Muslim men divorcing wives with abandon by issuing the dreaded triple statement "I divorce thee" have blurred the clear Qur'ānic discouragement of divorce except as a last resort, although they may reflect what has been the painful reality for many women through the ages. It is said that for the Prophet divorce was a thing to be detested. The Qur'ān does have some specific words for those cases in which separation is absolutely necessary,[9] and on the basis of these words Islamic law has traditionally understood two specific kinds of divorce, *talaq* and *khul'*.

Talaq, divorce taken at the initiative of the man, is the most frequent form of separation. One kind of *talaq* is fully acceptable under the law; it can be either a single repudiation after the waiting period of three months to ensure that a wife is not pregnant, or three successive repudiations in three months. The triple repudiation, which is the utterance of the *talaq* three times in succession without the three-month waiting period, is technically legal although so undesirable as to be classed as sinful according to the fivefold division of deeds in Islamic law. It is fair to say that this kind of divorce has been used far too often, making the Western stereotype in this case not too far from the truth.

Divorce initiated by the wife is called *khul'*. While technically possible, this form of divorce has not been effected nearly as often in any Near Eastern country as has repudiation by the male, both because women often have not been informed of its possibility or have been prevented from carrying it out, and because, unlike *talaq*, it requires either a special stipulation in the marriage contract or must be made on the basis of specific grounds such as desertion, physical abuse, lack of maintenance by the husband, insanity, impotence, and the like.

In the contemporary Islamic world, divorce rates vary considerably from one country to the next. Muslim apologists insist that divorce is not nearly as common in Islamic countries as it is, for example, in the United States. This statement is generally true, although in some countries, such as Morocco, the rate is high and continues to grow. Often what is really only the breaking of the engagement contract is included in divorce statistics, skewing the measure. Many countries are now considering serious changes in divorce procedures. The simultaneous triple repudiation generally has been declared illegal, and in many countries divorce initiated by either party, the man or the woman, must take place in the court of law. Other countries add special stipulations generally favorable to the woman. It remains true, however, that men can divorce for less cause than women, and often divorces hung up in courts with male judges can prove enormously difficult for women to gain.

In accordance with Islamic law, custody of the children traditionally has gone to the father at some time between the are of 7 and 9 for boys and between 7 and puberty for girls, depending on the legal school. This practice too is slowly changing, and in most areas women who have been divorced by their husbands are allowed to keep their sons until puberty and their daughters until they are of an age to be married.

It is considered one of the great innovations of the Qur'ān over earlier practices that women are permitted to inherit and own property. Non-Muslims have generally found great difficulty with the Qur'ānic stipulation that a woman is allowed to inherit property but that the inheritance should be only half that of a male.[10] According to the Islamic understanding, however, the rationale is precisely that which applies to the verse saying that men are in charge of women. Because women are permitted to keep and maintain their own property without responsibility for taking care of their families financially, it is only reasonable that the male, who must spend his own earning and inheritance for the maintenance of women, should receive twice as much.

Despite this rationale, it is true that women have not always been permitted to have access to the financial resources that the Qur'ān makes available to them. As in other areas of family law, such as the possibility of writing specific stipulations into the marriage contract for women, the failure to assume financial responsibility often has come through ignorance or willful cheating by male members of the family. Again we find that in many parts of the Muslim world attempts are being made to equalize the procedure for inheritance between men and women, particularly since women are playing an increasing role in the labor force.[11] To date, however, only Turkey in the non-Communist world and Albania and the Soviet Union among the Communist countries have discarded this Qur'ān-based law of inheritance.

According to the Qur'ān, women should not expose themselves to public view with lack of modesty.[12] It does not say that they should be covered specifically from head to toe, nor that they should wear face veils or masks or other of the paraphernalia that has adorned many Islamic women through the ages. The Qur'ān also suggests that the wives of the Prophet Muhammad, when speaking to other men, should do so from behind a partition, again for purposes of propriety.[13] It has been open to question whether this statement is meant to apply to all women. In the early Islamic community, these verses were exaggerated and their underlying ideas elaborated and defined in ways that led fairly quickly to a seclusion of women which seems quite at odds with what the Qur'ān intended or the Prophet wanted. When the community in Medina was established, women participated fully with men in all activities of worship and prayer. Soon they became segregated, however, to the point where an often-quoted hadīth (no doubt spurious) attributed to Muhammad has him saying that women pray better at home than in the mosque, and best of all in their own closets.[14] Today a number of contemporary Muslim writers are urging a return to the practices of the young Muslim community, with women no longer segregated from the mosque or relegated to certain rear or side portions as they generally have been, but participating fully in worship with men.[15]

The practice of veiling women, which still continues in many parts of the Islamic world, began during the period of the early conquests, when Muslims came into contact with the lands of Byzantium. Veiling was observed at that time in such places as Syria, Iraq, and Persia, and was taken into Islam particularly for urban and upper-class women. In general, veiling has not been common among Muslim village women, partly because they generally do not encounter strangers in that context, and partly because it would hinder them from various kinds of work in which they have traditionally been engaged.

Veiling and seclusion have been major factors in the lives of Muslim women, then, since the early days of the growth of the Muslim empire. Western observers of the Muslim world for centuries have been fascinated and horrified at stories of the harems (literally, "forbidden places") where women have been cut off from the social lives of males. Life in these female enclaves has provided material for studies of female compensaton and lines of authority and power. For the most part, the kind of enforced seclusion that characterized so much of the Muslim world for centuries is dying out, the economic realities of women in the labor force being one of the primary reasons. It must be recognized that for many Muslim women, seclusion was not entirely an evil. With freedom inevitably comes responsibility, and while some female voices in the Islamic world are crying loudly for an end to the kind of isolation and segregation that they see as demeaning,[16] others are recognizing that an end to seclusion can also mean assuming a major part of the burden of providing for the family, a worry that formerly rested primarily on the shoulders of the males.[17] Again, it should be stressed that this kind of seclusion has mainly characterized city rather than rural women.

What is popularly known as "veiling" is part of the general phenomenon of the segregation of women and yet is also distinctly apart from it. The two are increasingly seen as separate by contemporary Islamic women seeking to affirm a new identity in relation to their religion. Veils traditionally have taken a number of forms: a veil covering the face from just below the eyes down; a *chador* or *burka* covering the entire body, including the face, often with a woven screen in front through which women can see but not be seen; and a full face mask with small slits through the eyes, still worn in some areas of the Arabian Gulf. These costumes, so seemingly oppressive to Western eyes, at least have allowed women to observe without being observed, thus affording their wearers a degree of anonymity that on some occasions has proven useful.

The general movement toward unveiling had its ostensible beginning in the mid-1920s, when the Egyptian feminist Huda Sha'rawi cast off her veil after arriving in Egypt from an international meeting of women. She was followed literally and symbolically by masses of women in the succeeding years, and Egyptian women as well as those in other Middle Eastern countries made great strides in adopting Western dress. At the present time in the history of Islam, however, one finds a quite different phenomenon. Partly in reaction against Western liberation and Western ideals in general, women in many parts of the Islamic world are self-consciously adopting forms of dress by which they can identify with Islam rather than with what they now see as the imperialist West. Islamic dress, generally chosen by Muslim women themselves rather than forced upon them by males, signals for many an identification with a way of life that they are increasingly convinced represents a more viable alternative than that offered by the West.

This new form of dress, sometimes called *shar'i* (literally, "legal"), differs somewhat from country to country. In general, it is highly conservative, with arms covered to the wrists, legs covered either with a long skirt or with loose pants over which hangs a kind of tunic, and a scarf (not over the face) or a wimplelike covering on the head.[18] This dress is by no means universal, and when traveling across the Muslim world one still finds many women wearing local versions of very traditional dress and many continuing to dress as their Western sisters do. But modern Islamic dress is in evidence in Egypt, Turkey, Palestine, Syria, and even parts of the Arabian Gulf states such as North Yemen, a traditionally very conservative Islamic state. In Iran, the Islamic revolution under Imam Khomeini has reemphasized the chador, banned long ago by the Westernized government. To what extent the chador is approvingly chosen by Iranian women and to what extent it is an enforced product of the revolution remains to be seen.

We see, then, that while legal circumstances for women have undergone some significant changes in the past half-century, the dictates of the Qur'ān continue to be enormously influential in the molding of new laws as well as in the personal choices of Muslim men and women. It has been suggested that while the Qur'ān itself clearly improved circumstances over what they were for pre-Islamic Arabian women and in fact did establish a structure in which women were both protected and given clear rights and responsibilities, this situation changed for the worse in succeeded centuries. Contemporary Muslims are generally quick to point out that many of the hadīths describing the inferiority of women are spurious, that developments in the male-oriented community which led to the severe domination and seclusion of women were contrary to the dictates of the Qur'ān and the desires of the Prophet Muhammad for his community, and that the only way to establish a truly Islamic community with equal (if different) roles for women and men is to return to the Qur'ān and to hold as closely as possible to its formulations. This is not to say, however, that some Muslim women are not advocating radical changes for women of the sort that would be applauded by most Western feminists. I will return to that question shortly.

I have stressed here the insistence of the Qur'ān on the religious and spiritual equality of men and women. And aside from some unfortunate hadīths with very weak chains of authority suggesting that the majority of women will be in the Fire on the Day of Judgment because of their mental and physical inferiority,[19] religious literature in general, when talking about human responsibility and concomitant judgment, makes women full partners with men under the divine command to live lives of integrity and righteousness.[20] Nonetheless, as was suggested, early in the development of the community women began to find the mosque, the common place of worship, less and less accessible. As segregation became increasingly the pattern, it is not surprising to find that women, squeezed out of the more formal aspects of the Islamic faith, developed their own forms of religious response. Since God was conceived of as male and males generally were persons with whom women did not and could not interact in their everyday social lives, they often chose intermediary forms of religious response that were apparently more appropriate to their needs and conditioning.

One area in which this substitution took place was in healing and semimagical practices. Women have always been, and continue to be, primary agents in the relationship of humans to the world of spiritual powers. It is they who know how to ward off evil *jinn*, to cajole the spirits of the rivers and fields, to apply special formulae, and to appropriately display blue beads to challenge the power of the evil eye. These unorthodox practices served both to further isolate women from the formal rituals of the Islamic community and to give them an arena in which they could feel comfortable and in control. Despite periodic efforts to "clean up" such heterodox practices, they have been and continue to be a powerful part of the lives of many Muslims, especially women.

Of course, women do participate in many of the activities and duties considered incumbent on all good Muslims, but generally these practices have a somewhat different function for them than for men. Prayer for women, as we have said, is usually in the home rather than in the mosque, and does not necessarily follow the pattern of the regularized five times a day. Participation in the fast itself is normally the same as for the men (except when women are pregnant, nursing, or menstruating), but the particular joys of preparing the fast-breaking meals are for the women alone. While the husband determines the amount of money or goods to be distributed for almsgiving, another responsibility of all Muslims, it is often the wife who takes change of the actual distribution.

The last duty incumbent on Muslims after the testimony to the oneness of God and prophethood of his apostle Muhammad, the prayer, the fast, and paying the almstax is the pilgrimage once in a lifetime to the holy city of Mecca. Women do participate in this journey, and as transportation becomes easier and the care provided for pilgrims in Saudi Arabia becomes more regularized with modernization, increasing numbers of females join the throngs which gather to circumambulate the Kaaba at Mecca each year. For many women, however, this singular event may be only part of the meaning of pilgrimage. Yearly or more often, they make shorter journeys to the tombs and resting places of various persons considered to be among the saints of Islam. For Shi'ite Muslims, this journey may be to Kerbala or other shrines of Muslim leaders venerated as members of the houshold of the Prophet, while Sunnis visit innumerable large and small shrines to revere and talk with the deceased in their tombs.

Visitation of saints' shrines by longer pilgrimage or local visits is certainly not exclusive to women in Islam. Many men include such practices along with their observation of the more formalized aspects of the Muslim faith. This particular kind of religious experience has had a special meaning for women, however, and across the Islamic world one can find women spending long periods of time at shrine tombs, relaxing in a space in which none of the demands of their regular lives are put upon them. The shrine is a place in which women can be together, or alone can be in communication with a personage considered in some senses to be able to help them with the kinds of personal problems in which the high God may seem too remote to be interested.

Saints in Islam are both male and female. One is normally recognized as a saint not by any process of canonization but because of some miraculous deed(s) performed or through a dream communication after death with a living person requesting that a shrine be erected over his or her tomb. Often a woman is favored with these dreams and after the construction of the shrine she becomes the carekeeper of the tomb, a position of some honor and responsibility. Saints form a special category of person in the general Islamic understanding; unlike ordinary mortals, they are awake and very much conscious in their tombs after death. They are reported to be carrying on activities such as praying, reciting the Qur'ān, and responding to the greetings of their visitors. They are not actually worshipped, for that would be anathema in monotheistic Islam, but are considered to have a kind of special authority from God to help answer the requests of persons who come to them for assistance.[21]

While a man may be more likely to ask a saint for his or her intercession with God on the day of judgment or for strength in carrying out religious duties, women are more specifically interested in solving the immediate problems that trouble them in their daily lives. A study revealed that in Egyptian Nubia, for example, the problems more often brought to a saint were finding a husband for one's daughter, keeping one's husband from wanting to take another wife, illness or physical problems, retribution on another woman in the community who has been cruel or gossiping, and the like.[22]

The practice of saint veneration has been the object of puritanical scorn and wrath since the early days of Islam. Despite periodic efforts to purge it from the faith, however, it has continued to be a powerful force in the private and personal lives of countless Muslims. Even with the increasing numbers of women today who are consciously acknowledging their roles in the more formal structure of Islam by adopting Islamic dress and participation in the structured rituals, it seems clear that for many Islamic women relationships with saints and reliance on their assistance with the problems of life still plays a crucial role.

In addition to these more generalized practices, Muslim women in various parts of the world participate in certain activities that can be characterized as religious and which are more or less peculiar to women. In Egypt, the Sudan, and a few other areas, women (particularly middle- and lower-middle-class women) occasionally hold what are called "zār ceremonies," rituals designed to rid them of supposed spirit possession. Men may scoff at these activities, but generally are forced to come up with the money necessary for their wives to participate.[23] In most Muslim areas, activities related to spirit possession involve women generally or even exclusively. In Iraq some women enjoy hereditary positions as *mollas* (religious teachers). They receive money for such responsibilities as holding public sessions (*qrayas*) in which stories are read about the life of Hussain, the martyred grandson of the Prophet.[24] As with visitation to the tombs and the attendance at zārs, these are opportunities for women to meet together away from the home under the cloak of a traditionally sanctioned activity.

While women in the Islamic world have been segregated and secluded, and historically have been considered second-class citizens by the vast majority of males in the community, they have not been totally without power. They have been able to maintain a degree of control over their own lives and over the men with whom they live through many of the religious practices described above. The fact that they alone have the ability to bear children, the influence they continue to play in the lives of their sons, and the power they have over their son's wives are subtle indications that there are certain checks and balances on the obvious authority invested by the Qur'ān in men. From sexuality to control of the network of communications in the family to manipulation of such external agencies as spirits and supernatural beings, women have had at their control a variety of means to exert their will over the men in their families and over their own circumstances.[25] The subtle means of control available to women throughout the world have of course been exploited: withholding sexual favors (a questionable but often-quoted hadīth says that if a woman refuses to sleep with her husband, the angels will curse her until the morning),[26] doing small things to undermine a husband's honor such as embarrassing him in front of guests, indulging in various forms of gossip and social control, and the like.

In the Islamic world today, as was suggested in the beginning, there are an enormous number of currents going in various directions. Along with the kinds of comfort and power women achieve in more traditional ways and running parallel with some of the changes in the legal realities for women are rapid advances in education and employment opportunities. On the one hand, what is true for Muslim women in terms of education and entry into the work force in many ways is incidental to the fact of their being Muslim. On the other hand, male attitudes conditioned by the tradition of Islam, although not necessarily supported by the Qur'ān itself, have been and continue to be influential in determining what opportunities are available for women.

Until fairly recently, education for women in the Muslim world has been minimal. Girls were given the rudiments of an Islamic education, mainly a little instruction in the Qur'ān and the traditions so as to be able to recite their prayers properly. Beyond that their training was not academic but domestic. In the late nineteenth and early twentieth century, Islamic leaders awoke with a start to the reality that Muslims were significantly behind the West in a variety of ways, including technology and the education necessary to understand and develop it. Many of these leaders recognized that if Islamic nations were to compete successfully in the contemporary world, it had to be with the aid of a well-educated and responsible female sector. Thus, this century has seen a number of educational advances for women, and in some countries, such as Egypt, Iraq, and Kuwait, women constitute very significant numbers of the university population. Nonetheless, illiteracy in many Muslim nations continues to be high, and the gap between male and female literacy rates is even increasing in some areas. In Saudi Arabia, where at present the economic resources are certainly available, large numbers of Saudi girls are receiving a full education, though separated from boys, and are taught either by men through television transmission or by women.

In education as in most areas of life, the male understanding of women as encouraged by certain parts of the Islamic tradition continues to play an important role. The Qur'ān does state, along with the stipulation that women can inherit only half of what men inherit, that the witness (in the court of law) of one man is equal to that of two women. This unfortunately has been interpreted by some in the history of Islam to mean that women are intellectually inferior to men, unstable in their judgment, and too easily swayed be emotion.[27] Such perspectives are certainly not shared by all but nonetheless have been influential (and in some places are increasingly so today) in making it difficult for a woman to have access to the same kinds of educational opportunities that are available to men. Certain subjects are deemed "appropriate" for a woman to study, particularly those geared to make her the best and most productive wife, mother, and female participant in the family structure.

The prevalent view, confirmed by the Qur'ān, is that women should be modest and should neither expose themselves to men nor be too much in public places, where they will be subject to men's observation or forced to interact with males not in their immediate families. This view obviously has contributed to the difficulties of receiving a full education and of securing employment outside the home. More employment opportunities are open to women today than in the past, however, and in many countries women hold high-level positions in business, government, civil service, education, and other sectors. Statistics differ greatly across the Islamic world and are difficult to assess because they often fail to take into account the rural woman who may work full-time in the fields or other occupation outside the house but does not earn an independent salary.

It is also true that the economic realities of the difficult present time are coming hard against the traditional attitudes that the woman should remain in the home and not be part of the public work force. Increasing numbers of women are having to work to help support the family, often in factories and other heavy labor industries. Such realities are certainly not always liberating for women, of course, who have to struggle with home maintenance along with the pressures of the job. Day-care facilities for children are generally unavailable, and the extended family system which used to afford ready baby-sitting for all the children in the larger family is tending to break up. Fuller participation of women in the work force probably will lead to a raising of the traditionally low marriage age for young women.

While some Islamic women, then, are receiving a university education and are able to learn new skills and enter interesting and fulfilling professions, most of them are certainly not so fortunate. And the tightening economic realities may actually work against female advancement. As the need to go to work increases, many girls may in fact have to quit school. For many women, work does not mean the opportunity to have training in new areas because they are often channeled into professions which use their home-oriented skills as maids, food and textile industry workers, and the like.[28]

Saudi Arabia presents an interesting case study of the confrontation of Islamic ideas with contemporary reality. Women are greatly inhibited in the labor arena; because of conservative religious attitudes they must be veiled and covered, are not permitted to drive or even ride in a taxi with a strange man, and in general are unable to participate on the social and professional level with males. However, in a country in which production is both necessary and economically possible and which suffers from a lack of manpower, the use of women in the work force or increased importation of foreign labor seem the only two (both undesirable) alternatives. Thus more Saudi women are working, and because of their right to inherit, are accumulating very substantial amounts of money. It is interesting to note the rapid rate of construction of new banks exclusively for women in places like Jiddah and Riyadh.

The aforementioned Qur'ān verse about the witness of two women being equal to that of one man and the supporting literature attesting to female intellectual, physical (and in fact sometimes moral) inferiority have made it difficult for Muslim women to achieve equal political rights. In most Arab countries (except Saudi Arabia and certain of the Gulf States), as well as in most other parts of the Islamic world, women have now been given the vote. Centuries of passivity in the political realm, however, have made it difficult for women to take advantage of the opportunities now available to them. In some countries, such as Egypt, women are playing major political roles, but generally women politicians find little support from men or even from other women for their aspirations. This is not to underestimate the strong current in Islamic thinking which encourages the full participation of women in politics, as well as in the educational and professional fields.

Like an intricate and complex geometric pattern on a Persian rug or a frieze decorating a mosque, the practices, roles, opportunities, prescriptions, hopes, and frustrations of Islamic women are woven together in a whole. The colors are sometimes bold and striking, at other times muted and subtle. Some contemporary Muslim women are progressive and aggressive, no longer content to fit the traditionally prescribed patterns. Others are passive and accepting, not yet able to discern what new possibilities may be open to them, let alone whether or not they might want to take advantage of such opportunities. Some are Westernized as their mothers and grandmothers were and have every intention of staying that way, while others are increasingly clear in their feelings that the West does not have the answers and that Islam, particularly the Islam of the Qur'ān and the community of the Prophet Muhammad, is God's chosen way for humankind. For the latter, their dress, their relationships with their husbands and families, and their verbal assent to Islamic priorities reflect this conviction that the time has come to cease a fruitless preoccupation with things Western and to reaffirm their identity as Muslim women.

It is difficult for Western feminists to grasp exactly what the Muslim woman may mean by "liberation." For many Islamic women, the fruits of liberation in the West are too many broken marriages, women left without the security of men who will provide for them, deteriorating relations between men and women, and sexual license that appears as rank immorality. They see the Islamic system as affirmed by the Qur'ān as one in which male authority over them ensures their care and protection and provides a structure in which the family is solid, children are inculcated with lasting values, and the balance of responsibility between man and woman is one in which absolute equality is less highly prized than cooperation and complementarity.

The new Islamic woman, then, is morally and religiously conservative and affirms the absolute value of the true Islamic system for human relationships. She is intolerant of the kind of Islam in which women are subjugated and relegated to roles insignificant to the full functioning of society, and she wants to take full advantage of educational and professional opportunities. She may agree, however, that certain fields of education are more appropriate for women than others, and that certain professions are more natural to males than to females. She participates as a contributor to and decisionmaker for the family, yet recognizes that in any complex relationship final authority must rest with one person. And she is content to delegate that authority to her husband, father, or other male relative in return for the solidarity of the family structure and the support and protection that it gives her and her children.

That not all, or even most, Muslim women subscribe to this point of view is clear. And yet, at the time of this writing, it seems equally clear that, if Western observers are to understand women in the contemporary Islamic world, they must appreciate a point of view that is more and more prevalent. The West is increasingly identified with imperialism, and solutions viable for women in the Islamic community are necessarily different from the kinds of solutions that many Western women seem to have chosen for themselves. For the Muslim the words of the Qur'ān are divine, and the prescriptions for the roles and rights of females, like the other messages of the holy book, are seen as part of

God's divinely ordered plan for all humanity. Change will come slowly, and whatever kinds of liberation ultimately prevail will be cloaked in a garb that is—in one or another of its various aspects—essentially Islamic.

CONTRIBUTORS

ARVIND SHARMA (B.A. Allahabad 1958; M.A. Syracuse 1970; M.T.S. Harvard Divinity School 1974; Ph.D. Harvard University 1978) lectures at the University of Sydney, Australia. He has published several papers and monographs dealing with the position of women in Indian religions.

RITA M. GROSS is associate professor of comparative religions at the University of Wisconsin-Eau Claire. She received her Ph.D. from the University of Chicago for a dissertation entitled "Exclusion and Participation: The Role of Women in Aboriginal Australian Religion." She is coeditor of *Unspoken Worlds: Women's Religious Lives in Non-Western Cultures* and has written extensively on Hinduism and Buddhism. She has also been a leader in feminist scholarship and theology in North America and has many publications on these topics. Currently she is authoring a book on Buddhism and feminism. She is also very active in the area of Buddhist-Christian dialogue.

KATHERINE K. YOUNG is Associate Professor in the Faculty of Religious Studies at McGill University, Montreal, Canada. She received her M.A. from the University of Chicago and Ph.D. from McGill University in the History of Religions with specialization in Hinduism. She has periodically studied and done research in India and has published in two main areas: religion in South India, and women in Hinduism. She is currently combining these two interests in her research on images of the feminine in Tamil Vaiṣṇavism with special reference to the poet-saint Āṇṭāḷ. The McGill Studies in the History of Religions is appearing under her general editorship.

NANCY SCHUSTER BARNES received her A.B. in history from the University of Michigan in 1960 and her Ph.D. in Sanskrit and Indian studies from the University of Toronto in 1976. Her dissertation was on early Mahāyāna Buddhism in China and India and included a translation from Chinese of a very ancient Mahāyāna sūtra, The Question of Ugra the Householder. She also studied Indian languages and literature, and Chinese, Japanese, and Tibetan at the University in Göttingen, Germany, from 1964 to 1966.

From 1970 to 1980 she was a member of the faculties at the Hartford Seminary Foundation in Hartford, Connecticut, and at Wesleyan University in Middletown, Connecticut. She taught a variety of courses on Buddhism as well as on other Asian religions, philosophies, and art.

Her publications include:

"Changing the Female Body: Wise Women and the Bodhisattva Career in some *Mahāratnakūṭa Sūtras.*" *Journal of the International Association of Buddhist Studies* 4, no. 1 (1981): 24–69.

"Yoga Master Dharmamitra and Clerical Misogyny in Fifth Century Buddhism." *The Tibet Journal* 9, no. 4 (1984): 33–49.

"The Bodhisattva in the *Ugraparipṛcchā,* an early Mahāyāna Buddhist Sūtra." In *New Paths in Buddhist Research,* ed. A. K. Warder. Durham, N.C.: The Acorn Press, 1985.

"Striking a Balance: Women and Images of Women in Early Chinese Buddhism." In *Women, Religion, and Social Change,* ed. Y. Haddad and E. Findly. Albany: State University of New York Press, 1985.

BARBARA REED is assistant professor of religion at St. Olaf College, Northfield, Minnesota. She received a Ph.D. in religion from the University of Iowa in 1982 and also did graduate work in Chinese philosophy at National Taiwan Normal University (Taipei, Taiwan). Her primary interest is religious symbolism in the Chinese Buddhist and Taoist traditions.

DENISE L. CARMODY received her Ph. D. from Boston College in 1970 in the philosophy of religion. She has taught at Boston College, Notre Dame of Maryland, Pennsylvania State University, and Wichita State University. Since 1985 she has been the head of the Department of

Religion at the University of Tulsa, Tulsa, Oklahoma. Her major recent publications include *Women and World Religions* (Nashville: Abingon, 1979) and *Seizing the Apple: a feminist spirituality of personal growth* (New York: Crossroad, 1984).

ROSEMARY RADFORD RUETHER is the Georgia Harkness professor of applied theology at the Garrett-Evangelical Theological Seminary and a member of the graduate faculty of the joint program in theological and religious studies of Northwestern University in Evanston, Illinois. She is the author or editor of twenty books and numerous articles on the subject of Christian theological history and social justice. She has written on such topics as sexism and racism, economic exploitation, and war and peace. Among her recent books is *Sexism and Godtalk: Toward a Feminist Theology* (Beacon Press) and a three-volume documentary history entitled *Women and Religion in America* (Harper and Row). Dr. Ruether holds the Ph. D. degree in classics and patristics from the Claremont Graduate School in Claremont, California. She is a frequent lecturer on university campuses and church conventions, and has been actively involved in movements for social justice for twenty years. She is married and is the mother of three children.

JANE I. SMITH has been associate dean for academic affairs and lecturer in Islamic studies at Harvard Divinity School. She is the author of several books on the religion of Islam, including *The Islamic Understanding of Death and Resurrection* (with Yvonne Y. Haddad). She is the editor of *Women in Contemporary Muslim Society,* and has also written numerous articles on the historical and present circumstances of Islamic women. As associate director for the Center for the Study of World Religions at Harvard, she was editor of the center's "Studies in World Religions" publications series. She has traveled widely throughout the Middle East and other parts of the Islamic world, and has participated in Muslim-Christian dialogue sessions abroad and in the United States. One of her particular interests is interpreting current movements among Muslim women to American audiences. As of 1987 she will be Dean and Vice President at the Iliff School of Theology in Denver.

THERESA KELLEHER received her B.A. in Asian Studies from Manhattanville College, and then completed work for her M.A. in Chinese literature at the University of Hawaii as an East West Center grantee. She received her Ph.D. in Chinese thought from Columbia University in 1982, with a dissertation on the life and journal of a fifteenth century Neo Confucion, Wu Yü-pi, and his guest for sagehood. She is currently assistant professor of Religion and Asian Studies at Manhattanville College. Her present research interests focus around traditional Chinese instructional literature for women and children.

NOTES

INTRODUCTION

1 See *Women in China: Current Directions in Historical Scholarship*, edited by Richard W. Guisso and Stanley Johannesen (Youngstown: Philo Press, 1981), ix.

2 *The American Heritage Dictionary of the English Language*, edited by William Morris (New York: American Heritage Publishing Co., 1969), 961.

3 See also Janet Sayers, *Biological Politics: Feminist and Anti-feminist Perspectives* (New York: Tavistock Publications, 1982), pp. 65–104 for a survey of the various theories that have argued for male dominance and patriarchy on the basis of the comparatively greater size, strength and aggression of men. She presents the challenge to such views on the basis of historical, anthropological, psychological and sociological data and concludes that the scientific evidence establishes that "as in baboon societies, so in human societies male dominance is a learned phenomenon, a response to the material conditions of life: conditions that vary both historically and crossculturally" (82).

4 See Erich Fromm, *The Forgotten Language* (New York: Holt, Rinehart and Winston, 1951); Bruno Bettelheim, *Symbolic Wounds: Puberty Rites and the Envious Male* (Glencoe, Ill.: The Free Press, 1954); and Rita M. Gross, "Menstruation and Childbirth as Ritual and Religious Experience among Native Australians," in *Unspoken Worlds: Women's Religous Lives in Non-Western Cultures* edited by Nancy A. Falk and Rita M. Gross (San Francisco: Harper & Row, 1980).

5 Ever since Freud's discussion of penis envy as a possible and very probable consequence of the way girls deal with the discovery of the genital sex differences, this theory has been related to the symbolic significance of the penis in male-dominated societies and its corollary that the castration complex defines the entrance of the female child into the patriarchal symbolic order. I think that we need to take into account the biological factor of sexual differences to have a complete account of human psychology, male as well as female, though that analysis may differ from Freud's account. But by the same token I think that we must also take account of the male child's difficulty in early childhood to separate from the mother and

form a male identity as well as later castration anxiety related to the discovery that they lack a womb with its life-producing capacities. For perhaps the most repressed thought embedded in male psychology is womb envy, which has conveniently been hidden through male culture and definitions of male supremacy over the ages. If the powers of the mother and the womb served at some stage of human evolution or male development to threaten male identity in comparison to the dramatic power and life-affirmation of female biology, then there are good reasons to think that men tried first to come to terms with this reality through myth and ritual as in some tribal societies, but with the development of extreme male dominance came to repress and to compensate for this realization. Obviously, if a woman learns to resolve the discovery of genital differences so must men for a healthy psychology. But while girls begin to focus on the creation of a child and thus come to an appreciation of female biology, men have tended to define their identity in part by subordination of women culturally to gain a positive self-esteem. The resolution, however, has not been successful. Men remain subject to castration anxiety when a woman appropriates both biology and culture for fully actualizing her human potential.

6   The terms Brahmanical Hinduism and early Brahmanism are used here to distinguish early Aryan ethnic religion in India with Brahman leadership from the later uiversal religion which may be called Hinduism albeit still with Brahmanical leadership, especially in orthodox circles and their spheres of influence.

7   *The American Heritage Dictionary*, p. 450.

8   I am deeply indebted to a lecture given by Jane Smith on "Women as Participants in the Early Muslim Community" (McGill University, October 28th, 1986).

9   I wish to thank my associates at McGill for their valuable comments on my draft. My special appreciation goes to Paul Nathanson in this regard.

10 The quotations by the contributors to this book which are found in this introduction were drawn from the manuscript prior to final editorial changes.

HINDUISM

1   Brahmanical values have tended to define the ideals of Hindu society, mainly because the texts have been written by Brahmans; these values have also considerable influence on other sectors of the population through the process termed Sanskritization. In South India, however, a different kinship system based on cross-cousin marriage has given rise to different ideal roles for women, and although some Sanskritization exists even there, the analysis of women in Hindiusm must be qualified by the region under consideration. For purposes of this essay the focus will be the

prevailing Brahmanical values as they are found in North India or more technically, outside the areas where kinship is based on cross-cousin marriage.

2   One should distinguish between the person who commits the act of con-cremation and the act itself. Thus one uses the form *satī* (with the diacriti-cal mark) to denote the person and *sati* (without the diacritical mark) to denote the act. The discussion is based on Alaka Hejib and Katherine K. Young "Towards Recognition of the Religious Structure of the Satī," a paper delivered at the American Oriental Society, 1978.

3   The following discussion first appeared in my article "From Hindu Strī dharma to Universal Feminism: A Study of the Women of the Nehru Family" (Young 1983a).

4   See *Women's Development* 1978, 71–93, for charts illustrating the follow-ing trends: a decline in the ratio of women to men since 1901; a lower ex-pectation of life for women as compared to men; and a lower rate of literacy than men (18.7-per cent for women compared to 39.5 per cent for men). The number of women in the Lok Sabha (parliament) has decreased from 35 in 1962 to 19 in 1977, and the percentage of women working to the total female population has radically declined sincd 1911 as well.

Lalonde (1985), in her analysis of national development and the changing status of women in India, notes that higher status "was found in the southern states, supporting a cultural theory of the influence of a long-standing North/South dichotomy" (ii); that this dichotomy corresponds to different systems of kinship in North and South India (53) so that certain practices common in the North, "such as greater distance between natal and conjugal homes, lower age at marriage, unequal relationship between affines, giving of large dowries, the low position of new brides in their in-laws' homes, banning of widow remarriage, and low levels of economic participation among women, can have unfavourable repercussions on female status relative to males"(106), whereas in the South there are "relatively low sex ratios, lower infant and child mortality, later age at marriage, lower marital fertility, and lower over all fertility" (54). Lalonde's analysis reminds us once again that textual study of Hindu women based on Sanskrit texts reflects primarily the North Indian kinship system, though these texts certainly influenced other regions.

BUDDHISM

1   One of the most famous of these outbursts, found in the Pali canon of the Theravāda school, is this pathetically humorous accusation: "Even when ... stricken or dying, a woman will stop to ensnare the heart of a man" (A.III.67; GS.III.56–57).

2   I disagree with Diana Paul (1979, 5ff), who feels that the view of woman as "temptress or evil incarnate" was a significant attitude in early Buddhist

literature. I believe that a careful reading of most texts judged to be misogynist clearly reveals that it is a man's or a woman's own lustfulness
which is being denounced rather than the person who is the object of
that lust.

3   One of the most ill-tempered condemnations of women found in the Pali
canon deals directly with this issue of power and leadership. Ananda asks
the Buddha why women do not assume positions of leadership in an
assembly or in business enterprises, and the Buddha replies that it is
because they are uncontrolled, envious, greedy, and weak in wisdom
(A.II.82–83).

4   There were prominent nuns, especially in the earlier centuries of the
saṃgha, but even then they appear not to have been noticed as much as the
monks. When King Pasenadi (Prasenajit) of Kośala wanted to converse
with a wandering monk or a Brāhmaṇa, he could find none, and so settled
for a learned nun instead. To his surprise, she delivered an elegant lecture
to him on the nature of the enlightened one, the Buddha (S.IV.374–80).

5   Some Pali sūtras which offer specific advice to women are A.II.202–5;
III.36–37; IV.91–93; and S.IV.238–51. A sūtra which offers similar advice
to a male householder is D.III.180–93. On some economically independent
women, see Horner 1930, 75–76, 345ff.; and Davids 1909, 47–49, 134–
47.

6   An excellent explanation of what these processes are and how they work
can be found in Gomez (1976), especially pages 141–44.

7   A.IV.91–93 offers an interesting sidelight on "women's thoughts." Here
the Buddha lectures a young woman on seven kinds of wives, among them
some who lust after other men, some who are lazy or destroy a husband's
wealth, others who are loving, who serve, or who are true friends. But best
of all is the wife who is calm and pure in heart, endures everthing, obeys,
and is fearless and without wrath: she is the dāsī-wife, wife like a slave. But
as one can see, the dāsī's virtues are essentially those of the renunciant
who has become freed of desires and pursues the spiritual path single-
mindedly.

8   The story is retold by Weiler (1962, 247–48) and by Har Dayal (1932, 184).
Ksemendra adds that Rukmavatī was reborn later as the famous hero
Satyavrata (better known as Mahāsattva), who offered his body to a striving
tigress about to consume her cubs. In the story of Rukmavatī, after she has
cut off her breasts, the god Śakra appears and marvels at her determination.
Thereupon Rukmavatī utters the truthful affirmation (satyādhiṣṭhāna,
satyakriyā) that she had felt no hesitation before her amazing action, and
thus she causes her body to change magically into that of a man. (The
narrative theme of magical change of the female body is dealt with elsewhere in this chapter. On the connection between the theme of sexual
transformation and the truth act, see Schuster 1981.) Especially interesting
in Rūpāvatī or Rukmavatī's story is her own deliberate act of "unwomaning" herself by cutting off her breasts, which she follows by magically

transforming herself into a male. No religious reason is indicated for this sex change. But surely this striking act of violence symbolizes her abandonment of the traditional female role of nurturing mother so that another woman can survive and remain a real mother. This fascinating story deserves further study.

9 For some other sūtras containing the change-of-sex theme and for further references, see Paul (1979) and Schuster (1981).

10 The Vimalakīrtinirdeśa (Lamotte 1962, ch.7) and Śūrangamasamādhisūtra (Lamotte 1965, 172-78) are very explicit about the illusory nature of sex distinctions. In the latter text, the god Gopaka, who used to be a mortal woman, says that those who are established in the Mahāyāna do not see any difference between man and woman, that all phenomena (dharmas) have a "single flavor." Once, he says, "I had a female body, and that was according to my resolve, and now that I have a male body I have not destroyed nor abandoned the characteristics of a female body."

11 See Paul 1979, 219. Since according to Buddhist literature the lakṣaṇa of the mahāpuruṣa are also possessed by a universal monarch (rājācakravartin), who is primarily a secular character who fathers 1,000 or more sons (Sn.106; D.I.88; D.III.16, 161-62; M.II.134; Kāśyapaparivarta, T.vol. XII, no.350, p.191.b.16-19; von Stäel-Holstein 1926, 119-21), it is likely that the penis of the mahāpuruṣa sheathed "like a stallion's" (Mahāprajñāpāramitāśāstra, Lamotte 1949, 1:274-75) is in the cakravartin's case a mark of virility. The Buddha is a father, too, however—father of his daughters and sons in the dharma, who are born of his mouth, that is, of the truth he teaches: see Thig. 31 and 59 (Davids 1909, 37, 141); D.III.84; Sn.109, verse 557; Mahāprajñāpāramitāśāstra, Lamotte 1949, 1:456-57. In the Buddha's case, the sheathed penis probably symbolizes that his genital virility is controlled and contained and is replaced by his *oral* "virility." The mark of the long, broad tongue is closely connected with the mark of the sheathed penis in the earliest textual references to the mahāpuruṣalakṣaṇa. The tongue is the mark of one who speaks the truth, according to the Mahāprajñāpāramitāśāstra (Lamotte 1949, 1:456-57).

12 It is worth recalling here the story of Rūpāvatī or Rukmavatī, recounted above: Rupāvatī cuts off her breasts, "unwomaning" herself, and then by an act of truth undergoes sexual transformation. The young girls in our Mahāyāna sūtras accomplish their "unwomaning" without violence, but the significance is the same: they too sever all connections with woman's traditional role as mother, and they do *not* take up a traditional man's role to replace it.

13 Paul believes that the ten-*bhūmi* (ten-stage) scheme was accepted in most of the Mahāyāna-sūtras she translates and describes, certainly those grouped together in her chapter 5, "The Bodhisattvas with Sexual Transformation." But in the absence of evidence within a given sūtra for acceptance of a bhumi theory, I do not think we are justified in assuming that it was adhered to, particularly in early Mahāyāna texts.

14 Most of the nuns in the Bi-qiu-ni zhuan lived in the area of modern-day Nanjing and were active during the southern dynasties of Song, Qi, and Liang.

15 Cissel (1972, 90) says the nuns who were appointed samgha-director or precentor of the capital region under the Song and Liang dynasties had authority only over the nuns in the city, not over the monks. I find, however, that the text of the Bi-qiu-ni zhuan is ambiguous on this point.

16 Paul (1979, 282) cites Zhi-yi's commentary on the Lotus Sutra; the commentary makes the interesting statement that all the females in the heavens of Śakra, Brahmā, and Māra attained Buddhahood in their female bodies without sexual transformation. Thus, this text asserts that in three of the "five ranks" in which females are supposed to be unable to exist, there is a multitude of female Buddhas. Buddhahood itself is, as we have seen, the fifth of those "five ranks."

CONFUCIANISM

1 This cosmological orientation is articulated most extensively in the "Appendices" of the Book of Changes, the ritual texts (especially the "Record of Music" in the Book of Rites), and in the writings of the early Confucian philosopher Hsün Tzu. It is not that strong in works such as the Analects and Mencius.

2 Later this sequence was speeded up such that all the ceremonials to do with the parents-in-law occurred on the second day of the bride's arrival, and the presentation to the ancestors was held on the third day, rather than in the third month.

3 Though divorce was permitted, it rarely occurred because of the system of concubinage which underlay the marriage system. It was permissible for the husband to bring in other women to the household, and if he were displeased with his principal wife, he could allow her to stay but ignore her. One of the duties of the principal wife was to act kindly to these concubines. Any children born to the concubines were officially hers, and concubines could not participate in the ancestral sacrifices.

4 I base the following discussion on my reading of the Chinese text, as well as on the English translation by Nancy Lee Swann and Marina Sung's discussion of the text in her "The Chinese *Lieh-nü* Tradition."

5 The only thing we know about the author of this text is that her family name was Ch'eng (Chinese women have never taken their husband's name, but have always kept their family name, even though it is a patriarchal society), and that she was married to a court official named Ch'en Miao. For a more detailed discussion of the contents of this and the Analects for Women, see my "How to be the Perfect Woman: Chinese In-

structional Texts for Women," a paper presented at the annual meeting of Asian Studies on the Pacific Coast, June, 1986.

6   Sung Jo-chao was the second of five daughters of a high court-official. Supposedly her elder sister wrote it, but she took upon herself the job of disseminiting it. Refusing to marry, she spent most of her life lecturing to the women at court.

7   A standard history of women in China remarks that two of the most popular texts for women for most of Chinese history were Pan Chao's Instructions for Women and Sung Jo-chao's Analects for Women (Ch'en 1970, 185).

8   Confucians connected one's posture to one's moral character. Thus to slouch or lie on one's side would undermine the type of upright, square behavior to which one should aspire. The outer reflects on the inner. The blind musicians here are supposed to be chanting moral lessons which the baby inside the womb absorbs.

9   Few of the women in this collection have their own names. Most are known as "the mother of," "the wife of," "the daughter of," or "a resident of."

10 Mark Elvin, Susan Mann, and Ann Waltner have discussed the matter of chastity in Late Imperial China from the social, economic, political, and cultural perspectives. See Mark Elvin's "Female Virtue and the State in China," Susan Mann's two excellent unpublished papers, "Suicide and Chastity: Visible Themes in the History of Chinese Women" and "Widows in the Kinship and Community Systems of the Qing Period," and Ann Waltner's piece, "Widows and Remarriage in Ming and Early Qing China."

11 The most notable of these are Phyllis Andors, The Unfinished Liberation of Chinese Women, 1949–80, and Kay Ann Johnson's Women, the Family and Peasant Revolution in China.

CHRISTIANITY

1   Washington, D.C.: University Press of America, 1981. French edition, 1968.

2   All the members of the inclusive language lectionary committee of the National Council of Churches have received letters threatening their lives and those of their families. One member of the committee, Dr. Susan Thistlethwaite of the Chicago Theological Seminary, has studied the themes that have appeared in the "hate mail" she has received as a result of her work on the committee. The most frequent theme is one which correlates the concept of God as Father with a concept of absolute control and sovereignty over human affairs. Fear and horror is expressed at the idea of a female image of God, which is identified with the loss of authority and power.

3 Paul K. Jewett, *Man as Male and Female* (Grand Rapids: Eerdmans, 1975).

4 See Constance Parvey, "The Theology and Leadership of Women in the New Testament," in *Religion and Sexism*, ed. R. R. Ruether (New York: Simon and Schuster, 1974), 139.

5 Acts 21:8f. See Elisabeth S. Fiorenza, "Word, Spirit and Power: Women in Early Christian Communities," in *Women of Spirit*, ed. R. R. Ruether and E. McLaughlin (New York: Simon and Schuster, 1979), 39–44.

6 Didache 11:3–15:2.

7 See Fiorenza, "Word, Spirit and Power," 33–37. See also *In Memory of Her: A Feminist Theological Reconstruction of Christian Origins* (New York: Crossroads, 1983), 218–36.

8 Romans 16:7. See Fiorenza, "Word, Spirit and Power," 34–35. See also B. Brooten, "Junia, Outstanding among the Apostles," in *Women Priests. A Catholic Commentary on the Vatican Declaration*, ed. Swidler and Swidler (New York: Paulist, 1977), 141–44.

9 Romans 16:1ff: Fiorenza, *In Memory of Her*, 170–72.

10 Fiorenza, *In Memory of Her*, 217–18. See also H. Fischel, "Story and History; Observations in Greco-Roman Rhetoric and Pharisaism," in *American Oriental Society MidWest Branch Semi-Centennial Volume*, ed. D. Sinor (Bloomington: Indiana University Press, 1969), 74ff.

11 Fiorenza, *In Memory of Her*, 251–70.

12 Philadelphia: Westminster, 1983.

13 See Robin Scroggs, "Paul and Eschatological Woman," *JAAR* (Sept. 1972), 253ff; also *JAAR* (Sept. 1974), 532ff.

14 See Fiorenza, *In Memory of Her*, 53–56.

15 "Acts of the Martyrs of Lyons and Vienne," 41, in Herbert Musurillo, *The Acts of the Christian Martyrs* (Oxford: Clarendon, 1972), 75.

16 Stevan Davies, *The Revolt of the Widows: The Social World of the Apocryphal Acts* (Carbondale: Southern Illinois University Press, 1980), 95–109.

17 See, for example, Logion 114 of the Gospel of Thomas, where Jesus says: "See I shall lead her and make her male, so that she too may become a living Spirit resembling you males. For every woman who makes herself male will enter the Kingdom of Heaven."

18 See, for example, Leander of Seville in the preface to his *Institutes of Virginity*, where he speaks of the Christian virgin in the following words: "forgetful of her natural feminine weakness, she lives in manly vigor." See also Gregory Nyssa's life of his sister Macrina, where he says that he hesitates to call her a woman because she so transcends the weak female nature and approximates that of the male. (*Life of Macrina*, in *Asetical Works: Fathers of the Church*, vol. 58 [Washington D.C.: Catholic University Press, 1967]).

19 Aristotle, *The Generation of Animals*, II, 4, 20–21.

20 Thomas Aquinas, *Summa Theologica*, Pt. I, Q. 92, art. 1.

21 An example is the twelfth-century life of Christina of Markyate. See Eleanor McLaughlin, "Women, Power and the Pursuit of Holiness in Medieval Christianity," in Ruether and McLaughlin, *Women of Spirit*, 108ff.

22 Lina Eckenstein, *Women Under Monasticism: Saint Lore and Convent Life. A.D. 500–1500* (Cambridge University Press, 1896), 152–53.

23 Joan Morris, *The Lady was a Bishop* (New York: Macmillan, 1973), 16–23.

24 Eckenstein, *Women Under Monasticism*, 162–81, 238ff., 256ff.

25 See Ruth Liebowitz, "Virgins in the Service of Christ: The Dispute over the Active Apostolate for Woman during the Counter-Reformation." in Ruether and McLaughlin, *Women of Spirit*, 138–40.

26 E. M. McDonnell, *Beguine and Beghard in Medieval Culture* (New Brunswick, N. J.: Rutgers University Press, 1954), 194–95.

27 Marjorie Reeves, *The Influence of Prophecy in the Later Middle Ages: A Study of Joachimism* (Oxford: Clarendon, 1969).

28 Marjorie Reeves, *Joachim of Fiore and the Prophetic Future* (New York: Harper and Row, 1976), 50–51.

29 See Joan Kelly-Gadol, "Did Women Have an Renaissance?" in *Becoming Visible: Women in European History*, ed. Bridenthal and Koonz (Boston: Houghton Mifflin, 1977), 137ff.

30 Alice Clark, *The Working Life of Women in the 17th Century* (London: n. p., 1919).

31 Martin Luther, "Lectures on Genesis, Gen. 3:16," in *Luther's Works*, vol. I, ed. Jaroslav Pelikan (St. Louis: Concordia Publishing House, 1958), 202–3.

32 Edmund S. Morgan, *The Puritan Family: Religion and Domestic Relations in 17th Century New England* (Westport, Conn.: Greenwood Press, 1966), 13 and passim.

33 See Rosmary S. Keller, "New England Women: Ideology and Experience in First Generation Puritanism, 1630–50" in *Woman and Religion in America*: vol. 2: *The Colonial and Revolutionary Periods*, ed. R. Ruether and R. Keller (San Francisco: Harper and Row, 1983), 136–39.

34 William Perkins, *A Discourse on the Damned Art of Withchraft* (London: n. p., 1596).

35 Joyce L. Irwin, *Womanhood in Radical Protestantism, 1525–1675* (New York: Edwin Mellen Press, 1979), 210–14. See Also E. Thomas, "Women and the Civil War Sects," in *Past and Present* XIII (1958), 42–62.

36 Irwin, *Womanhood*, 170–78.

37 Mabel Brailsford, *Quaker Women, 1650–1690* (London: Duckworth and Co., 1915). See also Elaine Huber, "A Woman Must Not Speak: Quaker Women in the English Left Wing," in Ruether and McLaughlin, *Women of Spirit*, 153ff.

38 See Rosemary Ruether and Catherine Prelinger, "Women in Sectarian and Utopian Groups," in Ruether and Keller, *Women and Religion in America*, vol. 2, 261, 283–88.

39 See Keller, "New England Women," in Ruether and Keller, *Women and Religion in America*, vol. 2, 165–75.

40 Ruether, "Women in Sectarian and Utopian Groups," in Ruether and Keller, *Women and Religion in America*, vol. 2, 279–81.

41 Ibid., 278.

42 Keller, "New England Women," 141, 176–83.

43 Carol Karlsen, *The Devil in the Shape of a Woman: The Witch in 17th Century New England* (Ph.D. diss., Yale University, 1980).

44 Jacob Boehme, *Mysterium Magnum: An Exposition of the First Book of Moses called Genesis*, vol. 1, trans, John Sparrow (London: John M. Watkins, 1924), 121–33.

45 R. Ruether, "Women in Utopian Movements," in *Women and Religion in America*: vol. 1: *The Nineteenth Century*, ed. R. Ruether and R. Keller (San Francisco: Harper and Row, 1981), 60–61.

46 See "Condorcet's Pleas for the Citizenship of Women," *Journal de la Societe de 1789*, July 3, 1790. English translation: *The Fortnightly Review* 13:42 (June 1870), 719–20.

47 Sarah Grimké, "Letters on the Equality of the Sexes and the Condition of Women" (1836–37), in *Feminism: The Essential Historical Writings*, ed. M. Schneir (New York: Vintage, 1972), p. 38.

48 Ibid.

49 "Declaration of Sentiments and Resolutions: Seneca Falls, July 19, 1848," in Schneir, *Feminism: The Essential Historical Writings*, 82.

50 Carolyn Gifford, "Women in Social Reform Movements," in Ruether and Keller, *Women and Religion in America*, vol. 1, 301–2, 325–28.

51 See Letha Scanzoni, "The Great Chain of Being and the Chain of Command," in *Women's Spirit Bonding*, ed. Janet Kalven (New York: Pilgrim Press, 1984), 41–55.

52 See E. L. Mascall, *Women and the Priesthood of the Church* (London: The Church Union, Literature Association, n. d.).

53 The *Baptism, Eucharist, Ministry* document of the World Council of Churches (WCC), accepted at the Vancouver Meeting of the WCC in 1983, commits Protestants to a traditional concept of the three-fold ministry as the formula for ecumenical relations with Roman Catholicism and Eastern Orthodoxy, a formula that also lends itself to the oft-stated assertion in such circles that "women are a barrier to ecumenical relations." This perception has been confirmed in conversation with Constance Parvey (Cambridge, Mass.), who conducted the "Community of Men and Women in the Church" study for the WCC Faith and Order Commission between 1978 and 1982.

ISLAM

1 Nabia Abbott, "Pre-Islamic Arab Queens," *The American Journal of Semitic Languages and Literatures* 17 (January 1941) 1–22. See also, A. F. L. Beeston, "The Position of Women in Pre-Islamic South Arabia," *International Orientalists' Congress* 22, 2 (1951), 101–06.

2 See, for example, Gamal A. Badawi, "Woman in Islam," in *Islam: Its Meaning and Message,* ed. Kurshid Ahmad and Salem Azzam (Leicester: The Islamic Foundation, 1975,) 131–35.

3 "Say: He is God, the One and the Only, God the Eternal, Absolute" (Surah 112:1–2). "Then, when one blast is sounded on the Trumpet, and the earth is moved, and its moutains, and they are crushed to powder at one stroke— on that Day shall the Event come to pass" (69:13–15).

4 Sadiq Hasan Khān, *Husn al-uswa* (Cairo: Matba'ah al-Imām, n.d.), 117.

5 Surah 4:3.

6 Surah 5:6.

7 Surah 65:4.

8 See Nadia H. Youssef, "The Status of Fertility Patterns of Muslim Women" in *Women in the Muslim World,* ed. Lois Beck and Nikki Keddi (Cambridge: Harvard University Press, 1978), 69–99.

9 Surah 2:226–30; 65:1–2.

10 Surah 4:11–12, 177.

11 It is estimated, for example, that women in Saudi Arabia now own somewhere between 25 and 50 percent of the property in major cities such as Jiddah and Riyadh.

12 Surah 24:31.

13 Surah 33:53–59.

14 Ahmad Galwash, *The Religion of Islam,* vol. 1 (Qatar: Education and Culture Ministry, 1973), 155–56.

15 See, for example, Ahmad Sakr, *al-Khutab* (Ann Arbor: Taleemul Islam Publications, 1977).

16 See, for example, Fatima Mernissi, *Beyond the Veil* (New York: Schenkman Publishing Company, 1975).

17 See, for example, B. Aisha Lemu and Fatima Heeren, *Women in Islam* (Islamic Council of Europe, 1978), 13–18.

18 John A. Williams, "A Return to the Veil in Egypt," *Middle East Review* 11, 3 (1979), 49–59.

19 Ahmad Ibn Hanbal, *Musnad,* vol. 1 (Cairo: al-Matba'ah al-Maymaniyah, 1895), 137.

20 See Jane I. Smith and Yvonne Haddad, *The Islamic Understanding of Death and Resurrection* (Albany: State University of New York Press, 1981), Appendix B.

21 Farid Māhir, *Karmāmāt al-awliyā'* (Cairo: al-Matba'ah al-'Alimiya, 1971), 85–90.

22 Nawal al-Messiri, "The Sheikh Cult in Dahmit," in *Nubian Ceremonial Life*, ed. John Kennedy (Berkeley: University of California Press, 1978), 61–103.

23 Lucie Wood Saunders, "Variants in Zar Experience in an Egyptian Village," in *Case Studies in Spirit Possesssion*, ed. Vincent Crapanzano and Vivien Garrison (New York: John Wiley and Sons, 1977), 177–91.

24 Robert A. and Elizabeth W. Fernea, "Variations in Religious Observance among Islamic Women," in *Scholars, Saints and Sufis*, ed. Nikki R. Keddie (Berkeley: University of California Press, 1972), 391–95.

25 See, for example, Daisy Hilse Dwyer, "Women, Sufism and Decision-Making in Moroccan Islam," in Beck and Keddie, *Women in the Muslim World*, 585–98.

26 Yvonne Haddad, "Traditional Affirmations Concerning the Role of Women," in *Women in Contemporary Muslim Societies*, ed, J. I. Smith (Lewisburg: Bucknell University Press 1980), 70.

27 See, for example, "Al-Azhar, Islam, and the role of Women in Islamic Society," *The Islamic Review* 40, 8 (August 1952), 2–4.

28 See Fatima Mernissi, "The Patriarch in the Moroccan Family: Myth of Reality," in *Women's Status and Fertility in the Muslim World*, ed. James Allman (New York: Praeger Publishers, 1978), 312–32.

BIBLIOGRAPHY

INTRODUCTION

Ames, Roger T. 1981. "Taoism and the Androgynous Ideal." In *Women in China: Current Directions in Historical Scholarship*, ed. Guisso and Johannesen. Youngstown: Philo Press, 21-47.

Guisso, Richard W. 1981. "Thunder Over the Lake: The Five Classics and the Perception of Woman in Early China." In *Women in China: Current Directions in Historical Scholarship*, ed. Guisso and Johannesen. Youngstown: Philo Press, 47-63.

Guisso, Richard W., and Stanley Johannesen. eds. 1981. *Women in China: Current Directions in Historical Scholarship*. Youngstown: Philo Press.

Sagan, Eli. 1985. *At the Dawn of Tyranny: The Origins of Individualism, Political Oppression, and the State*. New York: Alfred A. Knopf.

Sanday, Peggy Reeves. 1981. *Female Power and Male Dominance: On the origins of sexual inequality*. London: Cambridge University Press.

Sayers, Janet. 1982. *Biological Politics*. London: Tavistock Publications.

Sung, Marina H. 1981. "The Chinese Lieh-nü Tradition." In *Women in China: Current Directions in Historical Scholarship*, ed. Guisso and Johannesen. Youngstown: Philo Press, 63-75.

Tsai, Kathryn. A. 1981. "The Chinese Buddhist Monastic Order for Women: The First Two Centuries." In *Women in China: Current Directions in Historical Scholarship*, ed. Guisso and Johannesen. Youngstown: Philo Press, 1-21.

Waltner, Ann. 1981. "Widows and Remarriage in Ming and Early Qing China." In *Women in China: current Directions in Historical Scholarship*, ed. Guisso and Johannesen. Youngstown: Philo Press, 129-147.

Weber, Max. 1951. *The Religion of China.* New York: The Macmillan Company.

TRIBAL RELIGION

Ashley-Montague, M.F. 1937. "The Origin of Sub-Incision in Australia," *Oceania* 8 no.3: 193–207.

Abbie, A.A. 1909. *The Original Australians.* New York: American Elsevier Publishing Co.

Bell, Diane. 1983. *Daughters of the Dreaming.* North Sydney, N.S.W., Australia: McPhee Grible/ George Allen and Unwin.

Berndt, Catherine H. 1950. "Women's Changing Ceremonies in Northern Australia," *L'Homme: Cahiers d'Ethnologie de Geographique et de Linguistique.* 1:1–85.

———. 1964. "Women and the 'Secret Life.'" In *Aboriginal Man in Australia,* ed. R.B. and C.H. Berndt. Sydney: Agnus and Robertson.

———. 1974. "Digging Sticks and Spears, or, the Two Sex Model." In *Women's Role in Aboriginal Society,* ed. Fay Gale. 64–84. 2nd ed. Canberra: Australian Institute of Aboriginal Studies.

———. 1981. "Interpretations and 'Facts' in Aboriginal Australia." In *Woman the Gatherer,* ed. Frances Dahlberg, 153–203. New Haven: Yale University Press.

Berndt, Ronald M. 1951. *Kunapipi: A Study of an Australian Aboriginal Religious Cult.* New York: International Universities Press.

———. 1952. *Djanggawul: An Aboriginal Religious Cult of North-Eastern Arnhem Land.* London: Routledge and Kegan Paul.

Berndt, R.M. and C.H. Berndt. 1951. *Sexual Behavior in Western Arnhem Land.* New York: Viking Fund Publications in Anthropology, No. 16.

———. 1964. *The World of the First Australians.* Chicago: University of Chicago Press.

Elkin, A.P. 1938/1964. *The Australian Aborigines.* Garden City, N.Y.: Doubleday and Co., The Natural History Library, Anchor Books.

Falk, Nancy A. and Rita M. Gross. 1980. *Unspoken Worlds: Women's Religious Lives in Non-Western Cultures.* New York: Harper and Row.

Gale, Fay. 1974. *Women's Role in Aboriginal Society.* Canberra: Australian Institute of Aboriginal Studies.

Gould, Richard A. 1969 *Yiwara: Foragers of the Australian Desert.* New York: Charles Scribner's Sons.

Gross, Rita M. 1975. *Exclusion and Participation: The Role of Women in Aboriginal Australian Religions.* Chicago: Unpublished Ph.D. dissertation.

———. 1977. "Androcentrism and Androgyny in the Methodology of History of Religions." In *Beyond Androcentrism: New Essays on Women and Religion,* ed. Rita M. Gross, 7–21. Missoula, Mont.: Scholars Press.

————. 1980. "Menstruation and Childbirth as Ritual and Religious Experience among Native Australians." In *Unspoken Worlds*, ed. N.A. Falk and R.M. Gross. New York: Harper and Row.

————. 1983. "Women's Studies in Religion: The State of the Art, 1980." In *Traditions in Contact and Change: Selected Proceedings of the XIV International Conference, IAHR*, ed. Peter Slater and Donald Wiebe, 579–91. Waterloo, Ontario: Wilfrid Laurier University Press.

Howitt, A.W. 1904. *The Native Tribes of South-East Australia.* London: MacMillan.

Kaberry, Phyllis. 1939. *Aboriginal Woman: Sacred and Profane.* Philadelphia: Blakiston Co.

McConnell, Ursala H. 1957. *Myths of the Munkan.* Melbourne: Melbourne University Press.

Meggitt, M.J. 1965. *Desert People: A Study of the Walbiri Aborigines.* Chicago: University of Chicago Press.

Mountford, Charles P. 1965. *Ayers Rock: Its People, Their Beliefs and Their Art.* Honolulu: East-West Center Press.

Mountford, Charles P., and Allison Harvey. 1941. "Women of the Adnjamatana Tribe of North Flinders Range, South Australia." *Oceania*, 12, no. 2: 155–62.

Parker, K. Langlah. 1905. *The Euahlayi Tribe: A Study of Aboriginal Life in Australia.* London: Archibald Constable and Co.

Piddington, R. 1932. "Karadjeri Initiation." *Oceania* 2, no. 1: 46–87.

Roheim, Geza. 1933. "Women and Their Life in Central Australia." *Journal of the Royal Anthropological Institute of Great Britain and Ireland* 43: 207–65.

Spencer, Baldwin, and F.J. Gillen. 1968 reprint. *Native Tribes of Central Australia.* New York: Dover Publications.

Warner, W. Lloyd. 1958. *A Black Civilization: A Social Study of an Australian Tribe.* Rev. ed. New York: Harper Torchbooks.

HINDUISM

Allen, Michael. 1982. "The Hindu view of Women," in *Women in India and Nepal,* ed. Michael Allen and S.N. Mukherjee. Canberra: Australian National University, 1–20.

Altekar, A.S. 1962. *The Position of Women in Hindu Civilization.* Delhi: Motilal Banarsidass.

Babb, Lawrence A. 1975. *The Divine Hierarchy: Popular Hinduism in Central India.* New York: Columbia University Press.

Basu, Jogiraj. 1969. *India of the Age of the Brahmanas.* Calcutta: Sanskrit Pustak Bhandar.

Behari, Bankey. 1970. *Minstrels of God.* Part 1. Bombay: Bharatiya Vidya Bhavan.

Chandra, M. 1973. *The World of Courtesans.* Delhi: Vikas Publishing House.

_____. 1958. *Constitution of India (as modified up to the 1st April).* Delhi: Government of India Press.

Dutt, Romesh C. 1969. *The Ramayana and The Mahabharata.* New York: Everyman's Library.

Falk, Nancy Aver, and Rita M. Gross. 1980. *Unspoken Worlds: Women's Religious Lives in Non-Western Cultures.* San Francisco: Harper and Row.

Freeman, James M. 1980. "The Ladies of Lord Krishna: Rituals of Middle-Aged Women in Eastern India," *Unspoken Worlds: Women's Religious Lives in Non-Western Cultures,* ed. Nancy Aver Falk and Rita M. Gross. San Francisco: Harper and Row, 110–127.

Gandhi, Indira. 1981. *My Truth.* Delhi: Vision Books.

Hejib, Alaka. 1980. "The Concept of Sacrifice in Understanding Hindu Women." Paper presented to the International Association for the History of Religions, Winnipeg.

_____. 1982. "Wife or Widow? The Ambiguity and the Problems Regarding the Marital Status of the Renounced Wife of a Samnyasi." *Yoga Life* 13, 11: 3–14.

Hejib, Alaka, and Katherine K. Young. 1978a. "Power of the Meek *(abalā):* A Feature of Indian Feminism." Paper presented to the American Academy of Religion, New Orleans.

_____. 1978b. "Towards Recognition of the Religious Structure of the Sati." Paper presented to the American Oriental Society.

Jacobson, Doranne. 1980. "Golden Handprints and Red-Painted Feet: Hindu Childbirth Rituals in Central India," In *Unspoken Worlds: Women's Religious Lives in Non-Western Cultures.* San Francisco: Harper and Row, 73–94.

Jacobson, Doranne, and Susan S. Wadley. 1977. *Women in India: Two Perspectives.* New Delhi: Manohar.

Jayal, Shakambari. 1966. *The Status of Women in the Epics.* Delhi: Motilal Banarsidass.

Kalelkar, Kakasaheb, ed. 1960. *Bapu's Letters to Ashram Sisters.* Ahmedabad: Navajivan Publishing House.

Kane, Pandurang Vaman. 1974. *History of Dharmasastra.* 5 vols. 2nd ed. Poona: Bhandarkar Oriental Research Institute.

Lalonde, Gloria. 1985. "National Development and the Changing Status of Women in India." M.A. Thesis, McGill University, Department of Anthropology.

Mādhavānanda, Swāmi, trans. 1965. *The Br̥hadāraṇyaka Upaniṣad: With the Commentary of Śaṅkarācārya.* Calcutta: Advaita Ashrama.

Mukherjee, Prabhati. 1978. *Hindu Women: Normative Models.* New Delhi: Orient Longman.

Nikhilananda, Swami, trans. 1942. *The Gospel of Sri Ramakrishna.* New York: Ramakrishna-Vivekananda Center.

Müller, F. Max. 1878. *Lectures on the Origin and Growth of Religion.* London: Longmans, Green, and Co.

Obeyesekere, Gananath. 1984. *The Cult of the Goddess Pattini.* Chicago: The University of Chicago Press.

Orr, Leslie, n.d. "Origins and Meanings of the Devadāsī Institution: An Approach Through the Early Literature of South India." Unpublished manuscript.

Pandit, Vijaya Lakshmi. 1979. *The Scope of Happiness: A Personal Memoir.* New Delhi: Vikas Publishing House.

Paul, Diana Y. 1979. *Women in Buddhism: Images of the Feminine in Mahāyāna Tradition.* Berkeley: Asian Humanities Press.

Report of a seminar of women legislators by the Gandhi Peace Foundation in collaboration with the Indian Council of Social Science Welfare, Government of India, and UNICEF. 1978. *Women's Development: Some Critical Issues.* New Delhi: Marwah Publications.

Sarasvati, Svami Satya Prakash, and Satyakam Vidyalankar, trans. 1977. *Ṛgveda Saṁhitā, with English Translation.* Vol. 1. New Delhi: Veda Pratishthana.

Shankaranarayanan, S., trans. 1968. *Glory of the Divine Mother (Devīmāhātmyam).* Pondicherry: Dipti Publications.

Shastri, Shakuntala Rao. 1959. *Women in the Sacred Laws.* Bombay: Bharatiya Vidya Bhavan.

———. 1969. *Women in the Vedic Age.* Bombay: Bharatiya Vidya Bhavan.

Upadhyaya, Bhagwat Saran. 1974. *Women in Ṛgveda.* New Delhi: S. Chand & Co.

Vaidya, P.L. 1962. *The Vālmīki Rāmāyaṇa* Vol. 2, The Ayodhyākāṇḍa. Baroda: Oriental Institute.

Vasudev, Uma. 1974. *Indira Gandhi: Revolution in Restraint.* Delhi: Vikas Publishing House.

Wadley, Susan S. 1980a. "Hindu Women's Family and Household Rites in a North Indian Village," *Unspoken Worlds: Women's Religious Lives in Non-Western Cultures.* San Francisco: Harper and Row, 94–110.

Wadley, Susan S., ed. 1980b. *The Powers of Tamil Women.* Syracuse: Maxwell School, Syracuse University.

White, Charles S.J. 1980. "Mother Guru: Jñānananda of Madras, India," In *Unspoken Worlds: Women's Religious Lives in Non-Western Cultures.* San Francisco: Harper and Row, 22–39.

Young, Katherine K. 1979. "The Beguiling Simplicity of a Dot." *Arc* 6, no. 2: 8–10.

———. 1981. "The Buddha's Attitude to Women." *Arc* 8, no. 2: 20–25.

———. 1982a. "Why are Hindu Women Traditionally Oriented to Rebirth Rather Than Liberation (mokṣa)?" In *Third International Symposium on Asian Studies.* Hong Kong: Asian Research Service.

———. 1982b. "Sexual Bisection at the Divine/Human Intersection: Reflections on the Hindu Couple as God and Goddess Incarnate." Paper presented to the Conference on Religion in South India.

———. 1983a. "From Hindu Strīdharma to Universal Feminism: A Study of the Women in the Nehru Family,"In *Traditions in Contact and Change: Selected Proceedings of the XIV Congress of the International Association for the History of Religions*, ed. Peter Slater and Donald Wiebe. Toronto: Sir Wilfrid Laurier Press.

———. 1983b. "Śrīvaisnava Feminism: Intent or Effect?" In *Studies in Religion/ Sciences Religieuses*, 12-2, 183–190.

Young, Katherine K. and Arvind Sharma. 1980. *Images of the Feminine in India: A Course Outline*. Sydney: Department of Religious Studies, University of Sydney.

BUDDHISM

Altekar, A.S. 1956. *The Position of Women in Hindu Civilizaton*. Delhi: Motilal Banarsidass.

Beyer, Stephan. 1973. *The Cult of Tārā: Magic and Ritual in Tibet*. Berkeley: University of California Press.

———. 1974. *The Buddhist Experience: Sources and Interpretations*. Encino: Calif.: Dickenson Publishing Co.

Chavannes, Édouard, trans. 1962. *Cinq Cents Contes et Apologues, Extraits du Tripitaka Chinois*. 4 vols. Paris: Adrien-Maisonneuve.

Chen, Kenneth. 1964. *Buddhism in China, A Historical Survey*. Princeton: Princeton University Press.

Cissell, K.A. (Kathryn A. Tsai). 1972. *The Pi-ch'iu-ni chuan: Biographies of Famous Chinese Nuns from 317-516 C.E.* Ann Arbor, Mich.: University Microfilms.

Conze, Edward, trans. 1973. *The Perfection of Wisdom in 8,000 Lines and its Verse Summary*. Bolinas, Calif.: Four Seasons Foundation.

Davids, C.A.F. Rhys, trans. 1909. *Psalms of the Sisters*. London: Pali Text Society.

Davids, T.W. Rhys, and H. Oldenberg, trans. 1881-85. *Vinaya Texts*. Sacred Books of the East, vols. 13, 17, and 20. Oxford University Press. Reprint. 3 vols. Delhi: Motilal Banarsidass. 1965-68.

de Jong, J.W. 1974. "Notes on the Bhiksunī-vinaya." In *Buddhist Studies in Honour of I.B. Horner*, ed. L. Cousins et al. Dordrecht: Reidel Publishing Co.

Falk, Nancy. 1974. "An Image of Woman in Old Buddhist Literature—the Daughters of Māra." In *Women and Religion*, ed. J. Plaskow and J.A. Romero. Missoula, Mont.: Scholars Press.

_____. 1980. "The Case of the Vanishing Nuns: The Fruits of Ambivalence in Ancient Indian Buddhism." In *Unspoken Worlds*, ed. N. Falk and R. Gross. San Francisco: Harper and Row.

Forte, A. 1976. *Political Propaganda and Ideology in China at the End of the 7th Century*. Naples: Instituto Universitario Orientale.

Gomez, L.O. 1976. "Proto-Mādhyamika in the Pali Canon." *Philosophy East and West* 26, no. 2:137–66.

_____. 1977. "The *Bodhisattva* as Wonder-Worker." In *Prajñāpāramitā and Related Systems: Studies in Honor of Edward Conze*, ed. L. Lancaster. Berkeley: Berkeley Buddhist Studies Series, no. 1.

Har Dayal. 1932. *The Bodhisattva Doctrine in Buddhist Sanskrit Literature*. London: Routledge and Kegan Paul. Reprint: Delhi: Motilal Banarsidass, 1970.

Horner, I.B.. 1930. *Women Under Primitive Buddhism*. London: George Routledge.

Hurvitz, L. trans. 1976. *Scripture of the Lotus Blossom of the Fine Dharma*. New York: Columbia University Press.

Kabilsingh, C. 1984. *A Comparative Study of Bhikkunī Pāṭimokkha*. Varanasi: Chaukhambha Orientalia.

Kajiyama, Y. 1982. "Women in Buddhism." *Eastern Buddhist*, n.s. 15, no. 2: 53–70.

Kasahara, K. 1983. *Nyonin Ōjō Shisō no Keifu*. Hisashimurayama: Kyōikusha.

Kasuga, R. 1966. "Nyonin Jōbutsu to Nannyo Byōdō." *Indōgaku Bukkyōgaku Kenkyū* 15, no. 1: 125–30.

Klein, Anne C. 1985. "Nondualism and the Great Bliss Queen: A Study in Tibetan Buddhist Ontology and Symbolism." *Journal of Feminist Studies in Religion* 1, no. 1.

Krishnasvāmi Aiyangar, S. 1928. *Maṇimekhalai in its Historical Setting*. London: Luzac and Co.

Lamotte, E. trans. 1949-80. *Le Traité de la Grande Vertu de Sagesse de Nāgārjuna (Mahāprajñāpāramitāśāstra)*. 5 vols. Louvain: Université de Louvain Institut Orientaliste.

_____. 1962 *L'Enseignement de Vimalakīrti*. Bibliothèque du Muséon, vol. 51. Louvain: Université de Louvain Institut Orientaliste.

_____. 1965. *La Concentration de la Marche Héroïque (Śūraṃgamasamādhisūtra)*. Vol. 13 of *Mélanges Chinois et Bouddhiques*. Bruxelles: Institut Belge des Hautes Études Chinoises.

Levering, M.L. 1982. "The Dragon Girl and the Abbess of Mo-Shan: Gender and Status in the Chan Buddhist Tradition." *Journal of the International Association of Buddhist Studies*. 5, no. 1: 19–35.

Li, Jung-hsi, trans. 1981. *Biographies of Buddhist Nuns: Pao-chang's Pi-chiu-ni chuan*. Osaka: Tohokai.

Macy, J.R. 1977. "Beyond Wisdom: Mother of All Buddhas." In *Beyond Androcentrism*, ed. Rita Gross. Missoula, Mont.: Scholars Press.

Nam-mkha'i snying-po. 1983. *Mother of Knowledge: The Enlightenment of Ye-shes mTsho-rgyal.* Translated by Tarthang Tulku. Berkeley: Dharma Publishing.

O'Flaherty, W.D. 1980. *Women, Androgynes, and Other Mythical Beasts.* Chicago: University of Chicago Press.

Paul, Diana. 1979. *Women in Buddhism.* Berkeley: Asian Humanities Press.

_____. 1980a. *The Buddhist Feminine Ideal.* AAR Disseration Series 30. Missoula, Mont.: Scholars Press.

_____. 1980b. "Empress Wu and the Historians: A Tyrant and Saint of Classical China." In *Unspoken Worlds*, ed. N. Falk and R. Gross. San Francisco: Harper and Row.

Ray, R.A. 1980. "Accomplished Women in Tantric Buddhism of Medieval India and Tibet." In *Unspoken Worlds*, ed. N. Falk and R. Gross. San Francisco: Harper and Row.

Schuster, N. (Nancy Barnes) 1981. "Changing the Female Body: Wise Women and the Bodhisattva Career in some *Mahāratnakūṭasūtras.*" *Journal of the International Association of Buddhist Studies* 4, no. 1:24–69.

_____. 1984. "Yoga Master Dharmamitra and Clerical Misogyny in Fifth Century Buddhism." *The Tibet Journal* 9, no. 4:33–46.

_____. 1985a. "The Bodhisattva Figure in the *Ugraparipṛcchā.*" In *New Paths in Buddhist Research*, ed. A. K. Warder. Durham, N.C.: The Acorn Press.

_____. 1985b. "Striking a Balance: Women and Images of Women in Early Chinese Buddhism." In *Women, Religion, and Social Change*, ed. Y. Haddad and E. Findly. Albany: State University of New York Press.

Sharma, Arvind. 1978. "Can There Be a Female Buddha in Theravāda Buddhism?" In *Women, Literature, Criticism*, ed. H.R. Garvin. Lewisburg, Pa.: Bucknell University Press.

Staël-Holstein, A. von. ed. 1926. *The Kāçyapaparivarta, A Mahāyānasūtra of the Ratnakūṭa Class.* Shanghai: Commercial Press.

Tay, C.N. 1976. "Kuan-yin: The Cult of Half Asia." *History of Religions* 16, no. 2:147–77.

Thurman, R.A.F., trans. 1976. *The Holy Teaching of Vimalakīrti, a Mahāyāna Scripture.* University Park and London: The Pennsylvania State University Press.

Topley, M. 1975. "Marriage Resistance in Rural Kwangtung." In *Women in Chinese Society*, ed. M. Wolf and R. Witke. Stanford: Stanford University Press.

Tsai, K.A. (=Kathryn A. Cissell). 1981. "The Chinese Buddhist Monastic Order for Women: the First Two Centuries." In *Women in China*, ed. R.W. Guisso and S. Johannesen. Youngstown, N.Y.: Philo Press.

Tsultrim, Alliane. 1986. *Women of Wisdom.* London: Arkana.

Waldschmidt, E. 1926. *Bruchstücke des Bhiksuniipratimoksa der Sarvāstivādins.* Leipzig: Deutsche Morgenländische Gesellschaft.

Warren, H.C. Trans. 1972. *Buddhism in Translations.* Harvard Oriental Series, vol. 3. 1896. Reprint. New York: Atheneum.

Wayman, A. and H. Wayman, trans. 1974. *The Lion's Roar of Queen Śrīmālā*. New York: Columbia University Press.

Weiler, R.W. 1962. "The Buddhist Act of Compassion." In *Indological Studies in Honor of W.N. Brown*, ed. E. Bender. New Haven: Yale University Press.

Willis, J.D. 1985. "Nuns and Benefactresses: The Role of Women in the Development of Buddhism." In *Women, Religion, and Social Change*, ed. Y. Haddad and E. Findly. Albany: State University of New York Press.

Yamamoto, K., trans. 1973. *Mahāyāna Mahāparinirvāṇasūtra*. 3 vols. Ube City, Yamaguchi-ken: Karinbunko.

CONFUCIANISM

Andors, Phyllis. 1983. *The Unfinished Liberation of Chinese Women, 1949-1980*. Bloomington: Indiana University Press.

Chan Wing-tsit, trans. 1967. *Reflections on Things at Hand: the Neo-Confucian Anthology*. New York: Columbia University Press.

Ch'en-Tung-yüan. 1937 *Chung-uo fu-nü sheng-huo shih*. Shanghai: Commercial Press.

Chu Hsi, ed. 1173. *Chin-ssu lu*. Ssu-pu pei-yao edition.

_____. 1187. *Hsiao-hsüeh*. Ssu-pu pei-yao edition.

Elvin, Mark. 1984. "Female Virtue and the State in China," *Past and Present* 104 (Aug. '84). 111–152.

Guisso, Richard. 1981. "Thunder over the Lake: the Five Classics and the Perception of Women in Early China." In *Women in China*, ed. Guisso and Johannesen. New York: Philo Press.

Handlin, Joanna. 1975. "Lü K'un's New Audience: the Influence of Women's Literacy on Sixteenth-Century Thought." In *Women in Chinese Society*, ed. Wolf and Witke. Stanford: Stanford University Press.

Empress Hsü. d.u. *Nei-hsün*. In *Nü ssu-shu*, ed. Wang Hsiang. Naikaku bunko 1844 edition.

Johnson, Kay Ann. 1983. *Women, the Family and Peasant Revolution in China*. Chicago: University of Chicago Press.

Kelleher, Theresa. 1986. "How to be the Perfect Woman: Chinese Instructional Texts for Women." Unpublished paper.

_____. d.u. *K'ung-tzu chia yü*. Ssu-pu pei-yao edition.

Legge, James, trans. 1966 reprint of 1923 ed. *The Four Books: Confucian Analects, the Great Learning, the Doctrine of the Mean, and the Works of Mencius*. New York: Paragon.

_____. 1967 reprint of 1885 ed. *Li chi, Book of Rites*. Edited by C.C. Chai and W. Chai. 2 vols. New York: University Books.

Liu Hsiang. d.u. *Lieh-nü chuan*. Ssu-pu pei-yao edition.

Mann, Susan. 1984. "Suicide and Chastity: Visible Themes in the History of Chinese Women." Unpublished paper.

_____. 1984. "Widows in the Kinship and Community Systems of the Qing Period." Unpublished paper.

O'Hara, Albert. 1945. *The Position of Women in Early China.* Washington, D.C.: Catholic University Press.

Pan Chao. d.u. *Nü-chieh.* In *Nü ssu-shu,* ed. Wang Hsiang. Naikaku bunko 1844 edition.

Steele, John. 1966 reprint of 1917 ed. *The I-li, or Book of Etiquette and Ceremonial.* Taipei: Ch'ung Wen Publishing Co.

Sung, Marina. 1981. "The Chinese *Lieh-nü* Tradition." In *Women in China,* ed. Guisso and Johannesen. New York: Philo Press.

Sung, Jo-chao. d.u. *Nü lun-yü.* In *Nü ssu-shu,* ed. Wang Hsiang. Naikaku bunko 1844 edition.

Swann, Nancy Lee. 1932. *Pan Chao: Foremost Woman Scholar of China.* New York: Century Co.

Tung, Chia-tsung. 1970. "Li-tai chieh-fu lieh-nü te t'ung-chen." In *Chung-kuo fu-nü shih lun-chi,* ed. Pao Chia-lin. Taipei: Mu-t'ung Publishing Co.

Waltner, Ann. 1981. "Widows and Remarriage in Ming and Early Qing China." In *Women in China,* ed. Guisso and Johannesen. New York: Philo Press.

Wilhelm, Richard, trans. 1967. *I Ching, or Book of Changes.* Rendered into English by Cary F. Baynes. Princeton: Princeton University Press.

Wolf, Margery. 1975. "Women and Suicide in China." In *Women in Chinese Society,* ed. Wolf and Witke. Stanford: Stanford University Press.

TAOISM

Bauer, Wolfgang. 1976. *China and the Search for Happiness.* Tr. Michael Shaw. New York: Seabury Press.

Bodde, Derk. 1961. "Myths of Ancient China." In *Mythologies of the Ancient World,* ed. Samuel Kramer, 367-408. Garden City, N.Y.: Doubleday.

Chen, Ellen Marie. 1969. "Nothingness and the Mother Principle in Early Chinese Taoism." *International Philosophical Quarterly.* 9 no. 3:391–405.

_____. 1973. "The Origin and Development of Being (Yu) from Non-Being (Wu) in the *Tao Te Ching.*" *International Philosophical Quarterly* 13 no. 3: 403–17.

_____. 1974. "Tao as the Great Mother and the Influence of Motherly Love in the Shaping of Chinese Philosophy." *History of Religions* 14 no. 1:51–64.

Chow Tse-tsung. 1978. "The Childbirth Myth and Ancient Chinese Medicine." In *Ancient China: Studies in Early Civilization,* ed. David T. Roy and Tsuen-hsuin Tsien. Hong Kong: The Chinese University.

Eliade, Mircea. 1959. *The Sacred and the Profane.* Translated by W. Trask. New York: Harcourt, Brace and World.

Granet, Marcel. 1932. *Festivals and Songs of Ancient China*. New York: E.P. Dutton.

van Gulik, R.H. 1974. *Sexual Life in Ancient China*. Leiden: E.J. Brill.

Hou, Ching-lang. 1979. "The Chinese Belief in Baleful Stars." In *Facets of Taoism: Essays in Chinese Religion*, ed. Holmes Welch and Anna Seidel, 193–228. New Haven: Yale University Press.

Kaltenmark, Max. 1979. "The Ideology of the *T'ai-p'ing ching*." In *Facets of Taoism: Essays in Chinese Religion*, ed. by Holmes Welch and Anna Seidel, 19–45. New Haven: Yale University Press.

Lin Yutang. 1950. *Widow, Nun and Courtesan*. New York: John Day Co.

Liu T'ieh-yün. 1952. *The Travels of Lao Ts'an*. Tr. Harold Shadick. Ithaca: Cornell University Press.

Loewe, Michael. 1979. *Ways to Paradise: The Chinese Quest for Immortality*. London: Allen and Unwin.

Maspero, Henri. 1981. *Taoism and Chinese Religion*. Translated by Frank A. Kierman, Jr. Amherst: University of Massachusetts Press.

Miyakawa, Hisayuki. 1979. "Local Cults around Mount Lu at the Time of Sun En's Rebellion." *Facets of Taoism: Essays in Chinese Religion*, ed. Holmes Welch and Anna Seidel, 83–101. New Haven: Yale University Press.

Needham, Joseph. 1976. *Science and Civilization in China*, vol. 5, part 3. Cambridge: Cambridge University Press.

_____. 1983. *Science and Civilization in China*, vol. 5, part 5. Cambridge: Cambridge University Press.

Potter, Jack M. 1974. "Cantonese Shamanism." In *Religion and Ritual in Chinese Society*, ed. Arthur P. Wolf, 207–231. Stanford: Stanford University Press.

Saso, Michael. 1978. *The Teachings of Taoist Master Chuang*. New Haven: Yale University Press.

Schafer, Edward H. 1951. "Ritual Exposure in Ancient China." *Harvard Journal of Asiatic Studies* 14: 130–184.

_____. 1978a. "The Capeline Cantos: Verses on the Divine Loves of Taoist Priestesses." *Asiatische Studien* 32, no. 1:4–65.

_____. 1978b. "The Jade Woman of Greatest Mystery." *History of Religions* 17, nos. 3–4:387–98.

_____. 1980. *The Divine Woman: Dragon Ladies and Rain Maidens in T'ang Literature*. San Francisco: North Point Press.

Schipper, Kristofer. 1978. "The Taoist Body." *History of Religions* 17, nos. 3–4: 355–86.

Seidel, Anna. 1983. "Taoism." *Encyclopedia Britannica*, XVII: 1034–1044.

Sivin, Nathan. 1978. "On the Word 'Taoist' as a Source of Perplexity, With Special Reference to the Relation of Science and Religion in Traditional China." *History of Religions* 17, nos 3–4: 303–30.

Stein, Rolf. 1979. "Religious Taoism and Popular Religion from the Second to Seventh Centuries." *Facets of Taoism: Essays in Chinese Religion*, ed. Holmes Welch and Anna Seidel, 53–81. New Haven: Yale University Press.

Strickmann, Michel. 1978. "The Longest Taoist Scripture." *History of Religions* 17, nos. 3-4:331-54.

_____. 1979. "On the Alchemy of T'ao Hung-ching." *Facets of Taoism: Essays in Chinese Religions*, ed. Holmes Welch and Anna Seidel, 123-192. New Haven: Yale University Press.

Waley, Arthur. 1958. *The Way and Its Power: A Study of the Tao Te Ching and Its Place in Chinese Thought*. New York: Grove Press.

Ware, James R. 1966. *Alchemy, Medicine, and Religion in the China of A.D. 320: The Nei P'ien of Ko Hung*. Cambridge: M.I.T. Press.

Watson, Burton, ed. 1968. *The Complete Works of Chuang Tzu*. New York: Columbia University Press.

Welch, Holmes, and Anna Seidel, eds. 1979. *Facets of Taoism: Essays in Chinese Religion*. New Haven: Yale University Press.

Yu, Anthony C., trans. 1977-83. *The Journey to the West*, vols. 1-4. Chicago: University of Chicago Press.

JUDAISM

Adler, Rachel. 1978. "The Jew Who Wasn't There: Halacha and the Jewish Woman." In *Contemporary Jewish Ethics*, ed. Menachem Marc Kellner, 348-54. New York: Sanhedrin Press.

Berkovits, Eliezer. 1978. "The Status of Women Within Judaism." In *Contemporary Jewish Ethics*, ed. Menachem Mark Kellner, 355-74.

Bird, Phyllis. 1974. "Images of Women in the Old Testament." In *Religion and Sexism*, ed. Rosemary Ruether, 41-88. New York: Simon and Schuster.

Blumberg, Rae Lesser. 1976. "Kibbutz Women." In *Women in the World*, ed. L. Iglitzin and R. Ross. Santa Barbara: Clio Books.

Buber, Martin. 1966. *Hasidism and Modern Man*. New York: Harper and Row.

Christ, Carol, and Judith Plaskow, eds. 1979. *Womanspirit Rising*. San Francisco: Harper and Row.

Cohen, A. 1975. *Everyman's Talmud*. New York: Schocken Books.

Daly, Mary. 1978. *Gyn/Ecology*. Boston: Beacon Press.

Daube, David. 1978. "Biblical Landmarks in the Struggle for Women's Rights." *The Juridical Review* 23:177-97.

Epstein, Isadore. 1959. *Judaism*. London: Penguin.

_____. 1961, ed. *The Talmud*. London: Socino.

Goldenberg, Naomi. 1979. *Changing of the Gods*. Boston: Beacon Press.

Greenberg, Blu. 1976. "Judaism and Feminism." In *The Jewish Woman*, ed. Elizabeth Koltun, 179-92. New York: Schocken Books.

Hauptmann, Judith. 1974. "Images of Women in the Talmud." In *Religion and Sexism*, ed. Rosemary Ruether, 184-212. New York: Simon and Schuster.

Heilman, Samuel C. 1976. *Synagogue Life.* Chicago: University of Chicago Press.

Herford, R. Travers, trans. 1962. *The Ethics of the Talmud.* New York: Schocken Books.

Koltun, Elizabeth, ed. 1976. *The Jewish Woman.* New York: Schocken Books.

Lahav, Pnina. 1977. "Raising the Status of Women through Law: The Case of Israel." *Signs* 31, no. 1:193–209.

Lipman, Eugene, ed. 1970. *The Mishnah.* New York: W.W. Norton.

McKenzie, John L. 1965. *Dictionary of the Bible.* Milwaukee: Bruce.

Mann, Denese Berg. 1979. *The Woman in Judaism.* Hartford, Conn.: Jonathan.

Neusner, Jacob. 1979. "Thematic or Systematic Description: The Case of Mishnah's Division of Women." In *Method and Meaning in Ancient Judaism.* Missoula, Mont.: Scholars Press.

Parrinder, Geoffrey. 1971. *A Dictionary of Non-Christian Religions.* Philadelphia: Westminster.

Plaskow, Judith. 1977. "The Feminist Transformation of Theology." In *Beyond Androcentrism,* ed. Rita Gross. Missoula, Mont.: Scholars Press.

Poupko, Chana K., and Devora L. Wohlgelernter. 1976. "Women's Liberation: An Orthodox Response." *Tradition* 15, no. 4: 45–52.

Sandmel, Samuel. 1972. *The Enjoyment of Scripture.* New York: Oxford University Press.

Scholem, Gershom G. 1961. *Major Trends in Jewish Mysticism.* New York: Schocken Books.

Swidler, Leonard. 1976. *Women in Judaism.* Metuchen, N.J.: Scarecrow Press.

_____. 1979. *Biblical Affirmations of Woman.* Philadelphia: Westminster.

Terrien, Samuel. 1985. *Till the Heart Sings.* Philadelphia: Fortress.

Trible, Phyllis. 1978. *God and the Rhetoric of Sexuality.* Philadelphia: Fortress.

Umansky, Ellen M. 1979. "Women in Judaism: From the Reform Movement to Contemporary Jewish Religious Feminism." In *Women of Spirit,* ed. Rosemary Ruether and Eleanor McLaughlin, 333–54. New York: Simon and Schuster.

Wiesel, Elie. 1978. *Four Hasidic Masters.* Notre Dame, Ind.: University of Notre Dame Press.

Wigoder, Geoffrey, ed. 1974. *Jewish Values.* Jerusalem: Keter.

Zborowski, Mark, and Elizabeth Herzog. 1962. *Life is With People.* New York: Schocken Books.

CHRISTIANITY

Børreson, Kari. 1981. *Subordination and Equivalence in Nature: The Nature and Role of women in Augustine and Thomas Aquinas.* Washington, D.C.: University Press of America.

Brailsford, Mabel. 1915. *Quaker Women, 1650-1690.* London: Duckworth and Co.

Bridenthal, R. and C. Koonz, ed. 1977. *Becoming Visible: Women in European History.* Boston: Houghton Mifflin.

Clark, Alice. 1919. *The Working Life of Women in the 17th Century.* London: n.p.

Davies, Stevan. 1980. *The Revolt of the Widows: The Social World of the Apocryphal Acts.* Carbondale: Southern Illinois University Press.

Eckenstein, Lina. 1896. *Woman Under Manasticism: Saint Lore and Convent Life A.D. 500-1500.* Cambridge: Cambridge University Press.

Fiorenza, Elizabeth S. 1983. *In Memory of Her: A Feminist Theological Reconstruction of Christian Origins.* New York: Crossroads.

Irwin, Joyce L. 1979. *Womanhood in Radical Protestantism, 1525-1675.* New York: Edwin Mellen Press.

Jewett, Paul K. 1975. *Man as Male and Female.* Grand Rapids: Eerdmans.

Karlsen, Carol. 1980. The Devil in the Shape of a Woman: The Witch in 17th Century New England (Ph.D. dissertation, Yale University).

MacDonald, D.R. 1983. *The Legend and the Apostle.* Philadelphia: Westminster.

Mascall, E.L. n.d. *Women and the Priesthood of the Church.* London: The Church Union, Literature Association.

McDonnell, E.M. 1954. *Bequine and Beghard in Medieval Culture.* New Brunswick, N.J.: Rutgers University Press.

Morgan, Edmund S. 1966. *The Puritan Family: Religion and Domestic Relations in 17th Century New England.* Westport, Conn.: Greenwood Press.

Musurillo, Herbert. 1972. *The Acts of the Christian Martyrs.* Oxford: Clarendon.

Pelikan, Jaroslav., ed. 1958. *Luther's Works.* Vol. I. St. Louis: Concordia Publishing House.

Perkins, William. 1596. *A Discourse on the Damned Art of Witchcraft.* London: n.p.

Reeves, Marjorie. 1969. *Joachim of Fiore and the Prophetic Future.* New York: Harper and Row.

Ruether, R.R. ed. 1974. *Religion and Sexism.* New York: Simon and Schuster.

———, and E. McLaughlin, ed. 1979. *Women of Spirit.* New York: Simon and Schuster.

———, and R. Keller. 1983. *Woman and Religion in America.* Vol. 2. San Francisco: Harper and Row.

Schneir, M. ed. 1972. *Feminism: The Essential Historical Writings.* New York: Vintage.

Sparrow, John. trans. 1924. Jacob Boehme, *Mysterium Magnum: An Exposition of the First Book of Moses Called Genesis.* Vol. 1. London: John M. Watkins.

Swidler, L. and A. Swidler. 1977. *Women Priests: A Catholic Commentary on the Vatican Declaration.* New York: Paulist.

Additional bibliographical details are contained in the notes.

ISLAM

Abbott, Nabia. 1941. "Pre-Islamic Queens". In *The American Journal of Semitic Languages and Literatures* 17: 1–22.

Ahmad, Kurshid, and Salem Azzam. ed. 1975. *Islam: Its Meaning and Message.* Leicester: The Islamic Foundation.

Allman, James. ed. 1978. *Women's Status and Fertility in the Muslim World.* New York: Praeger Publishers.

Beck, Lois, and Nikki Keddie. ed. 1978. *Women in the Muslim World.* Cambridge: Harvard University Press.

Beeston, A. L. F. 1951. "The Position of Women in Pre-Islamic South Arabia." In *International Orientalist's Congress* 22 (2): 101-106.

Crapanzano, Vincent, and Vivien Garrison. ed. 1977. *Case Studies in Spirit Possession.* New York: John Wiley and Sons.

Galwash, Ahmad. 1973. *The Religion of Islam.* Vol. 1. Qatar: Education and Culture Ministry.

Hanbal, Ahmad Ibn. 1895. *Musnad.* Vol. 1. Cairo: al-Mataba'ah al-Maymania.

Keddie, Nikki R. 1972. *Scholars, Saints and Sufis.* Berkeley: University of California Press.

Kennedy, John. ed. 1978. *Nubian Ceremonial Life.* Berkeley: University of California Press.

Khān, Sadîq Hasan. n.d. *Husn al-uswa.* Cairo: Matba'ah al-Islām.

Lemu, B. Aisha, and Fatima Heeren. 1978. *Women in Islam.* Islamic Council of Europe.

Māhir, Farîd. 1971. *Karmāmāt al-Awliyā'.* Cairo: al-Matba'ah al-Aimiya.

Mernissi, Fatima. 1975. *Beyond the Veil.* New York: Schenkman Publishing Company.

Sakr, Ahmad. 1977. *al-Khutab.* Ann Arbor: Taleemul Islam Publications.

Smith, J. I. ed. 1980. *Women in Contemporary Muslim Societies.* Lewisburg: Bucknell University Press.

_____, and Yvonne Haddad. 1981. *The Islamic Understanding of Death and Resurrection.* Albany: State University of New York Press.

Williams, John A. 1979. "A Return to the Veil in Europe." In *Middle East Review* 11(3):49-59.

Additional bibliographical details are contained in the notes.

INDEX OF NAMES

SUBJECT INDEX

INDEX OF TERMS